Business on the Board

How the World's Greatest Game Can Build Better Leaders

J.K. EGERTON

Business on the Board
By J.K. Egerton

Cover Design by Chris Collins
Copyright © 2016 by J.K. Egerton

ISBN: 978-1-944177-53-9 (p)
ISBN: 978-1-944177-54-6 (e)

Crescendo Publishing, LLC
300 Carlsbad Village Drive
Ste. 108A, #443
Carlsbad, California 92008-2999

GetPublished@CrescendoPublishing.com

Message from the Author

It's been said that history teaches us that we learn nothing from history. We fought World War I to be the war that ended all wars. Yet a generation later we were fighting World War II. After World War II, we were involved in a Cold War that lasted more than forty years and now there is concern that we are heading for another deep chill.

One of the theories of the origins of chess is that a queen in India was tired of losing her sons to war and formed a counsel to invent a game that would substitute for war. For more than 1,600 years chess has prevailed over all the travails generated in the world. Chess, and in a small part this book, will give you a new perspective on how to figure out the situations you face, determine what needs to be done, and take the actions necessary to create a better reality.

For a personal message on how *Business on the Board* can improve your strategic thinking watch the "Look Inside" video at:
www.businessontheboard.com/videos/

To get access to the free content including a PDF copy of links in the book, bonus chapters, organization chart, and training materials enroll in complimentary "Inner Circle" membership at:
www.businessontheboard.com/enroll/

Once you have the password proceed directly to:
www.businessontheboard.com/free-content/

Thank you for purchasing my book and I hope you enjoy the read, but more importantly enjoy the journey.

J.K. Egerton

What People Are Saying About Business on the Board

As a financial literacy educator and creator of the *ThriveTime for Teens* money and life reality game for youth, I understand the power and effectiveness of teaching through games. It's exciting to see *Business on the Board* take a fresh new interactive and game-based approach to teaching the skills needed to be successful in business and in life. Specific business strategies and leadership skills are brought to life by the book through sharing the game of chess from the mind of a master.

Sharon L. Lechter CPA CGMA
Entrepreneur, Educator, and International Speaker
Author of *Think and Grow Rich for Women*,
Co-author of *Outwitting the Devil, Three Feet from Gold* and
the *Rich Dad Poor Dad* series

This book is an example of how collaboration can produce something extraordinary. Not to mention how the strategies and tactics can improve your life.

Berny Dohrmann
CEO Space International

Think outside the box! Business is a game and this book will teach you how to win it using the same strategies and tactics as those employed in chess.

Lois P. Frankel, Ph.D.,
Author of *Nice Girls Don't Get the Corner Office* and
Stop Sabotaging Your Career

Always glad when people share my story about the good decisions and the one bad decision I made. Making decisions will shape your life. This book gives you a place to deliberately practice making the best decisions using business strategies and tactics you need to succeed.

Aaron Young
Laughlin Associates, Inc.

I've been in the talent development arena for decades, and *Business on the Board* will be a game changer in the way business leaders think, decide, and execute.

Dr. Jeffrey Magee
Best Selling Author and Human Capital Developer

Never before in history has strategic thinking been more crucial for impact-driven businesses than in today's complex global economy. Ideally suited for managers who want more than 'good enough,' this book provides a systemic approach to executive decision-making that has tremendous implications for business and personal success.

Wendy Lipton-Dibner
President of Professional Impact, Inc. and
Best Selling Author of *Focus on Impact*

Every problem is a leadership problem. It all can be traced back to your decisions. *Business on the Board* will sharpen those decision-making skills and make you the envy of every leader.

Sherrin Ross Ingram
CEO of International Center for Strategic Planning

As an expert in the field of transformational leadership, and a musical conductor, I know leadership skills need to be learned through rehearsal. Whether you practice with sixteen chess pieces or hundreds of musicians your ability to practice will determine your level of success. This book will give you transformational, situational, and end-results based leadership training every time you conduct your business on the board.

Hugh Ballou
SynerVision International, Inc.

As a trusted advisor to business leaders, I know how important a strategic planning process is to my clients. The success of their team is based upon using this process. In *Business on the Board*, you will learn how to function as a team, playing every role a successful business needs to win. As the CEO, your success depends on how well the team works together to stay one move ahead of the competition while being strategically strong, tactically sharp, and making the decisions that win the game.

Harry Lay
Lay Professional Services, Inc.

Building alliances is critical in making your business a success. In *Business on the Board*, you will learn how alliances work with your chess pieces so you have the best chances of winning. Using those same alliance-building skills in your business will generate a "Value Proposition" that will be hard to beat.

Ed Bogle
Ideation Edge

I love the way *Business on the Board* uses technology to bring the games to life for the reader. I never knew business and chess were so connected. If I weren't busy building successful websites for my clients, I might be on the internet using chess to practice and improve my decision-making skills.

Ken Courtright
Business and Growth Consultant

After sitting in on a Business on the Board™ session, it changed the way I look at chess. Now I know why so many in the legal field use it to determine the strategies and tactics they use with their cases and their clients.

Jason Webb
JP Webb Legal Services

Wow, turning business into a game sounds like a winning move to me.

Greg S. Reid
Best Selling co-author of *Three Steps from Gold* and
Motivational Speaker

My experience in coaching hundreds of CEOs to build strong, sustainable, and scalable businesses has strengthened my conviction that planning, sequencing, and implementation are imperative if you want your business to succeed. *Business on the Board* helps you develop those skills through the power of gamification. It's a business simulator you can use time and again to deal with complex situations.

Paul Hoyt
Hoyt Management Group
Founder, The Awakened CEO System

You need the right mindset to see the possibilities in your situation, visualize the future you want, and make the moves of a champion to get the success you deserve.

Dave Austin
Author of International Best Seller, *Be a Beast* and
Founder of Extreme Focus

Table of Contents

Author Dedication and Advice

This book was possible only with the assistance and support of my family. To my wife, who, while developing her own career, endured this twelve-year journey of getting my business "off the runway and nose up." To my children, who at times pulled me away from the game and at other times played chess right next to me during a US Open. To my mother, who let me take spring break a week early to play in my first National Open chess tournament at the Stardust Hotel in Las Vegas—the start of a lifetime of tournament experience. To my father, who thought it better to "get a job" than spend my time going over chess books in the basement, but who was only too proud to watch his third-grade grandson trounce high school player after player in a national chess tournament. To my high school English teacher, who told me if I started a chess club, he would sponsor it. That was the spark that ignited the flame that continues to burn.

A GPS

Like the GPS I used to navigate the streets of Los Angeles while taking the cover photo, using technology to navigate this book will optimize the learning experience. Open a browser using the links displaying the game or video. Using your print edition facilitates reading the narrative while watching the game in progress. If you follow the links, it will feel like we are making the moves together. Download a free PDF file with all the links in the book from our website www.businessontheboard. com. In the e-book version the links will automatically direct you to the websites used in the book. There are numerous strategically placed diagrams in the book that make anything other than the print version of the book unnecessary. A chess-playing program on your phone, tablet, or laptop would be useful for playing over the moves. Of course, there is the traditional way of playing over the moves which is using a chess set and board.

The First Move

"Business is a game, the greatest game in the world if you know how to play it."

Thomas J Watson, founder of IBM

Inside my Las Vegas hotel room, I wrote about the damage caused by business leaders making bad decisions. Meanwhile, outside my room, sirens wailed and helicopters chopped the air of the night sky. Emergency responders feverishly worked the scene of an incident on "the Strip." A driver had decided to plow her car into pedestrians on the sidewalk, killing one and injuring dozens in the melee. At that moment, I stopped writing about business leaders who run Ponzi schemes, who send workers into unsafe coal mines, or who manufacture defective car parts. As the police and rescue workers brought order to the scene, I returned to my work. Later, the morning light brought the news I already knew. Chaos had reigned on the sidewalks below my room the night before, ending at the entrance of my hotel. And in other news that I could have predicted, I heard the report that another company had betrayed our trust. Toshiba had misstated earnings for years in an accounting scandal leading to 8,000 layoffs and $4.5 billion in losses. How is the insanity of a vicious driver any different from the typical destructive scenarios caused by failing leadership and bad decision-making?

You are a leader at any level if your decisions affect the lives of others. Decision-making is a skill. If you want to be good at it, you need to practice. Fortunately, there is a game that allows business leaders to practice and improve their strategic thinking and critical decision-making. It's a game where the mistakes you make will not get you fired or into trouble with authorities. It's the game of chess.

The integrity of decision-making has become so bad it has spawned the whistleblowing industry. There are reports that one individual has the potential to become a billionaire just by blowing a whistle on a mutual-fund family. Do decision makers know the decisions they are making are bad, or were they just unable to predict the future correctly?

An associate went to prison for fourteen months after he pled guilty to a charge, "he either knew or should have known about." Honest as the day is long, he made some decisions he thought were good (cooperating with law-enforcement authorities), but they were in fact bad. Similarly, a *Wall Street Journal* editorial detailed the travails of a midlevel project engineer who worked nearly ninety days in order to help stop the flow of oil during the Gulf Coast explosion. His decision to assist in the containment process was not as significant as deleting a text-message conversation that made him a cover-up target. Given his treatment by the Justice Department, first responders may just decide next time to walk away and let the Gulf fill up with oil.

I have met hundreds of people at conferences and forums who admit they know how to play chess but haven't played for years and are really bad at it. The reason they quit is that they don't play "chess for purpose." They invested time and effort to create a tool they still have. They misunderstand how that tool can positively change their lives by helping them make better decisions. The tool sits unused because they do not see how keenly it relates to business. Those misconceptions and reservations need to be replaced with valuable strategies and tactics that are used in business every day.

Keep it Simple, Easy to Remember, and Useful for the Future

I have kept this book as simple as possible and easy to remember, which makes it useful for the future. For subjects as complex as business and chess that is no small task. Information that cannot be recalled has no payback. Being "in the moment" allows information to be used when needed. A business meeting can parallel a game of chess. Meetings result in the exchange of information through conversation. A chess game exchanges moves and ideas in silence. Bringing an agenda, memos, or emails on a tablet to a meeting has no value if they haven't been read. A rated chess tournament prohibits bringing any materials to the board because this is a contest of your knowledge and skill. This is not a game where you can phone a friend or ask the audience for help. Your knowledge from previous play and study is your only lifeline.

You Make it so Easy

"If anyone takes your training and they don't understand chess when you're done, they'll never get it. You make is so simple to understand."

Attorney Comment

Chess for Purpose

Chess is the simulator for business decision-making, whether your business is for profit or not-for-profit. Thought leader Adam Braun, the author of *The Promise of a Pencil*, thinks companies that are not-for-profit should be classified as "for purpose." Chess for purpose means you are learning about the game because you know it will help you in other areas of your life, such as in your business career, your athletic endeavors, or your formal education. Chess for chess can be fun, but as with tennis, only a very few at the top can make a living at the game. I am sometimes asked, "What is the difference between a chess grandmaster and a large pizza? A large pizza can feed a family of four."

Looking back at my MBA studies, I learned the value of chess as a tool for developing leadership skills as each semester passed. The need for a leader to understand how and when all the resources fit together to make a functioning organization became increasingly obvious. Each component of the enterprise we studied was part of a corporate organization chart. With each entity reporting up through a chain of command, it's the picture of an organization structure, at least on paper anyway. The charts are designed to help company management see the picture of the organization, which helps locate resources and resolve issues.

Further inspection revealed that each entity was a component of a well-constructed game of chess. The CEO defeats the competition when the team is aligned properly to achieve company goals in such a way that resources are better managed through deployment of the correct strategies and opportunistic tactics.

Chess is a powerful metaphor for business. If a simulator provides value to an airline pilot in training, then chess adds value by simulating business activity on the board. According to game theory, chess is a sequential game played with perfect information by each participant. In business it may be unwise to wait for anyone, and often the first-mover advantage can last for years. Perfect information is never available when competitors are changing their strategies. Corporate strategies are valuable commodities, and thinking you know a competitor's intended move is risky.

Filling the Need for Another Business Book

Two books that explained how business relates to chess were written by a lawyer and a world chess champion. My book is different because I have expertise and experience in both business and chess. This book is about chess for the purpose of business. It has only five chess games spread over ten chapters. No chess player would be interested in so little game content. I don't explain checkmate until chapter 10, when the richest man in the world falls into it. I describe business risk management in chess, which is something I have never seen in the hundreds of chess books in my library.

People who want to understand how business and chess relate need to be led by someone who has practiced both disciplines at a reasonable level. But more importantly, that person has to connect the dots between the two to complete the job. I've played hundreds of United States Chess Federation (USCF) rated competitive chess games over forty-four years, achieving a master ranking in postal competition and Fédération Internationale des Échecs (FIDE) expert ranking. I have an MBA in finance. I have worked in corporate management and training, as well as information technology, for twenty-three years, starting my career teaching mathematics. I've coached and taught chess for twenty-three years, full-time for twelve. My students are improving their lives through chess, and now it's time to do the same for your business career by using chess for purpose.

The Power of Retrospection

In 1978, two twenty-two-year-olds were fresh out of college and sharing a cubicle at Proctor & Gamble's headquarters in Cincinnati. While both were bright and ambitious, knowing exactly where each was headed in their respective careers was certainly not predictable at the time. In retrospect, however, each has had his measure of success. Jeffery Immelt became CEO of General Electric in 2001. His cubicle mate was Steve Ballmer, the former CEO of Microsoft. If that cubicle isn't enshrined as a tourist attraction, it might be a good place to start your career.[1]

The book in your hands is my journey through the ranks of management. Part memoir, it recalls situations and decisions I made during my career. In practically every instance I was able to draw upon strategies and tactics from chess that I knew and studied. They were used with the intention of a chess move, and in some situations I had the advantage of knowing my next move. Predicting the future is impossible, which means that running a department of fourteen employees one day is pure speculation. It's more impressive to be in charge of thousands, but the leaders of larger organizations don't know every employee. They have their span-of-control chess pieces (direct reports) who are used to operate the business. The ability to look backward at my business and chess careers is intended to pay it forward to enhancing your business career.

Taking a Middle Management Perspective

My affinity is for the ranks of middle management. You're responsible for implementing the strategies directed from above while generating and executing strategies for your direct reports. Not much has been written or directed at how the rank of middle or functional management works in an organization. In the business game of chess, you're the king of your department while being a pawn to your director. A recent Gallup poll found that companies usually name the wrong person to be the manager. Their analytics suggest companies get the right talent for the job only 18 percent of the time.

Bad management in the middle ranks can cost billions of dollars each year, and can even result in the demise of a company. According to Gallup, "the only defense against this problem is a good offense, because when companies get these decisions wrong, nothing fixes it. Businesses that get it right, however, and hire managers based on talent will thrive and gain a significant competitive advantage."[2]

I wrote *Business on the Board* with the middle manager in mind because the midlevel of the company is where managers have the greatest opportunity to grow, combined with the greatest need to learn and practice new business skills. Developing a leader's mindset from the outset is the result of being exposed to the chess method of decision-making and its consequences. Managing sixteen pieces of plastic into a productive workforce is a fertile training ground for future success with a real workforce. Business books, like this one, offer a high value for the business student, supervisor, manager, executive, leader, or entrepreneur who someday wants to oversee an entire enterprise.

Tactical management decisions made while engaged in such activities as developing and evaluating employees, delegating responsibility, and protecting assets are comparable to the kinds of decisions players make on the chessboard. Taking over a management position is no different from taking over a chess game that is already in progress. Decision-making and its consequences need practice at every level within an organization.

8

A Place to Practice Business

There is no "practice" in business. Constantly working on the firing line means a potential win or loss with every decision. In large organizations, future leaders gain experience by moving from division to division, soaking up the knowledge from different areas of the company. However, this cannot be called "practice" because your career is on the line every step of the way. Chess is a powerful vehicle for practicing leadership, strategy generation, employee evaluation, and delegation.

Another skill chess develops is the ability to remain calm under pressure. An unforeseen move by an opponent strengthens the "carry on" mentality. Adversity in chess builds your ability to work in a pressure-cooker environment. Though not at the stress level of the airline pilot who manipulated his huge passenger jet into a perfect landing in the Hudson River, when your job and those of direct reports are affected by your next decision, that's pressure.

Everyone Starts Somewhere

How many people who watch Wimbledon or the US Open actually play tennis? Yet if they don't know how to play the game, how can they appreciate the athleticism and competition they are witnessing? I take the approach that having an appreciation of chess knowledge when applied to business situations will improve leaders and managers. Knowing how and where your employee pieces provide the most value transcends both domains. A question not to be asked when interviewing for your first management position is, "Do I need to know how to manage?" My boss knew I didn't have any management experience. He must have thought I would figure it out because he certainly didn't tell me how to do my job. Even though the sixteen employees I previously managed lacked a heartbeat, these pieces brought me years' worth of leadership experience my boss would not have known about.

Several years ago Dr. Lois Frankel, the owner of Corporate Coaching International, and I were working on a joint proposal for our training. I connected with Lois when a student's mother said I needed to read her book, *Nice Girls Don't Get the Corner Office*. Truthfully, it was not something that I would have pulled off the library shelf on my own. But after opening it up, I liked the book immediately. Women fall short because they treat business like a family event, trying to make sure everyone gets along. Learning to play chess is one of the suggestions she makes to women for how to get better at playing the game of business.

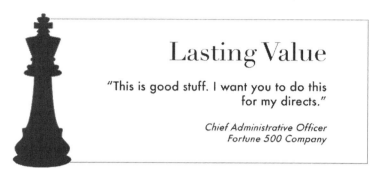

Lasting Value

"This is good stuff. I want you to do this for my directs."

Chief Administrative Officer
Fortune 500 Company

On the phone one day, I asked Lois the $64,000 question, "Do you play chess?" She replied that she knew how to play chess, but she chose to play tournament Scrabble® instead. It gave her the same competitive challenges of implementing strategies and tactics like a chess game. She related her strategy of purposely leaving a tile blank and letting her opponent use the tile so that she could then play off the word her opponent created, gaining an advantage. She used the decoy tactic to create a combination. Chess for purpose, in her life, was playing a word game that kept her strategically strong and tactically sharp. In my life, pursuing the MBA degree shortly after starting in management supplied another piece to the business and chess puzzle.

MBA Content Using Gamification

An advanced degree can add immeasurably to the success of a leader. Each course in my MBA program added a brick to my house of business knowledge. Completing your own business building helps you understand how each piece fits in the whole picture. A business degree has to cover the subject matter that business leaders use in their operation. To accomplish that, MBA programs use a method that has been successful in business schools and was rebranded from chess. The case method is the chess model of study. Look at a situation, determine what needs to be done, and then execute.

Instead of business cases this book uses chess games played by some of the best (world champions) and some good players (your author's opponents). If the moves can be turned into a story, and the links in the text are followed, it will be as if we are making the moves together. Along the way, I will bring up examples from athletics and business, but these will not be full-blown case studies. Instead, they will be briefs designed to illustrate a main point. One of the issues with business-case knowledge is it wanes over time. I can remember only several cases from the hundreds I reviewed during my study. The value of the chess model is remembering a previously played chess game because it could appear again in the next tournament. It literally comes to life again. Chess provides a continuous knowledge value-add because you can learn and improve after each move.

Making It Matter

Business on the Board is the first in a series of books focusing on different management disciplines. This book covers the full range of business management in order to sharpen your overall business acumen. Future books will allow for a deeper dive into the specific disciplines managers use every day. This series, while allowing me to tell my story, is served with the intention of improving your story.

An accelerating trend to the real path of riches and meaning is to give back to others to enjoy their success as well. Over the years I have trained thousands of people, from first graders to CEOs. All of them had a desire to learn. Chess allowed them not only to learn but also to practice what they were learning. The following diagram represents the land of opportunity for your future. To be strategically stronger and tactically sharper, while practicing good decision-making as a business leader, your best move starts with a journey that begins on the next page.

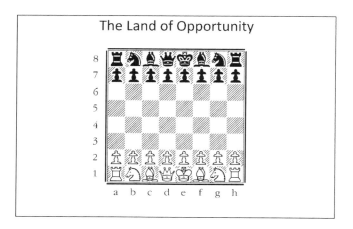

J.K. Egerton
Business on the Board

Chapter 1

Leadership—Starts With Your People

"Lead or Get out of the ..."

Who was rated the best chief executive on the planet? Andrew Grove, the late ex-CEO of Intel. However, what made him so special? What did Peter Thiel know about a better way to make purchases, which shook up the online e-commerce payment processing world? If your bank suffered huge losses under your watch, how would you keep your job and manage to turn that situation around? Jamie Dimon must have had a method to pull it off because that's exactly what he accomplished.

Any great leader will tell you the secret to business success isn't how much you know or how long you've been in business. There is no big secret to success other than this one fact: leaders who win know how to win.

Leadership training is a billion dollar industry built around a single goal: to teach you how to win. The subject occupies more than six shelves at my local community college. The book titles indicate leadership can be taught, leaders can be built, and leadership drives a company's success.

13

In *Lasting Leadership*, by Mukul Pandya and Robbie Shell, the success factors of twenty-five iconic business executives were revealed with one executive being declared "simply the best."

However, one thing the leadership books are short on is how to practice leadership. Serial entrepreneurs in the tech sector learn to run a business by practicing "fail fast, fail often." The idea is you learn from your mistakes. Tech start-ups are the perfect arena for learning leadership skills through mistakes because the small scale doesn't provide the resources to absorb many mistakes before the funding runs out. Each failure increases the entrepreneur's managerial skill set, so they are more likely to succeed with their next venture.

Winning

In business it's accomplished through your employees. In chess it's accomplished through your pieces.

Fortunately, you don't have to fail at business to learn how to succeed at business. Instead, you can learn how to organize and manage your people by studying the grandmasters and other strong chess players. The analogy between business and chess is so perfect that many management consultants use chess pieces and chess analogies when they promote their services. Adapting "chess for purpose" principles into their consulting practice can create a shared language and culture that unifies their global workforce or client base.

To succeed in business, you accomplish objectives through your employees. In the same way, chess victories come through the proper deployment of your pieces. If you understand how chess games are won and lost, you'll learn how businesses succeed and fail. The core strategies and tactics apply to both. Because chess is a game, you don't have much to lose. As a business simulator, chess teaches world-class decision-making.

Leadership Styles

Leadership comes in different styles and formats. It's based on values and experience. Leadership requires competency and character. Jack Welch, former chairman and CEO of General Electric, said that leadership is based on truth and trust. And he is right. But leadership styles are also based on the context of the situation. When given the opportunity to advance into a managerial or leadership role, chances are you will assume a preexisting situation. Your position was created, there was turnover in the position, and you are expected to take over. Most likely you will inherit the people along with your new title.

Leaders practice one of many leadership styles, or they may combine the styles in ways that best suit their needs. The three styles that directly relate to chess are transformational, situational, and results-based. These leadership styles are both personal and opportunistic.

Contexual Leadership Is...

• Transformational in the Opening
• Situational in the Middlegame
• Results-Based in the Endgame.

They are personal in the sense that the leader's personality falls into one or the other of the styles. For example, DISC analysis or other personality tests can help identify a manager's natural leadership style.

Leadership styles are opportunistic and exploit chances offered by immediate circumstances, not because of a general plan. Certain styles work better in different situations. Wise leaders may not be able to change their personalities, but they can introduce aspects of the other styles when needed. For example, a charismatic leader who is used to motivating the team to action may need to add an element of results-based leadership to train team members in new ways of doing things.

15

Transformational leaders focus on motivating their followers by imparting their devotion to achieving organizational goals. Transformational leadership works best in situations such as turnarounds or start-ups. Examples of transformational leaders include Gerstner's turnaround of IBM, Andrew Grove's leadership of Intel, or Fred Smith at Federal Express who, through his vision, designed the spoke-and-hub transformation of worldwide package delivery.

Situational leaders adapt their style to the people they lead. Situational leadership works in military operations where group dynamics are important and each situation has different demands. Situational leaders include General George S. Patton, who spoke to the level of his troops, and General George Custer, who during the Civil War fought right up on the front line with his troops, showing leadership in action.

Results-based leaders reverse traditional forward-looking approaches. They start with the end outcome in mind. Once end goals are identified, actions are undertaken that facilitate moving toward those desired objectives. Results-based leadership works best in situations where leaders can visualize the future and, by reasoning backward, create the actions necessary to achieve the desired end results. A results-based leader is Bill Gates, who had the ability to see the future of personal computing and then by reasoning backward took the necessary steps to make Microsoft the PC software leader.

Contextual Leadership

The optimal way to lead your team is to combine the best traits from each leadership style into a model I call contextual leadership. Leadership and management occur within a context of a given state of affairs. Management promotes you into an existing leadership position. As the leader, your first task is to assess what is right and wrong in your new situation so that you can make the changes necessary to move forward.

In Patrick Lencioni's *Five Dysfunctions of a Team*, Kathryn, the new and embattled CEO of the fictional company DecisionTech, took over a company that had initial success but floundered as competitors achieved more with fewer resources. Her situation was like jumping into a chess game in progress.

One of my favorite training exercises is to set up a chess opening position and let the participants play for several moves. Then I switch the players to a different board with another game in progress. They have to "pick up the pieces" of another situation, quickly figure out what is happening, and make the needed adjustments, just as Kathryn did with a series of off-site meetings. She determined which employee pieces she needed and which ones were creating problems and needed to be traded off. She also determined which employees needed new responsibilities to establish the trust that her team lacked to be effective.[1]

Leadership training builds upon competencies that must be practiced by the leader. Companies organize into divisions like separate chess games so that they can evaluate each leader on their own P&L. Playing concurrent chess games enables company results to be aggregated from all the games in progress. Each division head gets to exercise leadership while trying to win their own chess game without risking the entire enterprise. If the division does well, the future looks bright, but if their game results don't look promising, the division is in peril of being reorganized or sold off.

In *Building Leaders: How Successful Companies Develop the Next Generation*, Conger and Benjamin maintain:

> Leadership models have moved toward reframing the leader's principal role to that of a change agent. So a great number of today's competencies are concerned with implementing organizational change. The manager, who has these competencies, has a vision of the future, builds alignment, thinks strategically, plans proactively and implements with excellence.[2]

In *Lasting Leadership*, Pandya and Shell believe effective leaders manage their corporate cultures well, tell the truth, see opportunities that others miss, handle pricing and their brands, learn fast, and manage risk. Buried in the concluding chapter is the profound statement: "The single-most common skill these leaders have displayed is a knack for seeing into the future."[3]

What Leaders See

The ability of leaders to see the future and take advantage of trends is the basis of Max Bazerman's book, *The Power of Noticing: What the Best Leaders See*. He makes the case that when business leaders don't recognize trends and fail to drill down to generate analysis, huge problems occur.

JPMorgan Chase & Co. chairman and CEO Jamie Dimon fell into such a situation when his bank had losses generated by Bruno Iksil, the "London Whale" trader. Iksil earned the moniker thanks to the whale-sized, dangerous trading position he took as a London-based broker for the bank. Using the chess tactic of a skewer, where the more important piece steps aside and lets the lower-ranked piece behind take the hit or be captured, Dimon requested and accepted the resignation of JPMorgan Chase's chief investment officer. The CIO oversaw the risks taken by the bank's traders who suffered the loss. Meanwhile, the game went on with the king of JPMorgan Chase & Co. still at the helm.

Bazerman says, "Leaders often fail to notice when they are obsessed by other issues, when they are motivated not to notice, and when there are other people in their environment working hard to keep them from noticing."[4]

"Plausible deniability" is a hallmark of the presidency as a way to avoid fallout from poor decision-making or improper actions, especially by staff. President Nixon was preoccupied with the Vietnam War and developing Russian and Chinese relations, so he relegated much of the day-to-day work of domestic affairs to his direct reports. Although obsessed with stopping leaks to the press in his administration, Nixon didn't know what his chess pieces were doing to gather that information. Once Watergate broke, he was motivated not to notice by saying no one in his administration was involved in the break-in. Yet the day after the break-in, he was plotting how to cover up the affair in his office. In similar fashion, President Reagan was shielded from the Iran-Contra dealings by subordinates operating out of the White House who were working hard to keep him from noticing the weapons-for-hostages exchanges.

One way to notice is to think ahead. If you can see just one step ahead of the current situation, you may discover a different course of action.

BP CEO Tony Hayward missed such an opportunity when he suffered a lapse during a discussion with the media after the Gulf of Mexico oil-rig explosion. He said, "There's no one who wants this thing over more than I do. I'd like my life back." His mistake, of course, was focusing on himself rather than those affected by the immense oil leak that resulted from his company's mistakes. He didn't think ahead, and the backlash and the consequences of his words cost him his job. Anticipating the opponent's next move is a skill businesspeople and chess players share. Blame can also be awarded to his public relations "pieces" for not teaching him to focus on the apparent victims of BP's actions rather than himself in his press briefings. It should have been second nature to him to sympathize with the apparent victims (without admitting any wrongdoing).

In order to prevent predictable surprises, Bazerman recommends that leaders recognize the threat, prioritize the threat, and mobilize action against the threat. Chess players use that sequence of strategies often during the course of a contest. Their success is often determined by their ability to use their skills in taking preventive action against their opponent's threats.

Bazerman believes that noticing the threats in a situation is easier for outsiders. I couldn't agree more. During chess tournaments, I like to walk around and observe other games in progress. Sometimes I find a game where a player is deep in thought, and I notice a tactic or threat present with just a quick glance at their position. Because the player was too engrossed in analysis, their next move often overlooks the obvious threat in the position, and they suffer the consequences as a result.

Exhibiting Leadership Using Chess

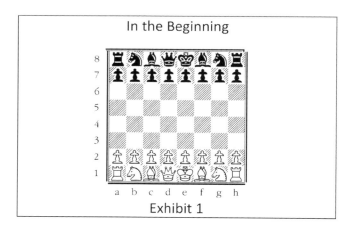

Exhibit 1

How can leadership be developed and practiced using chess pieces (employees) who have had the same capabilities for over 500 years? In the initial chess game set up in Exhibit 1, a leader sees the untapped potential of sixteen employees that have unique capabilities, skills, and deficiencies. It's a symmetrical situation where each leader has to make the most of the employees they have through the use of sound strategies while being tactically alert to how employees work together. A benefit of this business start-up is that the information you need is present in the position.

The leaders have no trade secrets or hidden knowledge on how the two companies will compete. White's advantage is moving first, but there are two schools of thought on that in business. The first-mover advantage can be negated by fast competitors who follow your trail then quickly gain the upper hand because they have let you blaze the way. This is true in chess as well. White moves first, but Black chooses the defense they prefer. Black gains the advantage of knowing how the defense will be set up while White has to be prepared to play against any Black defense.

The opening moves of a chess game require that the players exhibit the skills of a transformational leader. Sixteen employees wait on their leader to delegate responsibilities, give them meaningful tasks to accomplish, and form a team that can give them the best chance of winning. They have to create a company culture (aggressive or positional), have a role for each player on the team, and visualize the future at least to the point where every piece is involved in the game.

Seasoned players also know the terrain for which they will contend. They know where weaknesses in the initial formation can lead to an advantage. One such weakness is the square f7, which is guarded by the king. Beginning players love to attack that square and secure a quick checkmate victory in no more than four moves. The capabilities of each employee will be discussed in chapter 2 where we will review the resumes of each member of the team.

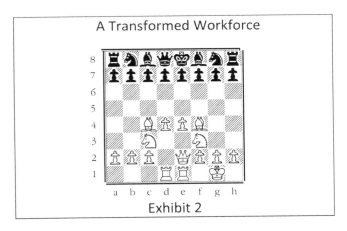

A Transformed Workforce

Exhibit 2

Take a few minutes to review Exhibit 2 to see if you can form some opinions about leadership. Targeted at the person who has no experience with chess, this diagram can form the basis for understanding how chess can develop leadership skills. What are the differences in the two sides?

Leadership at times can be hard to define, but just like the Supreme Court applied a rule to another less honorable subject, "I know it when I see it" applies in this case. White's leadership has transformed the employees into a force to be reckoned with. Black has been ultraconservative and not done anything with the employees.

Is this position possible? Yes, if Black brings out both knights and then returns them to their starting position. The initial phase of a chess game concerns the lack of mobility of the employees. Other than the two knights and the pawns, six out of eight back-rank employees cannot move and are thereby not contributing to the team effort. To see which moves are the best, go to our website: www.businessontheboard.com/videos, click on the VIDEOS tab, and watch "Getting Off to a Good Start." Using analytics, this video reveals the best two strategic moves used to start a game.

White has achieved several strategic objectives that will position the team to win the game. Like an entrepreneur starting up a business, White targeted a market segment of the board to occupy, developed resources, and managed risk. How did this player do that? White played for control of the four central squares of the board and dominated them. This player positioned pawns, knights, bishops, and rooks to advance and kept Black pushed up against the edge with little mobility. White developed every one of his employees. Not one piece on the back rank is on the original square from the start of the game. If a sign of good leadership is being able to develop subordinates, then White gets an A for effort. In contrast, Black has left the employees where they started.

Managing Risk

White managed the highest risk factor to the enterprise by removing his king from the middle of the board. He castled into a fortress where Black will find it more difficult to attack his king. Risk mitigation reduced the threat to the king but did not eliminate all risk because the king is always present on the board and subject to dangers of an attack (called check). A best-practice strategy in business or chess to manage risk is not to leave assets like employees or pieces unguarded or unprotected. Can you find the two pieces that White has on his team that do not have anyone protecting them? If they were captured, the opponent would have acquired them for free (hint: b2 & f4). In business you benefit from alliances with your employees, customers, and suppliers; they are designed to protect the operation. In chess, protect and guard your assets by forming alliances with your pieces.

Exhibit 2 was a contrived position used for illustrative purposes, but Exhibit 3 is not. It was taken from the highest level of play.

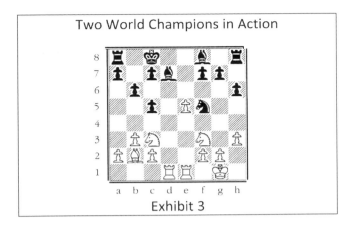

Two World Champions in Action

Exhibit 3

Both exhibits demonstrate leadership in action. Which player up to this point has demonstrated better leadership of their employees? The queens have been exchanged, and Black has two bishops since White traded one for a Black knight. Both sides have exchanged equal value, and neither has earned a profit for their efforts so far. Notice how White has situated his employees to garner the better position in both diagrams.

The White knights are centralized on c3 & f3. The rooks on d1 & e1 are "talking to each other," and the king is safe on g1. The rook on d1 has great play on the open d-file. Black has the liability of doubled pawns on the c-file while White's are all ready for action.

This game is one of the most important chess games ever played. It's the final game of the 2014 World Championship match between Magnus Carlsen and Viswanathan Anand. Why would Black, an ex-world champion who needs to win the game to stay in the match, aspire to a position where neither of his rooks or his black squared bishop has moved and his king is scrambling around in the center? Anand has seen this position before. He can visualize a future where even though White looks better, Magnus will not be able to make progress. Black will reorganize his forces and get right back into the game.

Measuring Leadership Using Chess

An important capability of a leader is to know the strengths and weaknesses of their associates. In chess, each piece has a unique capability that functions best in certain situations. At work, employees, coworkers, or competitors have unique skills and abilities. By taking time to understand how they work, you can maximize your interactions with them, enabling you to achieve peak performance. Leadership development using chess can be measured and tracked for progress. The moves made during even a casual game should be recorded so that they can be analyzed after the game.

The following questions can help evaluate your leadership skills at the board and on the job.

Chess Leadership Challenge	Business Leadership Challenge
1. Did you create an organizational environment with every piece contributing in fewer than twelve moves?	Has transformational leadership given every direct report responsibility within a reasonable time frame?
2. Can you describe what the role of each piece is in the game?	Do your employees know and execute their job descriptions?
3. Have you eliminated the highest risk factor in the game by castling the king to safety?	Are you managing systemic risk to the enterprise?
4. Are your pieces protecting each other, eliminating a common risk factor?	Are you managing employee risk factors?
5. Were you prevented from castling, and if so, how?	Has a competitor inflicted serious damage to your operation?
6. Do your games show you repeating the same patterns and getting the same results?	Are your leadership and management styles appropriate with your directs? Should they be adapted to the situation?
7. Are your visualization skills helping you see the consequences of the situation you are managing?	Are you using situational leadership to lead and manage in this unique position?
8. Are you losing to players you should be able to defeat?	Are competitors gaining ground? Did you ever have the advantage?
9. What causes inflection points in your games?	What causes your business to shift directions?
10. Are your mistakes strategic or tactical?	What company strategic or tactical mistakes have occurred?
11. Are you overlooking tactical opportunities available from the placement of your employees?	Were there tactical opportunities you did not see or did not take advantage of in your business?
12. Is it taking longer and getting harder to beat you?	Is results-based leadership securing your winning advantage?

A grandmaster-level computer, known as a chess engine, can generate moves and suggestions about better moves than the ones you chose. It is the equivalent of a consulting company available 24/7 to help navigate the difficulties in the position. This grandmaster-level analysis will identify what your play says about your underlying leadership and management skills. Insanity is doing the same thing over and over, expecting different results. In chess your mistakes are generally identifiable. It's rare for a player not to be able to castle at some point and is usually the result of a lack of adherence to good risk-management policies. The game Bachler versus Egerton in chapter 11 will clarify that situation.

Chess can help you identify your leadership style by identifying where, why and, how you position your workforce. Are you an aggressive, attack-at-every-opportunity player or a positional player? Decision-making in business, like many chess-move decisions, is often based on emotions instead of cold hard calculation. Keeping your emotions in check is a valuable skill that business and chess players cultivate.

Chess players compete in tournaments establishing a rating similar to a golf handicap or tennis rating. It becomes your competency credential in this domain. Business leaders use metrics like share price, ROI, and market share to establish their business rating. For aspiring business leaders, recognizing the ways your employees resemble the pieces on a chessboard, can provide a fresh perspective on how to get ahead.

Looking Back—Moving Forward

> Win in business with employees, in chess with pieces.

> Study the various leadership styles applicable to business.

> Invoke transformational, situational, and results-based leadership styles in chess.

> Transition to contextual leadership using the best traits from each style.

> Lead by visualizing the future.

> Drive results by understanding and utilizing the unique potential of each employee.

> ➤ Engaged employees strengthen a business; mobile chess pieces win games.

> ➤ Achieve lasting results by managing risk profitably.

To excel in your leadership position, the capabilities and limitations of your subordinates need to be understood. An effective leader will strengthen the team by studying the unique traits of their employees, which is next on our to-do list.

Chapter 2

Human Resources & Organizational Behavior—It's the Culture

"We the People..."

"Merrill Lynch brokers threaten to leave en masse" proclaims a business headline crossing the wires. That's old news from the Great Recession in the original Bank of America acquisition, right? Try the recent headlines when their brokers did not want to surrender promising leads on clients.

The United and Continental Airline merger confirmed airlines are not exempt from contention. United had a computerized, barcoded, state-of-the-art parts and maintenance system. Continental had a paper-based system. After the merger, of course they chose the paper-based system. Recently my wife and I were on a United plane anxiously waiting to depart on our Mexican vacation. The pilot came on and said they were waiting to replace a part in the cockpit, but he was having trouble getting the paperwork straight. I whispered to my wife, "This plane is in trouble." Sure enough, after five hours of delays and unsuccessfully replacing the autopilot system, the flight was canceled, and we lost one whole day of our vacation. That airline merger had been going on for years and still had issues.

It's the Culture

The large international bank where I worked for years acquired bank after bank. One thing that wasn't eliminated through the mergers, however, was the conflict generated from clashing cultures. Employees of an acquired organization can be redundant. They become "the save" the acquiring company calculated to justify the merger. Retained employees are converted to the acquirer's payroll system after the merger. In the merger, systems and methods are evaluated for a best-in-class status. It's natural for employees who remain after a merger to try hard to keep their culture intact. This is something that is seldom mentioned in the entire merger and acquisition activity: how will the two companies operate if they have different cultures after they merge?

You would think that after seven years everybody from Merrill Lynch that wasn't happy with Bank of America would have left. Years of merging activity should have made the skies even friendlier than they were. The real value after companies merge seldom meets expectations, and sometimes, as with Chrysler, it never works out and the companies divorce after giving it years to work.

Speaking at a THRIVE/Make Money Matter conference, David Bradford, the former executive of Novell, cited the differences between Novell and their acquired software company WordPerfect. The continuous infighting between sales organizations was just one symptom of conflict that was resolved only when WordPerfect was sold to Corel less than two years after the acquisition. The factor that puts these mergers at risk is culture.

Chess for centuries has generated its own culture. In some countries it is revered (Armenia), in some places it is ignored (USA), and in some it is banned (Iran). It's the same game, so how can it be so varied? It's part of the culture of that country. I still have students from India tell me I need to move the elephant when I pick up the bishop. It's part of their culture.

I'll Offer You a Draw

In 1999, Elon Musk's X.com and Peter Thiel's Confinity were locked in a heated battle to be the first company to supply eBay with an electronic payment system. Since four of the six PayPal founders had experience building bombs from their high school days, it wasn't surprising that one of their engineers came up with a plan to bomb X.com away. Instead, Mr. Thiel, a master-rated chess player, did what leading chess players do in the last round of every tournament. Rather than risk the possibility of losing it all, it's perfectly acceptable in chess to offer your opponent a draw. That means the two tournament leaders split the first and second prizes, resulting in a nice payday for both.

This merger idea could have been presented in the merger and acquisitions class of Mr. Thiel's law studies, but the impetus to hold on and fight to survive another day came from chess. X.com had cash reserves, and Confinity had the better product. So, fearful of a dot.com implosion in February 2000, the two met in a café and negotiated the draw, a fifty-fifty merger between the rivals. One month later the rivals merged and aligned their resources. As a result, the merged company survived the tech stock meltdown, yet the merger of cultures was anything but peaceful. Or as Ashlee Vance described the resulting scene: "The two companies tried hard to mesh their cultures with modest success. Groups of employees from X.com tied their computer monitors to their desk chairs with power cords and rolled them down the street to the Confinity offices to work alongside their new colleagues. But the teams could never quite see eye to eye."[1]

Two months after the merger Thiel quit. Intense technical debate over a Linux versus Microsoft platform led to a coup where Elon Musk was ousted and Peter Thiel returned as CEO. Where did Mr. Thiel get his experience to be a leading CEO? He practiced his leadership skills with sixteen pieces of plastic for years. He actively practiced leadership in August 2000 when he was in Minneapolis competing in the 2000 US Open Chess Tournament. The tournament was open to any player who paid the entry fee. Mr. Thiel got off to a rocking start before running into Grandmaster Yermolinsky, the eventual winner. All Thiel's games from the Open were published in online databases.

29

In what was the most lucrative draw offer ever made, the Musk and Thiel agreement did in fact generate a nice payday. In 2002, PayPal accepted a $1.5 billion offer from eBay, which made everyone involved very wealthy. Many of the original PayPal founders have since gone on to spawn other successful start-up companies with their proceeds. PayPal has been spun off from eBay and is now its own publicly traded company generating returns for current investors.

Differentiating Your Employees/Pieces

In *The One Thing You Need to Know...About Great Managing, Great Leading, and Sustained Individual Success*, Marcus Buckingham says that outstanding managers play chess. I'm sure he means "metaphorical" chess in their managing style with some real chess playing on their lunch hour. In class when he asks about the differences between chess and checkers, his students think chess is more difficult and more strategic. In my classes, I don't even compare the two games except to correct students that take a piece for not jumping or some such oddity. One significant difference is that checkers has been solved. Computers have determined that with best play for both sides the game ends in a draw. Even though chess computers are playing at a very high level, because of the vast order of moves (approximately 10^{120} possible moves), chess is still a long way—if ever—from being solved.

Even though Buckingham agrees with the difficulty and strategic observations, he doesn't think they convey the answer. Those with a chess background identify that in checkers all the pieces move alike. In chess all of them move differently. To be any good at chess you need to know how each piece moves, its relative strengths and weaknesses, and utilize that information in your overall game plan.

He says the management game is the same. Ordinary managers treat their employees like checkers. Everyone should have the same goals, motivations, learning styles, and personalities. Ordinary managers try to change or use the transformational leadership style with their checker-piece employees. They tell employees what is expected, help them when they need improvement, and reward those that conform to those behaviors desired and expected by management. The best mangers do the opposite of homogenizing everybody. According to Marcus Buckingham, "The one thing all great managers know about great managing is this: discover what is unique about each person and capitalize on it."[2]

Learning About Your Employees/Pieces on the Job

The strategy I used to become acquainted with my employees when I took over a management position was I asked each direct report to give me a copy of the resume they used to get hired by the company. That provided their prior work history. I contacted HR to produce a profile document that had all the current information on the employee, such as salaries, job titles, promotions, evaluations etc. When companies merge, they convert employees to one payroll system, often leaving the HR information behind or on a legacy system. Converting the data for all employees to a single reporting database is invaluable. Most HR systems have queries available to retrieve employee information. Having this information made it time for a one-on-one meeting.

In Mark Miller's *Chess not Checkers*, Brad, the new fictional CEO, would have known immediately that his administrative assistant was qualified to become the new marketing director with her resume and a profile document on his desk. Following my strategy, we need to take an in-depth inspection of the resumes of our chess employees that have already been hired.

Resume for His Royal Highness the KING

SUMMARY

I represent enterprise-wide risk to the entire organization. Nothing else matters if I am under attack. My teammates must guard me so that the enemy cannot checkmate me. If I am attacked and cannot block, move away, or capture the attacker, the game is over. Best utilization is to bide my time until the battle is winding down due to piece exchanges. Once the checkmate risk is abated, I head out into the middle of the board to assist where I can. My direct line movement of one square gives me access to any square on the board. I earn my keep by threatening, attacking, capturing, and defending. My permanent presence on the board helps the team win by assisting other pieces to checkmate the opposing king.

Work History

- Originally had a job title of ruler/general as one of the elements of ancient warfare in the Indian game of Chaturanga. In Persia my title became the king "shah" and opponents wanted my "mat" or death, so "checkmate" means "death to the king."

- Kings have played an influential role in history with King Ferdinand partnering with Queen Isabella to fund Christopher Columbus in his quest for a shortcut to India. (1492).

Objectives

- <u>Gain freedom to move</u>. At the start of the game, I am confined to a center position at the edge of the board, unable to move without a pawn moving first.

- <u>Castle into a protected position</u>. When the queen received her enhanced powers in the sixteenth century, it was risky for me to remain in the center of the board. A risk mitigation move called castling was introduced to get me safely into a fortified structure. Castling also activates a rook.

- <u>Avoid checkmate</u>. I am the only piece that remains on the board the whole game. I cannot deliver a check; I need the assistance of a rook or queen to checkmate the opponent's king.

Figure 1 shows the king in the center of the board at eight squares. This is a 62.5% improvement over the corner. Should he move to the center? *NOT* in the opening because he needs to stay safe from checkmates. But in the endgame, an active king can attack, defend, threaten, capture, and blockade.

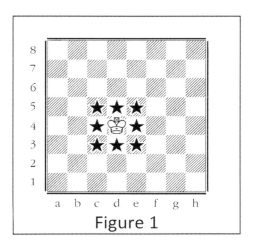

Figure 1

King Proficiency Footprint

3	5	5	5	5	5	5	3
5	8	8	8	8	8	8	5
5	8	8	8	8	8	8	5
5	8	8	8	8	8	8	5
5	8	8	8	8	8	8	5
5	8	8	8	8	8	8	5
5	8	8	8	8	8	8	5
3	5	5	5	5	5	5	3

Resume for Her Majesty the QUEEN

SUMMARY

The most powerful member of the team, I have experience in overwhelming the opposition with my power and agility. My direct linear movements allow immediate access to any square on the open board. I am capable of forming strong alliances with other pieces to develop and implement strategic projects and create a competitive tactical advantage, including checkmate.

Work History

- Originally had a job title of counselor (prime minister), one of the elements of ancient warfare in the Indian game of Chaturanga. Underwent a sex change in the fifteenth century from the king's male consort to the figure of a queen or a lady.

- Initially moved like the bishop but limited to only one square, which is half the power of the king. Queens have played an influential role in history. With the expanded powers of Catherine the Great and Elizabeth I, it's more than coincidence that the queen's power changed around 1500 AD. The promotion increased my power to the movement of the rook and bishop combined.

Objectives

- <u>Gain freedom of movement.</u> Prefer to use my ability to travel in eight different directions and operate where there are no pawns hindering my movements. An excellent attacker, I often provide the force necessary to end the game. I can play great defense for the team with my extensive board coverage and capabilities.

- <u>Avoid capture.</u> Frustrated at the start of the game being confined to the center edge of the board unable to move. Looking for a manager who understands my capabilities yet is not too careless with my assignments because if I am captured, the team usually loses.

- <u>Return to the game if captured</u>. A promoted pawn can request my return near the end of the contest in a winning moment. A satisfying assignment is when the king assists me in checkmating the opponent. I cannot checkmate alone and need another teammate to provide backup.

Figure 1 shows the queen maxing out at 27 squares in the center (d4, e4, d5, e5). An algebraic equation is queen = bishop + rook or $y = (2x + 7) + 14$ or $y = 2x + 21$ where x is the number of squares the queen is from the nearest side of the board.

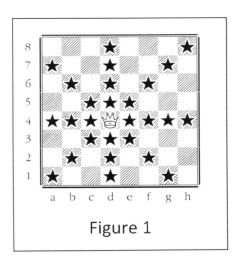

Figure 1

Queen Proficiency Footprint

21	21	21	21	21	21	21	21
21	23	23	23	23	23	23	21
21	23	25	25	25	25	23	21
21	23	25	**27**	**27**	25	23	21
21	23	25	**27**	**27**	25	23	21
21	23	25	25	25	25	23	21
21	23	23	23	23	23	23	21
21	21	21	21	21	21	21	21

Resume for the ROOK

SUMMARY
The second-most powerful member of the team, my straight-ahead attacking capability strikes fear in the enemy camp. No square is off-limits from a frontal or flank attack that occurs in one move. Prefer an unobstructed view of a rank or file where nothing hinders my direct line movements. Sequestered in the corner of the board, it will take patience and a proven plan to get me into the game. I can partner with other pieces to develop and implement strategic projects and create a competitive advantage, including checkmate. I am the other half of the castling move.

Work History
- Originally worked as a chariot during ancient warfare. One of the original pieces from the Indian game (600 A.D.) of Chaturanga that had chariots, horses, elephants, and foot soldiers, with a ruler and his minister.

- The Italian word "rocca" means "fortress," so when combined with the king's leap move, we build a fortress by castling. As the game progresses, I'm well positioned to defend my teammates and to take advantage of any enemy weaknesses that allow me to go on the offensive.

Objectives
- <u>Achieve a position that allows movement</u>. I loiter in the corner, unable to move without some of my teammates "getting off the bench" and preparing the way for my activity. Novice managers move the pawn in front of me up two squares and attempt a lift maneuver. Not advisable because you cannot castle with a moved rook and your opponent's bishops control a3 & h3.

- <u>Improve team performance</u>. Dramatically improved performance on any open file where there are no pawns blocking my way. It can be a central file or side file; just want to show my strength to the team by getting onto any open file. 7% increase in productivity for each extra square I control.

- <u>Move to the seventh rank.</u> I like to hang out on the seventh rank of a chessboard where all the pawns of my opponent reside. If I can get to the seventh, our team will have a significant—often winning—advantage. Figure 1 shows the rook in the center can go to 14 squares. An equation for the rook is a constant of $y = 14$, never varying its 14-square capability.

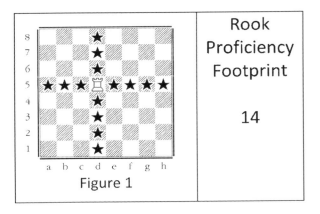

Figure 1

Resume for the BISHOP

SUMMARY

I am a quick-moving chess piece that has access to 50 percent of the chessboard. My diagonal movement confines me to either light or dark squares. This is not a limitation while there are two bishops on the team. Together we can control the entire chessboard. Proven ability to partner with other pieces to develop and implement strategic projects and create competitive advantage. Positioned next to the king and queen to provide advice about how our team should accomplish the goal of winning.

Work History

- Originally employed as an elephant, the "Beast of War," since elephant squadrons were standard components of the armies of ancient India.

- Due to the European preference of chess to replicate a king's court rather than a battlefield, the French made the piece a jester while the British made it a bishop. The absence of an elephantine figure in Europe transformed this piece into a powerful figure from the church around the fifteenth century. My unlimited diagonal moves were introduced in the sixteenth century, changing the strategy of the game.

Objectives

- <u>Help control the center</u>. I prefer to operate as close to the center as possible and where there are no pawns in my way. I cannot travel through any piece on the way to my destination. However, since pawns do exist and must remain on a dark or light square, I realize one of the bishops may be caught behind our pawns.

- <u>Gain freedom of movement</u>. At the start of the game, I am confined to the edge of the board, unable to move without a pawn move making way for my entrance to the game.

- <u>Execute a successful flanking maneuver when necessary</u>. A formation that emphasizes my strengths is when I flank or fianchetto my services down the longest diagonal of the board through the center.

Figure 1 has the bishop moving away from the side of the board gaining two squares each time. It reaches full potential in the center of the board at 13.

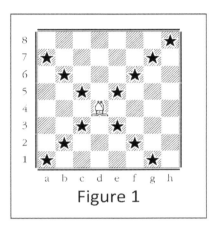

Figure 1

Bishop Proficiency Footprint

7	7	7	7	7	7	7	7
7	9	9	9	9	9	9	7
7	9	11	11	11	11	9	7
7	9	11	**13**	**13**	11	9	7
7	9	11	**13**	**13**	11	9	7
7	9	11	11	11	11	9	7
7	9	9	9	9	9	9	7
7	7	7	7	7	7	7	7

Resume for the KNIGHT

SUMMARY

A unique, powerful, experienced team member, I can travel across 100 percent of the chessboard. I am the battled soldier that fights for the kingdom. My nonlinear movement has me changing colors every move. I work in cramped positions because of my unique ability to leap over other chess pieces. Proven ability to partner with other pieces to develop and implement strategic projects and create competitive advantage by attacking behind enemy lines. Although able to traverse the entire board, quickness is not one of my strengths.

Work History

- The horse moved in the Sanskrit game precisely as the knight does in modern chess. For thirteen centuries this move has never varied. Peculiar to chess, it is a shibboleth that determines whether a board game is a descendant of chaturanga, the precursor of modern chess. Originally worked as a horse to pull the chariot that was located next to me in the corner. In the medieval European royal court I transformed from a horse into a knight riding a horse.

- Each move is a total of three squares: two in one direction and a third at a right angle. My movement creates an L-shaped path.

- I am a formidable fighting force, having singlehandedly won many campaigns. Particularly good at attacking two or three of my opponent's pieces (forking) and blockading enemy pawns.

Objectives

- Take advantage of my unique jumping ability. I operate whether anything is in my way because I can travel over any piece on the way to my destination. At the start of the game, I am the only piece on the edge of the board able to move without pawns moving.

- <u>Play offense and defense</u>. I can play offense and defense right from the early stages of the game. In the endgame, however, I cover only eight squares, so even with the help of the king, I cannot checkmate. Figure 1 shows the initial move for the knight to get to 8 squares. From the square (f3) he guards the kingside, controls half the center, and is ready to spring into an attack when the time is right. In the center, your knights are working 40 hours a week.

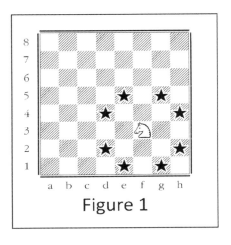

Figure 1

Knight Proficiency Footprint

2	3	4	4	4	4	3	2
3	4	6	6	6	6	4	3
4	6	8	8	8	8	6	4
4	6	8	8	8	8	6	4
4	6	8	8	8	8	6	4
4	6	8	8	8	8	6	4
3	4	6	6	6	6	4	3
2	3	4	4	4	4	3	2

Resume for the PAWN

SUMMARY

A limited-ability player that is willing to work hard—even sacrifice myself if necessary—for the team. My strengths are to protect the king in the castle and promote into another piece in the endgame. Any piece I take from the opposing team is a winning proposition. Our team seldom wins without using my services. André Philidor, one of the finest French chess players in the eighteenth century, knew about my ability and complimented my work, saying *"Pawns are the soul of chess."*

Work History

- Worked originally as a pikeman or foot soldier. My role is the army infantryman, providing the backbone of the forces. Infantry, cavalry, and artillery are expressed in chess as the pawns, the knights, and the rooks. People sometimes degrade my standing by saying, "I am just a pawn."

- In 1550 AD, I was given the capability to move up two squares, allowing my teammates to get into better positions. Unable to return to my original position, I expect to be captured in battle. The word "pawn" is indigenous to chess as it did not come from any other figure or game.

- Managers should know I do not like being alone (isolated), in front of other pawns (doubled), and behind other pawns (backward) where I am weak and subject to attack. Prefer working together with other pawns (connected), guarded by other pawns (protected), and without any opposing pawn between me and the last rank (passed). A passed pawn is often a winning advantage. A pawn on the board means we can still win.

Objectives

- <u>Move forward without leaving holes in the defense</u>. I have a "lust to expand" my way up the board. However, when I go past a square, I lose control over that square because I do not move backward. Leaving "holes" on the board is something my management is aware of.

- <u>Sacrifice myself willingly</u>. For centuries I have been offered free to my opponents in a Gambit. Willing to go along with the sacrifice for a positional or tactical advantage. My crowning achievement is advancing onto my opponent's first rank when I promote into another piece, usually a queen.

Figure 1 shows the pawn moving 1 or 2 squares forward onto any square with a star. Figure 2 shows the pawn's capturing ability, which derives from medieval battle formations. The pawn waits for something to come alongside, which it can then capture on the diagonal. Here the White pawn on d4 can capture anything that occupies c5 or e5. The pawn on f7, if advanced, usually promotes to a queen. It's poor strategy to move lots of pawns in the opening.

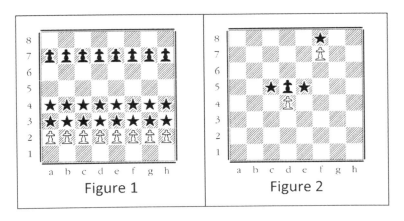

Figure 1   Figure 2

Establishing a Compensation System Using "Pay for Performance" Metrics

A key responsibility of human resources is to determine the pay practices of the company. In larger companies, that responsibility is left in the hands of the compensation department. They determine how the company will equitably pay their employees. If their pay is too low, employees leave for better opportunities. Pay too high, and the company will have the highest payroll in its industry. Some companies may want the highest pay in their industries to attract and maintain the best employees available. The key is for management to recognize that compensation is one of the tools they can use to build the kind of company they want. A low-price company will pay differently than a high-price/high-service company.

How do companies acquire information on what others in the industry and career tracks are paying? They join a professional organization like the American Compensation Association (ACA) and anonymously submit their pay information. This allows them to access the aggregated database of industry pay practices and technical tracks like engineers and computer specialists. There are also HR consulting firms that work with their clients to conduct specialized surveys of pay practice based on predetermined criteria.

Companies use this information to maintain control over what is usually their largest expense, labor costs. Consulting firms have access to this information and use it to generate statistics like how much it costs an airline to fly one passenger one mile compared to their competitors. In a competitive industry, the company with the higher labor costs has to reflect that cost in their prices in order to maintain profit margins unless they can compensate for their labor costs through higher productivity or cost-savings tactics in the other activities of the company. Higher prices can drive consumers into the arms of the competition. Companies usually do not want the distinction of highest costs and will negotiate with labor and suppliers to hold down increases to bring their costs closer to industry norms. Justifiably reducing labor costs doesn't always sit well with the employees. In specialized organizations, such as professional practices, engineering firms, and baseball teams, the return on investment for attracting and keeping the best talent justifies paying the highest salaries.

When I worked for an Occidental Petroleum (OXY) subsidiary, the new CEO instituted a pay freeze for one year for all salaried employees and gave himself a multimillion-dollar raise for doing that. He stated, "We are not in the business of hiring people." Pay scales or compensation systems are not perfect. Even if they are implemented properly from a top-down and bottom-up perspective, the pay system still doesn't resolve the issue of excessive executive pay. However, a well-thought-out pay structure can include the CEO's total compensation package so that it acts as a control on runaway compensation. This requires a strong board of directors willing to work with compensation experts and that knows how to say no. It also requires that the board understand the value of the talent they are purchasing when they hire a CEO. Sometimes it's worth paying millions to the new CEO if the ROI is in the tens of millions.

Pay for Performance

So what criteria can serve as the basis for valuing the employees on our team? In a company where an employee can make more sales, manage more people, or have more responsibility, they tend to receive higher compensation because they are generating more value for the company. In chess, it's how much the employee can accomplish, and that ultimate capability is found by being positioned in the center of the board. To see the connection between capability and value, go to our website, www.businessontheboard.com/videos, click on VIDEOS, and watch Pay for Performance.

Once the central location metrics are established, our "pay for performance" budget determines the value of our employees and how they should be compensated.

As proof that our employees resemble chess pieces not checkers, notice how each employee has a unique footprint that is well worth studying. Populate the Center Proficiency column in the following exhibit with the highest value from the Proficiency Footprint from the resume of each piece. Note that since the Q = R + B the combined center values should confirm that $27 = 14 + 13$.

Piece	Center Proficiency
♚	
♛	
♜	
♝	
♞	
♟	

Knowing each employee's proficiency will enable us to establish the relative value of each piece in relation to other members of the team. Even though this "pay for performance" salary budget has been set for centuries, for some reason the pieces don't seem to mind. Management has allocated working capital in salaries available to our employees in $9, $5, $3, and $1 denominations. One employee has an infinite value because he is not eligible for capture but a relative value of $3 expressed as $\infty/\$3$.

In line with the more valuable employee garnering a higher salary, the queen is the most proficient employee on our team, going twenty-seven places on the open board. She warrants the highest salary we can pay, which is $9. The rook has fourteen moves and gets a $5 salary, etc. The rest of our performance-based compensation system looks like this:

Piece	Center Proficiency	Relative Value
♚	8	$\infty/\$3$
♛	27	$9
♜	14	$5
♝	13	$3
♞	8	$3
♟	1	$1

The question becomes where did the seed capital come from to pay our employees? It's no different from Monopoly® where each player is given a $1,500 stake in the game. In business, investors dig into their own pockets or seek capital from various funding sources. Where did all the money in the mutual fund industry or hedge fund industry come from? People gave it to them from their paychecks or savings.

The following exhibit shows how $42 of working capital has been equitably invested in our employees in the following manner:

Piece	Accumulated Value
♚	$3
♛	$9
♜	$5x2=10
♝	$3x2=6
♞	$3x2=6
♟	$1x8=8
Total	3+9+10+6+6+8=$42

The relative values of our employees have been established. It's relative because at times their values can go up or down depending on the job they are doing and how well they are doing it. A pawn that is on the second row protecting the king is not as valuable as a pawn on the seventh rank that is ready to be promoted to a queen. Yet if the pawn that is guarding the king keeps him from being checkmated, then it has more value than a pawn that is about to reach a queening square.

Since the definition of accounting is the tracking of assets that have monetary value, by assigning a monetary value to our pieces, it is easier to account for them. We can also use these values for financial forecasting if we want to make an investment and sacrifice a piece for less than its equivalent value. If the investment works out, we will get more money back than we sacrificed. But because investments have risk, we could lose money on the deal as well. We'll see such a situation in chapter 5 where

Grandmaster Anand decides to give up a rook and receives only a bishop in return.

Managers generally have a feeling for what they pay their direct reports, but in the chess business it has to become "walking around knowledge." The value of your pieces has to be memorized. Every move made at a chessboard reflects the relative value of the pieces since the winner is usually showing a profit at the end of the game. That profit is then turned against the opponent and results in a checkmate or resignation.

But What About?

Some of my students have challenged these valuations. *If the queen is the rook and bishop combined, why isn't the queen worth 5 + 3 = 8?* The best answer I can give is that if you have a bishop it is confined to one color the whole game. The queen, by just sliding over one square, can become a bishop of the other color and attack both White and Black squares. The rook is a constant, so the queen is slightly more than a rook and a bishop. While the queen possesses the combined capabilities of a rook and a bishop, she enjoys a synergy that increases her value above and beyond the simple addition of one rook plus one bishop.

If the rook can go to fourteen squares and the bishop goes to thirteen, why is there so much discrepancy in their values? The bishop can use only 50 percent of the board. The rook can use 100 percent. The rook and the queen are considered major pieces and, with the king, can enforce a checkmate. The bishop cannot even check a king if he is on the other color. There is a "Rule of 5'" in chess: you need $5 or more to checkmate your opponent's king. If you don't have $5, you have insufficient material, and the game will end in a draw.

Some people believe the bishop is fractionally more valuable than the knight. Being long-range pieces, the two bishops can provide an advantage if the board is open. If it is all locked up with pawns, the knights can be more powerful because they can jump over any obstruction. The two bishops can be an advantage in the endgame because they can cover every square on the board. If it were definite that the bishop is worth more than the knight, you would never see one getting exchanged for the other, but that happens all the time in chess. It all depends on the position and comes through experience of knowing what your employees can do and what situation is the most beneficial to their abilities.

The king can never be captured, so how does he have a relative value? The king is always on the board. But once he is not worried about being checkmated in the endgame phase, he will leave the safety of the castle and become involved with attacking, defending, and capturing like any other piece. In the endgame, if you are not utilizing your king, you are essentially playing down a piece.

I have assigned the king an approximate relative value of $3 like the other minor pieces of the bishop and the knight. In chapter 6, we will see how Magnus Carlsen made better use of his king than Vishy Anand did with his king, which allowed Magnus to retain his world championship title.

Where did those budget numbers come from? These are historic values that have been associated with the chess pieces for centuries. They are usually associated with a pawn's value; for example, the queen is worth nine pawns, the rook is worth five pawns, etc. But what is a pawn worth? In business it can be a supreme mystery how the annual merit budget is established. Some years the company is profitable and raises are meager, and other lean years can generate the best increases. It's all relative, and as I experienced at OXY, it is management's discretion how much employees should be paid.

Looking Back—Moving Forward

- ➢ Hire the brightest, and develop a culture of accountability.
- ➢ Risking everything is for losers; a draw offer allows one to fight another day.
- ➢ Treat employees like chess pieces that have unique footprints and talents.
- ➢ Employees are not checkers who are one and the same.
- ➢ Constantly appraise the value of your employees, and pay for capability and performance.
- ➢ Invest the working capital ($42) of your employees in strategic, tactical situations.

With an appreciation of leadership styles and a familiarity with the abilities and values of our employees, the next item on our to-do list is an understanding of strategy and tactics. What is strategic thinking? How do we use it to turn sixteen angry pieces into an organized force that is up to any challenge?

Chapter 3

Strategy, Strategic Thinking, Tactics—In One Word

"What were you ...?"

"Advantage Agassi," announced the Wimbledon umpire, sitting in his raised chair high above the net at center court. It was no ordinary advantage. If Andre won the next point, he would be the year's men's champion. No one, not even Agassi himself, expected him to be in this position. It was time to return serve, and he had a strategy.

Quality strategic thinking and good decision-making ability, especially in business, are skills that every productive leader wants. These skills, like any others once developed, need to be practiced. But what do you practice with? How do you measure your results? How will you know if the decisions you make are the best ones, given the situation?

In my MBA degree program, the capstone course that pulled all the business content together was called "Policy." After completing all the content courses, it was time to view business from a 30,000-foot, big-picture view. My policy course used a book called *The Strategy Process* by Henry Mintzberg and James Brian Quinn that was two inches thick. Like all good scholarly writers, the authors defined their terms, and right on page five, they wrote: "A strategy is the pattern or plan that integrates an organization's major goals, policies, and action sequences into a cohesive whole. A well-formulated strategy helps to marshal and allocate an organization's resources into a unique and viable posture based on its relative internal competencies and shortcomings, anticipated changes in the environment, and contingent moves by intelligent opponents."[1]

If Andre had all those thoughts running through his prefrontal cortex inner voice, he would have dropped his racquet on the ground before match point even started. That definition matches closely an all-inclusive vacation. Is there anything that is not mentioned? It fills up a paragraph nicely, but once read, it is quickly forgotten. Such a definition suffers from focusing decision-making on known patterns or plans. For example, SWOT (Strengths, Weaknesses, Opportunities, and Threats) analysis is a great way to paint a picture of your company's current situation and potential. What it lacks is a way to reinvent the business by identifying "Blue Ocean" opportunities, the kind that change the nature of the space you play in. What happens when your bookstore has to compete with an invisible (to the local market) Amazon? Consider why Amazon even exists. Why didn't Sears or Target or one of the other big-box retailers anticipate shopping online and own the Amazon position? They had the money and the customers to make it happen. The Internet was up and running for at least five years before Amazon began operations.

In keeping with my introductory comments, it's best to keep your definition of strategy simple, easy to remember, and above all useful for the future. My simple one-word definition of strategy is "choice." Strategy is the choice of actions available to you given the situation. Notice the last part of the sentence because it's just as important as the first. Strategy changes as the situation changes. British Petroleum used far different strategies the day after the Gulf Coast explosion than the day before. The situation was different, and the old strategies no longer worked. Instead of business as usual, they went into disaster-recovery crisis mode. Some business decisions are better off made using the subconscious mind when an immediate response is called for. This is the same way world-class athletes, like Andre Agassi, make decisions. It will help you avoid the tendency to overanalyze and suffer "paralysis from analysis." That's a benefit of chess; you have to make a decision at some point based on the best information you have. You review the choices, analyze their value, pick the optimal one, make your move, and turn it over to your opponent. The faster you can decide, the more time you save on the clock.

Strategy Is Choice

Strategy is the choice of actions available to you given the situation.

Use the STOPS™ model Dr. Jeffrey Magee discusses in *The Trajectory Code*. **Stop** and see what issue you need to address. **Target** and think through why the issue is important. **Organize** options for addressing the issue. **Pick** which option is most viable and proceed. **Start** the process again to maintain your correct trajectory. Magee recommends applying his process to maintain the direction of your career while you remain on the correct path to your destination. These are the same steps chess players use on each move of the game. There is a fluid situation on the board, and if you want to checkmate your opponent, stay on the correct trajectory toward that goal.[2]

So what was Andre's strategy at match point that he revealed in his book, *Open*? It could have been: *I see my opponent is choking under pressure by double-faulting on his serve. Let's hope he does it again at match point.* Or he may have had a simple thought like, *Just get the ball over the net and see what happens.*

But he had choices in the matter. He had never been up championship match point at Wimbledon, and he knew at the time that he might never be in the situation again. So he decided to take full advantage and have no regrets by hitting the service return as hard and deep as he could so that his opponent would never get to the ball. The idea was: I'm going for a winner! Andre knew that in pressure situations, his opponent Goran Ivanisevic liked to serve up the middle of the court. So Andre positioned himself for that service return, but Goran netted his first serve. It was second serve, and the crowd was on their feet.

Andre's strategy was this: "Return this serve with all your strength, and if you return it hard but miss, you can live with that. ... One return, no regrets, hit harder."[3] Goran served to Andre's backhand. Andre's strategy was sound but his execution was weak, and his ball floated over the net where Goran was ready to hit a winning volley. Instead, Goran dumped the volley into the bottom of the net, and Andre was the Wimbledon champion. So in this case it was good enough to just get the ball over the net.

In business, you generate strategies in brainstorming sessions where the participants discuss ideas and list strategies for all to review. Or the firm can engage a consulting company with competitor industry knowledge to advise them on strategy generation. The best strategic planning approach is to combine a committee of in-house executives with outside consultants. The in-house team has the advantage of being close to the company's situation but the disadvantage of constantly working at the tactical level rather than the strategic. The outside consulting firm brings the latest thinking in strategic planning and can help focus the team on the 30,000-foot level where great strategies are born.

In the end, strategies derive from the phase of the game a business is in. Start-up mode, growth mode, and maturity mode have strategies that have been documented in business cases and practiced for years. The phases of a business are similar to the phases of a chess game and will be discussed in chapter 4 through chapter 6.

Larger companies may have a strategic planning and initiatives department that is responsible for reviewing situations in the marketplace. The purpose is to be ready to react if a business transaction (like an acquisition or merger partner) appears that they want to pursue or a new market is worth entering. They also may be investigating who might be interested in an asset or line of business they no longer want to maintain. Having previously looked at and analyzed their available choices, they know whether a deal is worth pursuing.

In chess a prepared variation is when one of the players analyzes the opponent's previous games at home ahead of the actual game. They are able to play out their strategically and tactically correct moves using no time while their opponent struggles to refute them by analyzing over the board. Many a chess match has been determined before the game begins because of the analysis one player did against the other. Players can attempt to steer the game into formations they know their opponent doesn't like. If your opponent likes to attack, play positional moves removing the tactics. If they like positional play, introduce "wild and crazy" tactical fireworks to take them out of their element.

In chess, the strategies may deal with improving an underperforming piece. In business, the strategies may focus on improving an underperforming division. Regardless of how the strategies are generated, they need to be listed and documented beyond brainstorming that takes place in strategy sessions. In chess the strategic alternatives under consideration are called candidate moves. A candidate move is a possible move that, from experience and reasoning, should be given serious consideration as a viable move to be played in the position. As chess players and business executives gain more experience, they become better at limiting how many candidate moves to consider.

Candidate Moves

In chess, possible strategies that are under consideration are called candidate moves.

This ability to limit the number of choices that must be considered is where humans and computers diverge in their analytic skills. Humans program computers with scenarios they want computers to analyze. These "models" then help business leaders determine what actions to consider. But if they don't program all the scenarios, there can be problems. When Congress asked AIG why their models never predicted that insuring so many subprime mortgages could backfire, they responded that their models assumed that the value of housing would always increase. Their models never incorporated the worst-case scenario because in the history of the housing industry such a collapse of homeowner equity had not occurred since the 1930s.

By failing to consider the basic principle of gravity that what goes up must come down, AIG fell into the trap known as "The Bigger Fool Theory." The idea is that a house (or anything else, for that matter) will continue to rise in price as long as a willing seller can find a willing buyer. When there are no more willing buyers, the last buyer (current owner) overpaid for the property and becomes a bigger fool than the person he or she purchased it from.

Computers with their vast calculating speeds consider many, if not all, the chess moves that can be played. Algorithms weigh the different possibilities and determine the best choice. Computer chess-playing programs have made incredible progress and now can beat 99.99 percent of all human players, including grandmasters. So that should signal the demise of chess, right? Not a chance. Grandmasters use technology to improve their play by letting computers assist them in their analysis. Which grandmaster plays most like a computer? World Champion Magnus Carlsen takes that distinction. For humans, two or three candidate moves start to reach their limit. The experience of having seen a position before as Grandmaster Anand saw in chapter 1 is invaluable.

Strategic Thinking

Analysis of the choices available, determining which one is the best and committing to act on that choice.

Once the series of possible strategic alternatives is listed, the task shifts to analyzing which of the alternatives is the best. In business or chess, the best alternative is the one that gives the greatest chance of winning. My one word for strategic thinking is "analysis." Strategic thinking is analyzing the choices available, determining which one is the best, and committing to act on that choice.

Businesses use models that analyze the variables involved in a situation yielding the best move to make for their company. Faced with decision-making in uncertainty, companies rely on software that can drill down into different scenarios—often with a financial analysis helping make the final decision. Marketers can use a SWOT analysis to lead to a quality decision. Not all decisions reflect cool-headed, calculated analysis. Emotions play a big part in decision-making, and given the choices available in business or chess, staying away from trouble can be just as beneficial as pursing an attack. A legal example is a company that settles a suit out of court for a sum of money without admitting guilt or wrongdoing.

Today, companies use big data to conduct this type of research. By tapping into massive amounts of data, companies are able to predict their best moves to a much higher level of precision than previously possible. For example, in marketing, you use particular advertising on certain TV programs but not on others because viewers of the first show are more likely to buy. Online, banner ads pop up on your favorite news website because of your past buying patterns.

Creativity in Decision-Making

During my career, I was faced with occasional situations where none of the business or chess candidate moves looked all that appealing. In chess I have encountered positions where I see two or three reasonable moves to make in the situation, but they all have drawbacks. Since tournament chess matches are played with a time control using a clock, analyzing by jumping back and forth between variations without reaching a conclusion will lead to time trouble. It's frustrating when you repeat your analysis, looking for something you missed. In handling difficult, underperforming employees, sometimes there are no good moves. Coaching, warnings, and holding back pay increases or promotions are examples of moves that at the time don't work. As a manager, this is a time for creative action either to let the troublesome employee go or possibly require training or counseling to resolve any issues.

Strategy Versus Tactics

Two terms that are used almost interchangeably in business and athletics are "strategies" and "tactics." If we reopen my policy textbook, the definition of tactics is on the very next page: "Tactics are the short-duration, adaptive, action-interaction realignments that opposing forces use to accomplish limited goals after their initial contact."[4] The use and abuse of these terms doesn't seem any clearer after that.

I've heard strategies called "things you cannot see" and tactics "things you can hold." So if I am holding a bag of potato chips, is that a tactic? But maybe not opening it is a good strategy for weight loss.

I once had a discussion with a lawyer who said strategy is wanting to be a lawyer, and tactics are all the courses you have to take to get the degree. What is tactical about being conscripted into taking certain classes if you want to become a lawyer? There might be a strategic choice of courses that meet a requirement, or a tactical opportunity to take two courses at the same time, but that simply debases the terms. A tactical opportunity for a law student would be clerking for the Supreme Court or landing an internship at a prestigious law firm. It's semantics, but chess can help improve the distinction of the terms.

Chess nomenclature can help businesspeople with the definition of tactics. All the tactics in chess have names. Many of them, such as overworked piece, clearance, skewer, desperado, double attack, remove the defender, and pin, directly correlate to actions taken in business. Tactics don't always appear in a chess position or a business situation. My one-word definition of tactics is "opportunities." Tactics are opportunities that appear during the game or in the course of business that can dramatically change the outcome of the situation.

Tactics Are Opportunities

Tactics are business opportunities that become available through placement of your resources. In chess it's through the placement of your pieces.

The challenge for business leaders is to be tactically sharp by understanding what the tactics are and when they are present. Tactics are even more powerful when aligned over several moves in a combination that can end the game on the move if strong enough. The power of tactics will be on display in chapters 4-6 in the Carlsen vs. Anand game. In chapter 10, in the Gates vs. Carlsen game, Mr. Gates missed a "remove the defender" tactic and lost on the move.

One tactic that has business and chess implications is called "desperado." A desperado tactic in chess occurs when a piece about to be captured takes any available opponent piece of lesser value. It's the "I'm going down and I'm taking you with me" scenario. If a bishop can get a pawn on the way to being captured, you cut your loss to $2. I play the tactic in the Zepada vs. Egerton example later in this chapter.

In business, a desperado employee may be a whistle-blower who has nothing left to lose and reports the company for malfeasance. Some desperado employees go home, raid the gun cabinet, return to work, and settle their issues that way. Employees from an acquired company who don't see a future in the merged organization may get desperate since they have nothing to lose except maybe their severance.

In their book, *Strategy Rules*, David Yoffie and Michal Cusumano make the case that strategy is the overriding glue that holds a company together. The strategies deployed by Bill Gates at Microsoft, Andy Grove at Intel, and Steve Jobs at Apple included looking forward and reasoning backward, not betting the entire company, helping partners leverage their technology, and building the company from their personal strengths. The authors make a convincing argument about the strength of strategy, but this may just be a case of the subjects fitting the premise. I am reminded of the demise of the Amaranth hedge fund that made outsized natural gas futures bets. Investors in the fund found out way too late to make them whole with their funds. Ah, but not all was lost as Ann Davis, Henry Sender, and Gregory Zukerman pointed out, "But some investors have a keepsake. Amaranth once sent chess sets as year-end gifts, inscribed with a quotation from the late grandmaster Alexander Kotov: It often happens that a player carries out a deep and complicated calculation, but fails to spot something elementary right at the first move."[6] Strategy rules, but tactics prevail. Wars and football games are won in the trenches, not the sidelines.

Clarifying the Distinction between Strategy and Tactics with Chess

Strategy and tactics need to be used together to reach a winning position. Most people would agree that investing is a good strategy for creating and generating future wealth. How you invest your savings determines whether you will realize a gain or a loss. Investing opportunities (tactics) avail themselves, and you have to decide whether to pursue them or not. People gave money to Bernie Madoff, knowing that investing is a smart way to generate and preserve wealth. Investing with Bernie Madoff appeared as a tactical opportunity, one in retrospect they wish had never come along. His investors did not make a strategic mistake (investing is good); they made a tactical mistake of not evaluating how he was making his outlandish returns (Ponzis are bad).

In chess, tactical opportunities appear frequently, and they need to be evaluated regarding whether they are worth pursuing into some kind of an advantage. Strategy is always there; it's the tactics that come and go. Chess can help distinguish between a strategic mistake and a tactical error. Two of my United States Chess Federation (USCF) rated tournament chess games will demonstrate the difference between a strategic mistake and a tactical one. Both mistakes determined the final outcome of the game. Once the mistakes were made, because of the quality of my opponent's play, my game was lost.

Game 1 - A Losing Strategic Move

One of my challenges as I sat down for play in a suburban Chicago tournament was to make decisions critical to overcoming my highly experienced master-level opponent. We were scheduled in the first round of five games to be played over two days. Unfortunately for me, I didn't have my critical decision-making skills ready and working at the outset of the match. I learned that it's hard to sit down and analyze without warning up.

I may be putting the cart before the horse here. Strategies will be covered in chapters 4 through 6, and tactics in chapter 7. But if you have a chess background, you can play through the moves online to recall the strategies and tactics you have used in the past. If you have limited or no chess background, link to the following game and click on move 19 by pointing at that move in the list. This is the move and position where the strategic mistake occurs.

People who take my training ask if they need to know how to play chess. They don't want to get involved if they don't know how. My answer is that they have the opportunity to learn the most. If a management opportunity becomes available, are you going to respond with "I don't know how to manage, never done it"? Take the challenge. Those afraid of jumping into the water without swimming lessons can jump ahead to chapters 4 through 7 and come back to these two encounters later. Decisions, decisions …

Click on the following link to have the game Tyehimba vs. Egerton appear on your screen.

http://www.365chess.com/game.php?gid=1326246

Tyehimba, Bem (2230) - Egerton, James [B82]
Oak Park Master Challenge (1), 1996

Click through the first six moves to the following diagram.

1.e4 c5 2.Nf3 d6 3.d4 cxd4 4.Nxd4 Nf6 5.Nc3 a6 6.f4 Qc7

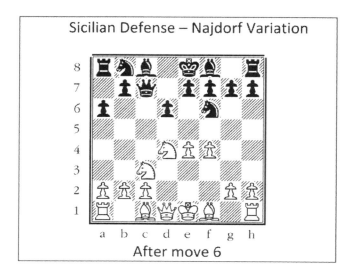

My defense to White's king-pawn opening move is called the Sicilian Defense. White usually plays on the kingside of the board and Black on the queenside. The Sicilian is the most active defense, and each player is going to deploy his employees to critical squares. 5...a6 was a preventive move keeping a White piece out of b5. Named after Grandmaster Miguel Nadjorf, this defense has been used by world champions for years.

Move six is the fork in the road for this defense. Both players had used only seconds in making their opening moves, which were played from preference and memory. White chose to advance his f-pawn two squares and set up a formation that will eventually attack my king's castle—not the most popular, but playable. This stage of the business game was about targeting a segment of the market to control (the center) and employee development.

Click through the next five moves to the following diagram after move eleven.

7.Bd3 e6 8.a4 Nc6 9.Nf3 Be7 10.0–0 0–0 11.Kh1 Bd7

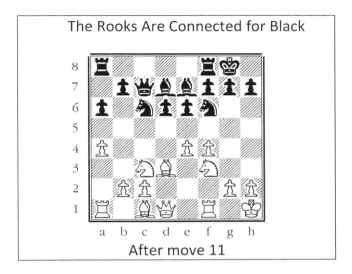

The Rooks Are Connected for Black

After move 11

Something similar to the leadership diagram from chapter 1 developed. In this game, however, as Black I didn't let my opponent get all the good territory on the board. Notice my rooks were "talking to each other," and White had yet to make that happen.

I've developed my minor pieces and followed good business practice of risk management. I mitigated the risk to my king by castling. With my resources deployed, I was engaged in the business of attacking my competition and looking to generate a profit or competitive advantage.

Click through the next six moves to the following diagram after move 17.

12.Qe1 Nb4 13.Qg3 Nxd3 14.cxd3 Rfd8 15.Be3 b5 16.a5 Qb7 17.Nd4 b4

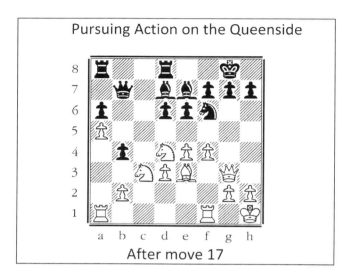

After move 17

White developed his bishop on the g1-a7 diagonal and set his intentions on getting it to b6, a weak square on my queenside. White ignored that my knight attacked his bishop on d3, so for an even exchange he allowed me to capture it—so much for the bishop being worth more than the knight. I expanded on the queenside, not worrying about exchanges by advancing my b-pawn. I threatened his $3 knight with my $1 pawn, so White will move the knight or lose $2. The result will be either a lost knight or a knight out of position. Either way, I gain an advantage.

A Game Theory Moment

In game theory, strategic moves contain threats, promises, or commitments. A threat takes the form of "do what I say or else." This is a promise: "If you do A, I will cooperate and do B." That doesn't happen very often in chess—maybe offering a draw to your opponent or repeating a move three times. A commitment is an unconditional pledge to make a certain move. Again, unless it's a forced recapture, such cooperation or pledging is rare in chess or business. I was using the game-winning threat of "move your knight or you lose it."

18.Na4 Bxa4 19.Rxa4

White moved his knight to the a-file, intending to outpost it on b6, a location where no pawn would be able to remove it. That would be a job for one of my pieces. Thinking that if the knight got to b6 it would paralyze my queenside activity, I overreacted and made my position worse by taking the knight. The three scenarios for facing a threat are described in chapter 9 under the "Legal" section. This is an instance of overestimating the power of White's knight.

Being the lower-rated player with over 32:1 odds against winning this game, I caved into the fear of my master-strength opponent instead of playing the board. I should have let him put the knight on b6 because it lacked support from his other pieces. I also gave my advantage of the two bishops back and missed the best move with 18...e5 hitting in the center when moves like 19. Nf5 Bxf5 20. exf5 Rac8 gave me a lasting advantage. My analysis didn't reflect reality and played off poor emotional reasoning. If good strategic thinking leads to better decision-making, it was not on my radar at the moment.

Strategic Moves

"Strategic moves aren't acts of desperation - they're moves that are added to an existing game and can change the outcome of a game dramatically."[7]

A teaching moment here is to be very careful with your emotions as a manager. That instinctive move you want to make may well be the right one, but if it is, you should be able to confirm it before you move with a little planning and clear-headed thinking. One business example is when a midlevel manager is invited to the boardroom to present a plan for their department. You're playing with the big people, and you have to bring your best game. It's a fearsome challenge, but you have to check your fear before you enter the boardroom.

Inflection Point of the Game

19...d5?

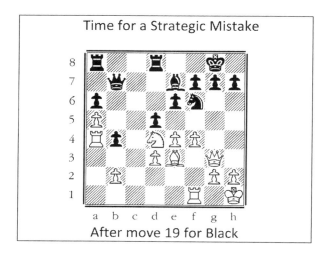

Time for a Strategic Mistake

After move 19 for Black

A critical moment (a.k.a. an inflection point, according to Mr. Grove) had just occurred. After this move, the game edged firmly to White's advantage. In retrospect, my move 19...d5 was a strategic mistake. The purpose was to open up the center of the board, giving my pieces better scope. On a capture, my rook on d8 gets better, and his weakness on d3 is attackable.

If I wanted to open up the position, my opponent wanted to keep the center closed. He had a perfect move to do that. My move was a strategic and not a tactical mistake since it was my choice to open up the center of the board. My strategy was faulty because opening the center was not guaranteed. I had played d5 in many of my Sicilian Defense games but only after I had played e5. Here e5 is an open square, which my opponent was able to powerfully occupy with one of his pawns.

20.e5 Ne8

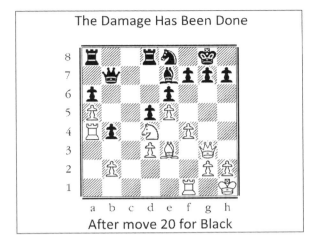

The Damage Has Been Done

After move 20 for Black

Learning to Anticipate

A skill that proficient business-people and chess players have is the ability to anticipate their opponent's next move. My intention was to open up the position, but instead my move allowed my opponent to close up the position. All the action will take place around my king. Even more important, my move allows my opponent to drive away my knight on f6, making it easier for him to attack my king by removing one of the best defenders of the castle.

Employee utilization should have guided my candidate move selection here. Instead of retreating the knight to the back rank, 20...Nh5 attacking the White queen and 21...g6 defending the knight with the possibility of helping to defend against the attack was a better formation to play. Click through the rest of the moves to see how quickly my game collapses.

My next several moves are strategically incomprehensible. In retrospect, I was under the influence that if I exchanged more pieces, his attack would go away. A good general strategy when under attack is to exchange forces, but here I was just exacerbating his attack. The last piece I should have exchanged was my bishop, which left me with weaknesses on the black squares. But I did it and had to live with the consequences.

The Auditor's Report
The Scoreboard

Each player has exchanged three minor pieces and a pawn. The accountants have made the appropriate entries and aren't concerned about the capital since each player has received "book" value for their players. An evaluation of the position shows that while material assets are even, Black is strategically lost.

Chess originated in the days when scoreboards did not exist. Imagine a basketball game without a scoreboard. Without knowing the score, who is winning, and how much time is left, the game becomes an exercise in frustration. The scoreboard for a chess player is kept in their head. It's one of the reasons chess is a difficult spectator game. The game could end on any move, so a scoreboard would just be relative. However, you can bet the players know the score!

White – 10 Black – 10

The remaining moves were:
**21.f5 Qd7 22.Raa1 Bc5 23.f6 Bxd4
24.Bxd4 g6 25.Qg5 Rdc8 26.Qh6 Rc2
27.Rf3 Rac8 28.Rh3 1–0**

After my strategic mistake on move 19, my game was lost. My opponent did more with his employees than I did with mine. The significant difference in our playing abilities (ratings) showed with my critical lapses in judgment. Trading off my black square bishop and not keeping it on f8 let White post his pieces wherever he wanted. Before move 19, the grandmaster chess-playing computer gave me a slight advantage. Move 19 was an inflection point that started an unrecoverable downtrend, which eventually led to checkmate.

Game 2 - A Losing Tactical Move

The next game demonstrated a losing tactical mistake on my part. Played twelve years later at the US Open in Dallas, Texas, it was the fourth round game. Once the tactic appeared in the situation, an inflection point occurred, and my game never recovered from the downtrend. The deciding tactic in this game has a bona fide business application. A "trapped piece" quickly determined the outcome of the game. In business, a trapped employee is one locked into a position that has no chance for advancement or movement. It may be a trapped financial trader who is locked into losing positions that cannot be unwound. If the situation doesn't change soon, the employee can go desperado and leave for another opportunity. Sometimes the employee stays, leading a quiet life of desperation like a chess piece that sits on the same square move after move. Once a chess piece is trapped, the opponent will try to attack and win it. Once a tenuous financial position is exposed (trapped), competitors take advantage by buying opposite positions, exacerbating the loss of the financial trader. My bishop went desperado, but it didn't change the final results.

Click on the following link, and choose the first game on the list to have the game Zepeda vs. Egerton appear on the screen. The second small icon under "View" on the left opens the game in a new window for best viewing.

http://chesstempo.com/gamedb/player/56420

This is a different database (one of several that include my games). This site also includes analytics to the right. It shows the most common moves in the positon with the winning percentages. This is a valuable tool for players who want to get better in the opening. In business, it's having a system that tells you what the best practice is in the situation you are facing—not a bad idea to have the answer key while you are taking the test. Access to this type of online data is why tournament chess has become vigilant about technology not being used in over-the-board games.

Zepeda, Lorena (2161) - Egerton, James (2045) [B90]
US op 109th Dallas (4), 05.08.2008

1.e4 c5 2.Nf3 d6 3.d4 cxd4 4.Nxd4 Nf6 5.Nc3 a6 6.Be3 Ng4

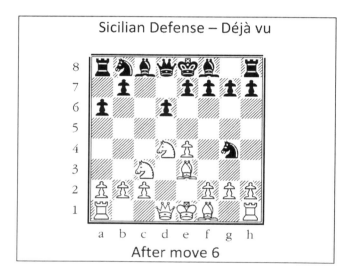

Sicilian Defense – Déjà vu

After move 6

The first five moves were exactly the same as the previous game. This is how the players pick up time on the clock, making their first several moves in seconds. Here White chose the most popular alternative on move six, called the English Attack against the Sicilian Najdorf. I decided to chase after the bishop, and White allowed me to capture it, giving me an easy equality right out of the opening. Notice the White queen cannot capture my knight on g4 because the bishop on c8 is protecting it. That would be a $9 vs. $3 capital loss in her game.

A Draw Is a Draw Is a Draw

A silly way to end the game here is to bring the bishop back to c1, Black returns his knight to f6, the bishop comes to e3, the knight attacks it again with Ng4, return and repeat a third time for a draw. Nobody does that, right? In McShane versus Nakamura, Las Vegas, 2015, that's exactly what was played in a big-money tournament. The players were not allowed to draw in fewer than thirty moves, but the director had to let the result stand. Nakamura went on to win the $100,000 first prize in part because of this quick draw. Because players have to pay their own way into chess tournaments, taking the draw allows them to share a reasonable payoff. Spectators, however, want to see action, not a quiet agreement before things happen.

Until chess can overcome this obstacle, major sponsors will shy away from chess competition. Imagine at 3-all in the first set of the Wimbledon final if Novak called Roger up to the net and offered a draw and he took it. When I played over these moves in my class, a young lady in the back of the room stood up and exclaimed, "That's ridiculous," which broke the entire class into laughter. Yes, it's ridiculous; however, in business, it may be the best strategy and is no different from Peter Thiel offering Elon Musk a draw when they merged to form PayPal.

Click through the next six moves to the following diagram after move 12.

7.Qd2 Nxe3 8.Qxe3 e5 9.Nb3 Be7 10.g3 Be6 11.Bg2 0–0 12.0–0 Nd7

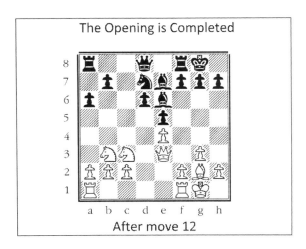

The Opening is Completed

After move 12

Both players have completed their opening moves, clearing out the back rank, castling, and developing all the minor pieces. Black was able to again get the bishop pair from White's weak 7.Qd2 move. The database shows that the most popular move here was 7.Bg5, saving the bishop. By flanking (fianchetto) her white square bishop to g2, it is classified as a bad bishop because the pawn on e4 blocks the diagonal. Black has a backward pawn on d6 on a half-open file, but experience has shown it is not easy to attack that pawn. Both kings have mitigated their risk, and now the players will maneuver (reorganize) the employees onto better squares. Management realizes their employees are not always in the best formations and reorganize on a regular basis.

Click through the next four moves to the following diagram after move 16.

13.Rad1 Nb6 14.Nd2 Rc8 15.h4 Bg4 16.Rc1 Rc6

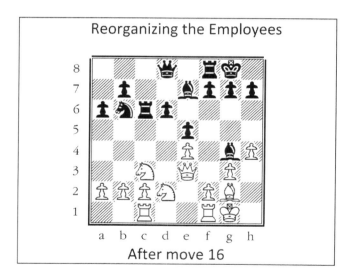

The players continued to put their employees on the best squares they can find. White put her knight on d2 to prevent my knight from getting to c4. White put her rook on d1, and my bishop promptly dislodged it with Bg4.

By playing 15...Bg4 however, I introduced one of the biggest risk factors in chess or business. I had an unprotected asset because the bishop on g4 had no backup. Employees work best when they form alliances, whether they are in sales or engineering. Good teamwork is a sign of a leader who knows how to get the best out of their employees.

Click through the next six moves to the following diagram after move 22.

17.b3 Qc8 18.Ndb1 Rd8 19.a4 Bf8 20.Qd2 Nd7 21.Nd5 Nc5 22.Na3 Ne6?

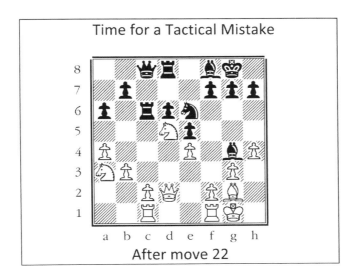

Time for a Tactical Mistake

After move 22

Both players had been reorganizing their employees by maneuvering them into better positions. I got significant pressure on the c-file when White moved up the b-pawn. She had an outpost on d5 for her knight, an example of exploiting the weakness of the e-pawn advancing because only my bishop or my knight could get the knight out of there. With my last move, I intended to position my knight to d4.

However, my move had definite drawbacks. I had interfered with the protection of the bishop from the queen on c8. I also had blocked any retreat the bishop on g4 could make. I had set myself up for a tactic. Can you see it? This position demonstrated why tactics are opportunities. If my opponent didn't see her opportunity on this move, I could take some evasive action and her opportunity would be gone. In business, leaders can be completely steeped in solid strategy, but as the Amaranth trader found out, an involved calculation can fail to spot something elementary on the first move.

23.f3! Bh5 24.g4 Bxg4 25.fxg4

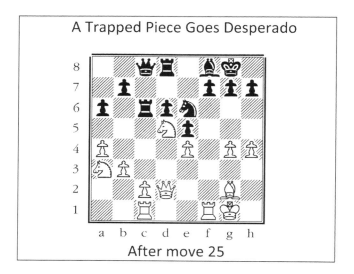

A Trapped Piece Goes Desperado

After move 25

Seeing the bishop had no retreat, White threatened it with a pawn. If the knight were not on e6 and this move were played, I could simply play 23...Bh3 and trade off the White square bishops because my queen on c8 was aligned with the bishop. My knight move created a tactical opportunity, my opponent saw it and took advantage of it, and the game for all intents and purposes was over.

Rather than let the pawn capture on h5 and get my bishop for nothing, I went desperado and took the pawn on g4, reducing my loss to $2. If I were to play this again, I would retreat to g6, then when h5 was played, I would capture the h5 pawn. That would leave her with a weak pawn on h5 and a compromised castle formation, giving some compensation for the lost piece. Having a $2 profit, White has a winning margin, and the remaining moves demonstrate her "technique."

The Auditor's Report
Each player exchanged one minor piece, and my opponent has a bishop for which I have a pawn. The accountants have made the appropriate entries showing that White is $2 ahead, a winning profit margin. Later, she increased that margin, and I resigned on move 46 totally lost.
White – 6 Black – 4

The remaining moves were:
25...Nd4 26.Qd1 b5 27.c3 Ne6 28.axb5 axb5 29.Nxb5 Ra6 30.c4 Qc5+ 31.Kh1 Rda8 32.Qf3 f6 33.Qc3 Rb8 34.Ra1 Rxa1 35.Rxa1 Qf2 36.Qe1 Qb2 37.Rb1 Qa2 38.Nb4 Qa8 39.Ra1 Qb7 40.Nd5 Nc5 41.Ra7 Qc8 42.Qg3 Ne6 43.g5 fxg5 44.Bh3 Rxb5 45.cxb5 Qc1+ 46.Qg1 1–0

Strategic mistakes in business can lead to tactical opportunities for competitors if they are able to seize the moment. Two mistaken financial strategies cost their companies billions of dollars while competitors gained at their expense.

Too Big to Fail

On a warm August afternoon, while much of Wall Street was off on vacation in the Hamptons, a story came across the wires that Russia was going to pay their workers instead of the interest on their bonds. This financial missile scored a direct hit on one firm in particular—Long Term Capital Management. Long a darling of Wall Street, they had all the banks in their back pocket and were led by PhD economists who were able to see the future through their models. LTCM was a big holder of Russian bonds. Unable to lose money because of the $100 billion they had under management, they were seen as too large an institution that had too many connections and partners to deal with financially to not live up to their agreements. Hence, they were too big to fail.

In chess, a strategic mistake is often followed by an opponent taking advantage of tactical opportunities created by the mistake. Once LTCM realized the precarious position they were in, it was time to unload some of those totally illiquid instruments. While their strategy up to that point had been successful, the firm was losing millions of dollars each day. One endgame exit strategy was to find a partner with which to merge. Any firm that was interested had to do their due diligence and inspect their portfolio. Once the books were opened and potential partners consequently left the deal on the table, a curious thing started to happen: the market was flooded with orders, taking the LTCM positions even lower. It seems other firms sensed a tactical opportunity and took advantage of the situation. That's similar to a poker player who reveals his hand to his competitor and then asks if they want to split the pot. The problem was if LTCM couldn't make good on their investments, the entire financial community would have been in chaos.

Postgame analysis of a chess contest is a way to reveal the reason for a loss. The epilogue of *When Genius Failed* provides the black box of what brought LTCM crashing down to earth. The Russian bonds were the spark that started the fire, but they, along with other positions, were only one-third of the firm's holdings and alone were recoverable. Swaps and equity volatility were two-thirds of the positions of the firm. LTCM became too big in these markets, causing a distortion of the efficiency they were trading. Add in a leverage of 30-1 meant they were leveraged and illiquid, which the author terms a version of Russian roulette. Their models were based on predictable past behaviors. According to Roger Lowenstein, "The professors overlooked the fact that people, traders included, are not always reasonable. ... No matter what the models say, traders are not machines guided by silicon chips; they are impressionable and imitative; they run in flocks and retreat in hordes."[8]

In a precursor to the 2008 financial crisis, the Federal Reserve became involved and mediated an agreement between fourteen financial firms to take over LTCM. After a matter of time, the positions were sold, the markets returned to normal, and a lesson that should have been learned about too big to fail had been lost. The only bank that refused to participate in the bailout was Bear Stearns. Federal Reserve Chairman Bernanke later coined the term "TITF—too interconnected to fail" as the reason that some banks cannot be allowed to enter bankruptcy. The term applied to LTCM, but it was the reason the Federal Reserve bailed out Bear Stearns in the 2008 financial crisis, allowing them to be acquired by JP Morgan Chase & Co. They were too interconnected to fail.

"A Complete Tempest in a Teapot"

In April 2012, a tempest in a teapot is what the CEO of JPMorgan Chase & Co. thought he was dealing with. After surviving the tumultuous 2008 financial crisis, the JPM CEO wanted his bank to boost profits, even if that meant taking more risk, so the bank applied a strategy to boost profits. The bank risk management requirement that anything over a $20 million loss was to be liquidated became a casualty. The positions taken by the London traders were originally designed to hedge against downside economic consequences from the positions the bank held from the Washington Mutual acquisition.

Cultural and technical differences between the London traders and New York risk managers exacerbated the problem. The new JPM strategy was to wind down the positions the London whale had acquired. Originally, Chief Investment Officer Ina Drew assured Mr. Dimon that the London trades were being properly managed but that they were getting squeezed by hedge funds. But just like Ms. Zepada noticed a tactical opportunity in our chess game, a hedge fund manager on this side of the Atlantic saw something out of alignment and immediately went into action.

Boaz Weinstein was a chess master at sixteen, a blackjack ace who has been banned from the Bellagio casino for card counting, and a credit derivative player in his mid-twenties. Scott Patterson and Serena Ng reported, "Colleagues say Mr. Weinstein believed his chess skill gave him an ability to see several moves ahead in trading. One day in 2005, a Russian employee on the trading desk challenged Mr. Weinstein to a 'Blindfold' chess match in which Mr. Weinstein would play with his back to the board. With more than 100 employees watching, some placing bets, Mr. Weinstein won in about two hours."[9]

Mr. Weinstein had made hundreds of millions in dollars of profits for Deutsche Bank in 2006-2007, earning a decade worth of profits while he was there. In the high stakes of financial markets, Mr. Weinstein had a record of his own as being the whale. In 2008 he was in charge of global credit trading for all of Deutsche Bank. He took positions in corporate bonds and protected them with credit-default swaps that insured against the bonds defaulting. But as the financial crisis deepened, banks and insurance companies backed away from issuing new swaps because by then Bear Stearns had been acquired by JPMorgan, Merrill Lynch was acquired by Bank of America, Lehman Brothers had gone bankrupt, and the government was taking over Freddie Mac, Fannie Mae, and AIG. The Deutsche Bank management, looking at all the losses piling up on Mr. Weinstein's trades, forced him to sell his positions, resulting in a $1.8 billion loss. He left the bank and started his own hedge fund called "Saba," which is Hebrew for "grandfatherly wisdom."

While chess playing and market expertise both require the ability to visualize the future, Mr. Weinstein doesn't think you need a chess background to be a good trader. But a tactical opportunity got him his first break into Wall Street, and it came about from his chess ability. Writing for the *New York Times*, Azam Ahmed stated, "Having failed to land a summer job at Goldman Sachs, Mr. Weinstein ran into a senior partner in the bathroom on his way out. The partner, a chess expert, had played Weinstein numerous times and quickly arranged more meetings for him."[10]

Like a master-level chess player waiting for a tactical opportunity, the Saba hedge fund manager was now playing the pieces in a finance game and began harpooning the London Whale. Boaz Weinstein started buying the positions that JPM trader Bruno Iksil was selling, and at first, they weren't profitable. He had to wait months to learn that Iksil was on the other side of the trading.. At a conference coordinated by William Ackman, the same shareholder activist that gave Bob McDonald at Proctor & Gamble his headache, Mr. Weinstein fired the shot across the bow of JPM that got everyone's attention. He announced his best trade at the moment was buying the same index that the London whale was shorting.[11] When the European debt crisis became an issue, his trades turned profitable and drove a multibillion-dollar hole into JPMorgan.

Back at JPM, Jamie Dimon retracted his statement about the seriousness of the $3 billion loss. He testified before Congress about what happened, agreed to huge fines for the lack of oversight, and used the skewer tactic on his chief investment officer. In her article "The Woman Who Took the Fall for JPMorgan," Susan Dominus documented how everyone knew someone had to take the fall for such a huge loss. In chess, when the king or more important piece cannot take the loss, they step aside, and the piece behind them takes the hit. In this case the CEO requested and received the resignation of his CIO. In February 2011, in front of hundreds of senior bank leaders, Mr. Dimon admonished them to be bold. He singled out his CIO as someone who was bold. Sixteen months later, boldness was a weakness, and she was gone. And who knew a whale could speak? In a letter he provided to financial publications recently, Mr. Iksil deplored being made the media scapegoat because his trades were "initiated, approved, mandated and monitored" by senior management.[12]

These financial examples show how strategy and tactics are related. Like the strategic mistake I made against Mr. Tyehimba, LTCM and JPM invoked a strategy that, without proper oversight became a disaster. Out of those strategic mistakes came tactical opportunities like Ms. Zepeda saw in my trapped bishop. Mr. Weinstein got more than a $3 bishop for his effort, but he first had to see the London whale was trapped to take advantage of the situation.

Looking Back—Moving Forward

➤ Strategy is the choice of actions in a situation.

➤ Consider strategic choices like candidate moves in chess.

➤ Strategic thinking is analysis of the choices under consideration.

➤ Tactics are opportunities that require detection and execution.

➤ Strategic moves contain threats, promises, or commitments.

➤ Inflection points occur in business and chess.

➤ Learning to anticipate is an acquired skill.

With strategy (choice), strategic thinking (analysis), and tactics (opportunities) in our rearview mirror, we'll combine those by taking our leadership and employee knowledge to the next level. My two chess games served as examples of a strategic and a tactical mistake, but the level of play was way beneath those of world chess champions. If we look up to the highest level, what can we learn from observing two world chess champions plying their trade? Certainly few if any of us will ever play chess at their level, but we would like to lead our companies the way they conduct their business on the board.

In the next three chapters we observe the play of Grandmasters Magnus Carlsen and Viswanathan Anand. There are pearls of knowledge to be gleaned from observing their play. We find those pearls by taking a deeper dive into the strategies they use, taking their game through opening (start-up), middlegame (growth), and endgame (maturity) modes. The last game of their match determining the 2014 world chess champion had everything on the line. Magnus has the title, which he took from Anand in 2013, and now Anand wants it back. The challenge? Make better use of your sixteen angry pieces—that's all.

Chapter 4

Opening: Leadership Phase – The Entrepreneurial Mode

"Lead us not into ..."

If you want to get out of Memphis, Tennessee, by air, you'd better board your plane before 8:00 p.m., or you'll be leaving in a container. At 8:00 p.m. the Memphis airport closes down to commercial traffic, shuts off the lights, and sends everyone home to a late dinner. But for some, dinner will have to wait because after 8:00 p.m. the airport becomes a nocturnal focal point of activity for thousands of Federal Express employees.

As the FedEx "Super Hub" springs to life, workers begin to process the nightly tsunami of packages bound for destinations all over the world. They unload the inbound containers and sort thousands of packages and envelopes into outbound containers according to their intended destinations. Out on the tarmac, workers load the outbound containers onto the awaiting aircraft. The departing planes then disappear into the night sky, making the promise of next-day delivery a reality.

On an average night, 2.2 million packages go through the hub. That's slightly more than the six that came through on the first night FedEx began operations.

FedEx accumulates statistics about volumes from the package pickups made during the day. They use this data to determine the size of the various aircraft needed to make their deliveries on time. How much time do they have available for the turnaround? The clock on the wall will tell you. Just like chess players have to make forty moves in two hours, FedEx employees have to move millions of packages before their clock expires.

The dream of next-day delivery would not be possible without the company having made a critical strategic decision during its opening phase of existence. Every day FedEx takes advantage of the principle of centralization. The idea of a central location where all the packages arrive, get sorted, and rerouted to their destination is the hub (and spoke) form of operation. During their early days, clients found it hard to believe that if a package needed to go from Chicago to Milwaukee it had to go through Memphis. So that was not a point that was brought to the customer's attention. Instead it was the promise: "When it absolutely, positively has to be there overnight."

I witnessed complexity being simplified in just hours during a management seminar conducted by FedEx. The successful nightly exhibition of teamwork results from placing their employees in the right position, which makes incredible things happen. Observing automated miles of conveyer belts handle the barcoded packages during the sort, where a piston punches a package off one conveyer belt onto another, is an impressive utilization of automation. Click the following link to see how that happens.

https://www.youtube.com/watch?v=v-Q7Tmw85Xs

The Principle of Centralization

The distance between San Diego, California, and Bangor, Maine, is 3,200 miles, a convenient number to divide by the eight files of a chessboard. Each file of a chessboard (denoted by the letters a-h) when overlaid on a map of the continental US yields a file 400 miles wide. The geographical center of the United States is Lebanon, Kansas, which means Lebanon is located at the intersection of the squares e4, d4, e5, and d5 on a chessboard. Memphis is about 750 miles southeast from Lebanon, 350 miles south and 400 miles east. Locating Memphis on a chessboard puts it on the e4 square right in the middle of the board.

The FedEx story is one of quick development and dogged pursuit. Determined that a central hub was the best way to operate economically, FedEx settled on a location before its launch on June 18, 1971. To select the hub, the company's founder, a charismatic CEO who demonstrated a transformational leadership style, knew that the site had to be south of the bad northern snowstorms and north of the coastal hurricanes. If you want to move a package from Seattle to San Diego overnight and your hub is in Miami, good luck with flight times and avoiding the disruptions of storms like Andrew and Katrina.

Originally located in Little Rock, Arkansas, the company's growth plans quickly revealed that their then current Adams Field facility was too small. The search for a new hub began. A nearby air force field lacked infrastructure and labor. But a little more than 100 miles up the road was Memphis, and it was perfect. It had the correct instrumented runway configuration, a bountiful labor market, and a developed city, which made the new home ideal. To be successful at chess, recognizing where to be positioned is paramount to gaining a competitive advantage.

The Importance of Employee Development

During his tenure at General Electric, if you couldn't find Jack Welch in his office, a good place to check was in a classroom where he groomed the future leaders of his company. Noel Tichy's book *Succession* describes Welch's role in reengineering the GE model of employee talent development at their training facility in Crotonville, New York. Tichy recalls that Welch wanted a "f****** revolution" to occur on how future talent should be developed at GE. Out with the old business case model and in with new GE-related, on-the-job, experience-building opportunities. Today, GE executive leadership training, known as corporate audit staff (CAS), is a five-year program, and only 2 percent finish the program. Because the program is loaded with client-based field experience, young potential executives spend typical 100-hour weeks on projects. Instead of competing against each other, collaboration with team-building and leadership training enables them to develop an extensive network of executive level contacts.[1] Tichy's premise is that companies who develop a pipeline of internal transformational leaders have the best record of successful corporate leadership transition. Even after leaving GE, Welch continues to champion the importance of employee development through his corporate business schools and books.

In line with the GE model, many successful companies now use a corporate university concept to groom their future leaders. Developing their employees internally is a best practice of leading companies. FedEx uses their Leadership Evaluation and Awareness Program (LEAP) to help identify and develop their management candidates.

Andre Agassi is also interested in the development of future employees. He built and operates a charter school in Las Vegas, Nevada, where accountability sets the foundation. Longer days generate 25 percent more time on task. Teachers have annual renewals, and with 1,000 kids waiting to enroll, students and parents know the value of their opportunity. What's missing is tennis courts because, according to Agassi, "The idea that I succeed at your demise doesn't fit the culture."[2] There is room to measure their results because Las Vegas ranks fifth in American school district size and last in students advancing to college. Andre's purpose after retiring from tennis is to focus on impact.

In her book, *Focus on Impact*, Wendy Lipton-Dibner defines impact as "the measurable difference you create in people's lives as the direct result of contact with you, your team and your company's message, marketing, products, and services."[3] To be successful at chess, developing the workforce under your control to make a measurable impact is a critical skill to master.

Managing Risk in Business or Chess

A matter of concern for every businessperson is the assumption of risk and how to manage it. The earliest risk-management record is from Babylon around 2100 BC. "Bottomry" was a form of insurance where a boat owner pledged the bottom of his boat for the money to buy cargo. If his ship sank, he did not have to pay the debt.[4]

Risk to a business can be external or internal. An external risk is a fire that destroys the operating facility. An internal risk is over projecting sales based on a management decision that loses money. While usually considered negative, risk can have a positive outcome. When a company like FedEx prevails over numerous implausible difficulties to become successful, it makes their reward all the more gratifying.

In *Changing How the World Does Business*, Roger Frock addressed how things would have been different if an adverse risk factor had happened at the wrong moment for FedEx. Among them, what if the Federal Reserve accepted the FedEx check-delivery proposal, what if United Parcel Service had agreed to pick up and deliver for FedEx, what if Pan Am had sold the planes FedEx needed to expand to someone else, what if Emery or UPS started immediate competition, what if the Arab Oil Embargo had a bigger impact, what if the banks had foreclosed, what if airline deregulation hadn't happened, and what if a planned *coup d'état* of the CEO had taken place?[5] Any of these "what ifs" would have doomed FedEx. There will always be risks that cannot be eliminated because innovation and all the risks that entails is a requisite for success.

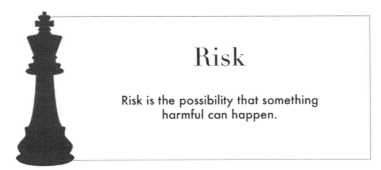

Risk

Risk is the possibility that something harmful can happen.

Assessing the risk is determining what the harm could be. Risk management means creating corporate policy and organizing, planning, controlling, and directing an organization's resources in order to avoid harm and mitigate harm if it occurs.

One of the best places to look for the risks associated with a company is in their annual report. Pages of documentation list the different risk factors that keep management awake at night. Risk management is discussed in the 2014 annual report for JPMorgan Chase & Co. under management's discussion and analysis. In the 2014 annual report for Occidental Petroleum, a global energy company, the risk factors are more external as they search for and acquire the resources the company needs to bring to market. In chess, players operate as their own risk manager. They determine the amount of risk they want to accept and whether it is ultimately enough to win the game.

Risk factors (RFs) of a large bank, international energy company, and a chess game:

JPMorgan Chase (JPM)	Occidental Petroleum (OXY)	Chess
Enterprise-wide	Commodity Pricing	King exposure to attacks
Credit	Restructuring	Undefended assets (files)
Market	Delays or Cost Overruns	1 or more unprotected pieces
Country	Governmental Actions	Weakened pawn formations
Model	Political Instability	Lack of mobility
Principal	Competitive Environment	Underdeveloped resources
Operational	Judgmental Reserves	2 or more pieces attacked
Legal and Compliance	Climate Change	Too much responsibility
Fiduciary	Catastrophes	Desperado competitors
Reputation	Cyber Attacks	Job duty interference
Liquidity	Reserve Addition Fluctuation	Reorganizing/Maneuvering
Cyber Security	Prices, Interest Rates, Credit	Sacrificing

When listed side-by-side, risk-factor commonalities of business to chess have numerous parallels. For JPM, an enterprise-wide risk factor is managing risk to protect the safety and soundness of the firm. The ultimate risk factor to the firm in chess is a king exposed to attack. Because he is the enterprise, if he is checkmated, operations cease immediately. To OXY, restructuring the company is like the reorganizing or maneuvering that chess players attempt with their pieces. The moves may or may not meet the requirement of being successful. JPM and OXY share the risk of countries within which they operate taking adverse actions to their firms.

Liquidity risk to JPM is not having the funding available to support its assets. In chess that would be immobile or underdeveloped resources unable to support the objective of winning. OXY faces a competitive environment; chess players must deal with desperado competitors who are competing to win. For OXY, political instability can lead to interference with the accomplishment of what they are attempting. In chess our own or our opponent's pieces can interfere with our objectives. The fluctuating commodity price of oil at OXY resembles a sacrifice in chess where the relative value of a piece is ignored if it generates a superior return like checkmate. At JPM and OXY, one person is not responsible for managing all of these risks; a chess player doesn't have that option.

Four Options for Managing Risk

Avoidance

When managing risk there are four options a business or chess player can follow. One is to avoid the risk altogether. Don't operate in that country or acquire a firm if the risk is too high. Don't give the company a loan if you think you will not be repaid. In chess the only way to avoid defeat is not play the game at all. Once the first move is made, it's game on, and if played to conclusion, your king may suffer the ultimate loss.

Mitigation

A second method is to mitigate the risk. In business, invoke and monitor processes that lessen the possibility of the risk occurring. At JPM set up a diversified portfolio of loans. At OXY operate in numerous locations so that if one country cuts off an oil supply, another can pick it up. In chess the biggest risk-mitigation factor is castling with the king. Get him to a safe harbor while the war rages on around him.

Transfer

A third method is to spread or transfer the risk to someone else. For business that means having insurance so that the risk resides with the insurance company. They can replenish the money needed to replace the lost assets if the risk occurs. In chess a risk transfer is to always keep a pawn on the team so that if it gets promoted, a queen can reappear on the board with a winning advantage. A material advantage in a chess game is a form of insurance. If during a game you are facing a raging attack and are ahead in material, one technique to break an attacker is to trade off or return the material to your opponent with a counter sacrifice. If you still have a better position after the trade, the material assets return to even but you have a promising future.

Acceptance

The fourth method is to accept the risk as you are able to live with it. At JPM, if a London whale wants to take risky positions, as long as the positions make money for the bank, it's fine. If they are losing trades, however, that is another story. At OXY if you want to drill offshore for oil, a platform explosion will always be possible. In chess if you don't want to castle and prefer to leave your king in the middle of a raging battle, then you will have to live with the consequences. The Bachler versus Egerton game in chapter 11 demonstrates the risks of that strategy.

Three Strategies in the Opening or Startup

In *Zero to One, Notes on Startups, or How to Build the Future*, Peter Thiel says, "A startup is the largest group of people you can convince of a plan to build a different future."[6] There are critical things great companies get right at the beginning. Thiel's law is this: "A startup messed up at its foundation cannot be fixed. Beginnings are special. They are different from all that comes afterward."[7] In chess, the opening of the game determines what comes after in the middlegame. If the opening gets messed up and your opponent takes advantage of your weak foundation, the game may be over. To lay the foundation correctly, businesses use different strategies, but three of the most common are used in chess. The shared strategies are targeting a market (where to play), allocating, and developing resources while managing risk. In business that translates to who is your target customer, what customer needs or wants are your resources satisfying, and can you mitigate risk long enough to be successful?

In chess three strategies in the opening or start-up phase used repeatedly are:

1. **Centralize** by playing for the center of the board for optimal team mobility.

2. **Develop** your pieces to occupy, control, or exert pressure across the board.

3. **Castle** with the king to address risk management to the most important asset.

The start of a chess game features a highly immobile workforce. In his leadership book *Chess not Checkers*, Mark Miller says, "The more pieces you involve in the game, the greater your chances of winning."[8] Only two of our eight pieces enjoy any freedom to move at all. From the "Getting Off to a Good Start" video you watched earlier, we know that grandmasters use only two moves regularly to start a game. Moving the pawn in front of the king or the queen up two squares increases the mobility count from two to five. Once the pieces have freedom to move, activating them according to their proficiency footprint continues to build a solid formation. Sequestering the king is the best way to establish longevity.

Transformational Leadership in Business or Chess

The transformational leadership style that Jack Welch used at GE and Fred Smith used at FedEx is needed to conduct a successful chess opening. Sixteen pieces are the largest group of employees you will ever have to build a different future. But without a vision from their leader on how each employee is supposed to architect a future, not much will be accomplished.

Blake had just become the fifth CEO in ten years at his new company. His employees were engaged, but he felt they weren't being led correctly. His mentor told him, "If you want to lead a high performance organization, you've got to play chess, not checkers."[9] Blake felt that his chess pieces were just randomly placed at various place on the board. The mentor also told Blake if he would leverage the unique capabilities of each employee under his control, it would increase his chance of victory.[10] Putting that advice into practice, Blake elevated his mythical company to success the way Kathryn did at DecisionTech because they both transformed the people working for them. It's time to watch two real leaders transform their identical workforces into a high-performance organization. They aren't going to accomplish that by playing checkers. They will do it on a chessboard during a world championship chess match.

Two World Champions Put It All on the Line

We're in Sochi, Russia, to observe game eleven of the 2014 World Championship chess match between Norwegian Grandmaster Magnus Carlsen and challenger Indian Grandmaster Viswanathan Anand. "Vishy" had the world champion title until 2013 when Magnus took it away in a match in Anand's homeland of Chennai, India. The next year, Anand played really well in a qualifying tournament, won the event, and was entitled to challenge Magnus. This was not because he was due a rematch. Anand deserved this because he finished ahead of the rest of the best of world-class chess grandmasters. There are only two games left in their twelve-game match, and Anand needs to win one of the last two to have any chance of regaining his title.

Click on the following link to have the game Carlsen vs. Anand appear on your screen.

http://www.365chess.com/game.php?gid=3918815

Carlsen, Magnus (2863) - Anand, Viswanathan (2792) [C67]
World Championship Sochi (11), 23.11.2014

1.e4 e5

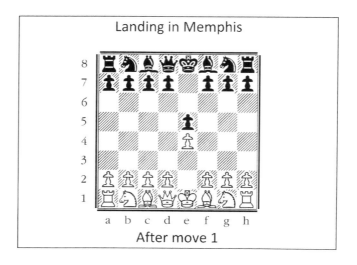

Landing in Memphis

After move 1

Magnus Moves His Pawn to Memphis

Magnus uses his king's pawn to put a stake right in the middle of the board. This is a move used successfully for centuries and is still going strong. Anand has numerous defenses at his disposal but chooses a double king-pawn response. In the days of Napoleon, these were the only moves known to be played.

2.Nf3 Nc6 3.Bb5 Nf6

All four of these moves demonstrate employee development. White developed a knight to f3 immediately, making the knight as proficient as possible. As stated on his resume, his job is to defend the upcoming castle formation. At the same time, he is on offense, threatening the pawn on e5. "Hey, 'Vishy,' want to give me your king-pawn?" asks the knight. There is only one good way to defend the e5 pawn, and of course, Grandmaster Anand found and used it by playing his knight to c6. 2...Nc6 is the best move because it:

1. Defends the e5 pawn
2. Develops a piece
3. Optimizes the knight's capability by moving it toward the center
4. Doesn't block any other teammate

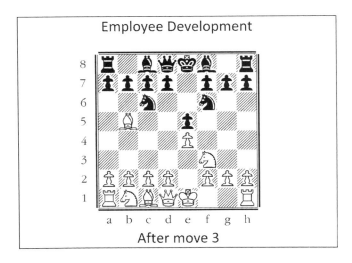

Employee Development

After move 3

Obstructing the development of other pieces on your team is not a good opening strategy. We will see Bill Gates fall into this situation against Magnus Carlsen in chapter 10. It is only the third move, and the interacting of the pieces has Magnus introducing the first tactic of the game. Known as the Ruy Lopez or Spanish opening, these moves are the most popular double king-pawn plan available. Anand delegated his knight on c6 with the responsibility of protecting the e5 pawn. That's his job for the moment. If he isn't on the board though, the pawn is unprotected. Magnus is threatening a "remove the defender" tactic. Like employees who quit or are fired, they immediately no longer have any responsibility to others at the company.

If the bishop captures the knight on c6, the White knight can capture the pawn on e5, realizing a $1 profit on move four. The bounty cannot be kept, however, if Black recaptures with the d-pawn. If White's knight proceeds to take the e-pawn, Black's queen arrives on d4 with a tactic called a "double attack." The knight and the e-pawn are both attacked, White moves the more valuable knight back to f3, and Black captures on e4 with check and can equalize easily.

The most popular alternative here has been 3...a6, putting the question to the bishop, which usually retreats to a4, and then the knight comes out to f6. Anand goes straight ahead with the employee developing move 3...Nf6, attacking White's pawn on e4 with what is known as the Berlin Defense of the Ruy Lopez.

At this point in game two of this match, Magnus played 4. d3 to protect the e4 pawn. He went on to win that game in thirty-five moves and took a one-game lead in the match. That game is at the following link:

http://www.365chess.com/game.php?gid=3917668

So why did Magnus mess with success? Why not repeat the same moves and win another game in the same manner? That's the psychology of chess at work here. Magnus appears to be convinced that Anand has found an improvement somewhere; otherwise, he wouldn't repeat the same moves.

Each player has a team of grandmaster coaches (called seconds) who work together to help their player make the best move at every turn. 4. d3 is a solid move that, once the white square bishop has been deployed, allows the black square bishop to head out as well. This is how each of the players deploys transformational leadership to implement their vision of how the team will be positioned to compete. It's a logical flow, like a football play that has been designed in the locker room, practiced on the field, and called during the game. These players have seen this play so many times they could make the moves in their sleep.

Magnus is preparing to mitigate the risk to his king by getting him safely into the castle. This is one of the benefits of king-pawn openings (called Open games) versus queen-pawn openings (called Closed games). White is able to mitigate his king risk earlier, and the battle can start in earnest. In this game Anand has another idea about what to do with his king.

4.0–0 Nxe4 5.d4 Nd6

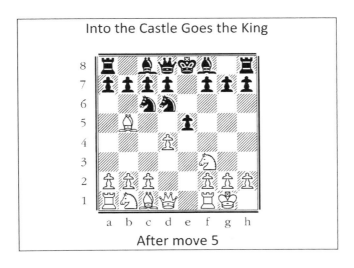

Into the Castle Goes the King

After move 5

Magnus ignored the threat to his king pawn and went ahead with castling. Having played and analyzed this position before, they both know that if Black tries to hold onto the pawn lead, he will just get further behind in development. By taking the pawn, Anand now has his king lined up on a semi-open file ready for the White rook to jump on e1.

Magnus takes advantage of his opponent keeping his king in the middle of the board by opening lines that target Black's king. Going after the king can involve giving up some material if your pieces can take advantage of that asset, which is the open e-file; hence, he plays 5. d4, which brings the other bishop into the game and further threatens to open up the center of the board. Anand is not comfortable with his knight on the e-file, so he retreats it to d6 with the first major game-threatening attack.

Do you see what he is attacking? When he moved his bishop to b5, Magnus created a serious risk factor in his game. It's the unprotected asset on b5. Anand is threatening to take the free bishop and create a winning profit margin of $3. Players at this level do not miss such silly threats. New players to the game miss them all the time.

What Do Those Numbers Mean?

You may have wondered what that letter and number combination [C67] means at the end of the title to this game. It's called the Encyclopedia of Chess Opening (ECO) classification number. The openings have all been categorized in a database, and if you want to look at games that have this position, then [C67] is the way to find them—just like the call number for finding a book in the library. The previous game had a different move with 4. d3, so it is classified as [C65]. And what are those large numbers next to their names? Those are their ELO chess ratings indicating the player's strength. It's their golf handicap, tennis rating, or bowling average, and Magnus has the highest rating in the world. Anand is not far behind, but he is the lower-rated player, which is based on recent tournament results and experience.

6.Bxc6 dxc6 7.dxe5 Nf5

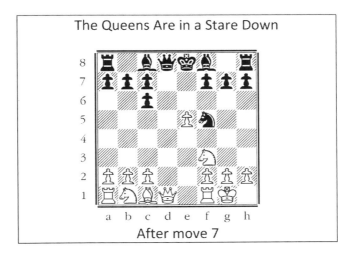

The Queens Are in a Stare Down

After move 7

Magnus, of course, saw his bishop was loose and traded it off for Black's knight. Black took it back with the d-pawn. Magnus captured on e5, getting his pawn back. That profit margin didn't last long. The Black knight on d6 was attacked by the pawn on e5. It must move and headed for f5. Now a situation where the queens are opposing each other on the d-file has occurred.

Should you trade or keep them on the board? That's the decision Magnus had to make.

8.Qxd8+ Kxd8 9.h3 Bd7

Magnus takes advantage of the queen trade, which denies Anand one of the best privileges of the game. The only way for Anand to recapture his queen is with his king, and once he moves, castling is lost. This position has to be to Magnus' advantage since there are plenty of forces left on the board to cause a wandering king problems.

95

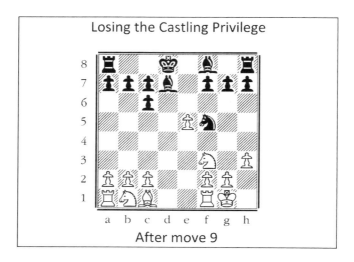

Losing the Castling Privilege

After move 9

Both players know that with the queens traded off, the king can survive in the center. One long-term reason the king is okay in the center is that the game will be entering the endgame before long. During the endgame, the king wants to be in the center. It's closer to Memphis where the king can exert his ability to move in any direction to full advantage.

Another reason to castle is to develop a rook and get them connected on the back rank. That is going to take some time, but Anand goes patiently about "castling by hand." He will make all the moves that make it look like he castled, but he'll have to make progress one move at a time instead of the quick two-piece move that Magnus made on move four. Anand knows that if Magnus cannot exploit his advantages, then within a few moves, his employees will be just as proficient.

Repeat or Break the Pattern?

9...Bd7 is new. In game seven of the match, Anand played 9...Ke8, and after 122 moves the game ended in a draw. For those willing to wade through the moves, here is the link.

http://www.365chess.com/game.php?gid=3918074

That was a thorough test of endgame skills by both players. One point to consider here is just how much energy these two players consumed sitting on the edge of their seats, analyzing and making all the moves needed to complete this game. To Magnus, it was "another lap in the race," which just got him closer to the finish line.

Reminiscent of the 2009 Federer vs. Roddick Wimbledon men's final match that was tied up through the fifth set, Andy Roddick had his serve broken for the first time in the seventy-seventh game of the Wimbledon men's final. That one break of Roddick's serve, after more than four hours and fifteen minutes of play on Center Court, was all that Roger Federer needed to take the fifth set and the title 16-14.

Usually after such a long, involved endgame, the next game features a quick draw where the players recover their energy levels for another game. By move twenty-eight in the next game, a bishop and knight endgame was peacefully played out to a forty-one-move draw. As Dr. Jim Loehr and Tony Schwartz describe in *The Power of Full Engagement*, busy executives as well as chess players know that "energy, not time, is the fundamental currency of high performance."[11]

In game nine of the match, the players again repeated the position up to move nine. That game ended in a twenty-move draw. Both players agreed to repeat the position three times to save their energy for another game. Each draw helped Magnus get closer to retaining his world championship title. The moves of that game can be found at this link:

http://www.365chess.com/game.php?gid=3918813

10.Nc3 h6 11.b3 Kc8

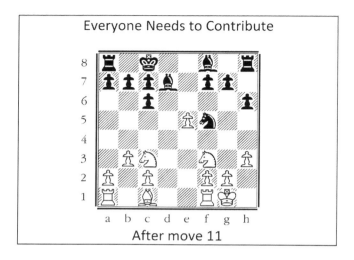

Everyone Needs to Contribute

After move 11

Employee development is still the current objective, even with the queens having departed. Black is going to untangle his back rank, and White will probe for any available weaknesses. Magnus positions his queen knight to its optimal position. Black prevented the White bishop from reaching g5 with his preventive (prophylactic) pawn push to h6. Each player is trying to deprive the other player from getting any significant advantage through placement of their employees. If Plan A is out, switch to Plan B. Magnus realized his bishop on c1 could not get to g5, so he decided to open up another diagonal for that piece. He will fianchetto his bishop and have it run right through the center of the board. Right now the pawn on e5 will limit the scope, but that pawn has potential to move. Black has a plan to place his king on b7 and slides him over yet another square on his journey to a safer place. Each player is still trying to transform his employees into their optimal positions.

12.Bb2 c5 13.Rad1 b6 14.Rfe1 Be6

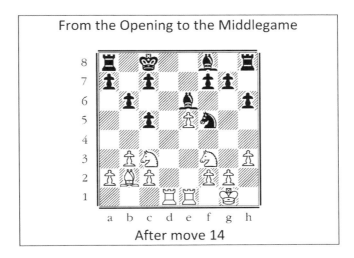

From the Opening to the Middlegame

After move 14

Magnus, as planned, moved his bishop to b2, clearing out his back rank for his rooks to get into the game. Black obstructed his black square bishop by pushing to 12...c5. With the two bishops, if Black can keep Magnus from getting a knight outpost, he has great chances. In an employee-enhancing display of power, Magnus moves his a-file rook over to the open d-file. This is the only open file on the board, and Magnus has his rook on it.

During a chess game, possession of an open file or diagonal can prove to be a valuable asset. Not too many moves into the future, this rook advances well into the competition's position. Black creates a square for his king on b7 to reside. Anand doesn't have to worry about creating any white square weaknesses because Magnus does not have a white square bishop anymore. He traded it on move six. Magnus activates his other rook, getting behind the e-pawn for support. Anand wants to move his king to b7, but right now he is guarding the bishop on d7, so he moves the bishop out of danger and stops the e-pawn for the moment.

> ## The Auditor's Report
> Both players have exchanged their queen, a minor piece, and a pawn. The accountants have made the appropriate entries and aren't concerned about the value of the lost capital since each player has received "book" value for their players. An evaluation of the position shows that material assets are even and each team has $29 worth of working capital still invested in the employees.
> White – 13 Black – 13

We have reached the Exhibit 3 position from chapter 1. Magnus has transformed every one of his employees into a purposeful force. The problem is that right now Black doesn't have any weaknesses and is slowly unwinding his position. Only one of four central squares is occupied, so that portends well for Anand's bishops, which like open diagonals. Every one of White's pieces has moved; three of Anand's are still on their original squares. Anand's team has analyzed this position and knows it is just a matter of time before his employees will be in a position to challenge Magnus' forces.

Looking Back—Moving Forward

➤ Lead your pieces with transformational leadership skills in start-up or opening mode.
➤ Prioritize centralization, employee development, and castling in the opening.
➤ Scrutinize your business game for risk factors.
➤ Circumvent risk by avoiding, mitigating, transferring, or accepting it.
➤ Visualize the power of either repeating or breaking a pattern.

➢ Maintain patience to get total contribution from each employee piece.

Businesses in start-up or opening mode have different needs and follow different strategies than their growing or mature counterparts. The leaders have a vision of how their business game will proceed, and often that means taking the company public and offering shares to investors. In the middlegame, attacking and defending create a unique situation requiring sound strategies, tactical awareness, and a different style of leadership. Even though the queens were traded, there is still plenty of challenge in making use of the angry pieces left. Magnus and Vishy are ready to lead their respective businesses into the middlegame.

Chapter 5

Middlegame:
Managing Phase - Making a Profit

"Right in the ... of something"

Attacks blasted across Bob McDonald's desk. Three years into his tenure as CEO of Proctor and Gamble (P&G), his efforts to continue with the initiatives of his successful predecessor were not going well. Poor economic conditions and cost-conscious consumers smashed sales for many of the P&G brands, and P&G's stock price flat-lined under his command. His main attacker was shareholder activist William Ackman. After having acquired a 1 percent stake in P&G, Ackman accused McDonald of being inept and demanded his removal. Even though Ackman's shareholder activism with JC Penney and Target had stumbled and eventually ran its course, McDonald decided on a different approach. He would confront his attacker face-to-face. As the story was told in the *Wall Street Journal*, "Ackman greeted McDonald with a 75-page litany of complaints about his three years at the helm of the consumer-products giant, poor results, eroding investor confidence and sagging employee morale."[1] Two P&G

board members were present at the meeting and afterwards, along with the rest of the board, gave McDonald a complete vote of confidence. All was quiet at the Cincinnati headquarters for the moment.

Being in the Middle

Centralization is often expressed as being in the middle. It's being in between the top layer of management and layers of the workforce. This book is directed toward managers in the middle of the organization. Openings in chess have been around for centuries, all committed to books where nothing new will be discovered. It's been done before. Endgames are categorized by what material remains on the board. The theory about the remaining pieces you have left requires expertise in using them to win the game. In business, start-up strategies are well known. Some lead to success, others to failure. Endgames determine the final outcome of a chess game or a business. So where is the action happening? What new stuff is being discovered? It happens when the game leaves the opening and transitions to the middlegame.

The middlegame is unresolved. It's where fresh, new ideas based on strategies and tactics occur. A company in its middlegame faces daily challenges where new ideas are needed to accomplish objectives. Based upon what has preceded in the opening, alternative strategies are undertaken because there is a unique situation present on the board. You're on your own. Every department directed by a middle manager is unique. You have unique employees that bring knowledge and skills to the department, thus requiring a different type of leadership. Being able to manage the situation is the new requirement. After all, it's called "middle management," not "middle leadership." Problems and issues need to be resolved in the middle since not everything should get pushed up the chain of command. That's the responsibility of middle management.

Middle managers take direction from top decision-level executives. They are expected to lead and implement the strategies and directives from above. But who is your boss in a chess game? It's your opponent. On certain days, the good bosses will go along with all your plans and create weaknesses you can exploit, such as knowledge they don't have. They can exercise poor judgement, resulting in an easy game. They can promote you and give you challenging assignments and corresponding rewards. They allow you to be the king running your own department.

But on a different day they can be the bad boss—the enemy that frustrates your plans by removing employees from your department during the game. They can make life difficult and deny you opportunities. They can dictate who is going to be on the team or who has to go. They can stymie your strategies while playing under-promotion tactics, like bringing in employees from outside the company to handle responsibilities. Your bad boss can cause your demise through a reorganization leading to resignation. You are a pawn on their chessboard.

In chess your compliant opponents can make it easy for you by misplaying their pieces, playing into your strategies, overlooking tactics in the position, or leaving assets unprotected. Their lack of experience can lead to an easy day for you at the office and a short one for your opponents.

Or your difficult opponents can dictate what you will be forced to do. They can frustrate your strategies, utilize tactical opportunities against you, and trade off your valuable pieces if it is to their advantage. They can reorganize their pieces to your detriment, which can lead to your demise through resignation. Sound familiar?

It doesn't seem that long ago when I was managing my systems department of twelve people that my boss came in and told me he was reassigning two of my employees to another project that was falling behind schedule. What about the systems they were working on? They can be on call for an emergency. Can I bring in a consultant? Will those employees ever come back? No and no. Once a piece is removed from the game, it doesn't come back unless through a promotion of a pawn. My boss was an opponent capturing the pieces I needed to win the respect of my clients and maintain their systems. Just like that, two of my employees were captured. In chess, you can lose only one employee per move.

In another instance, when my assistant left, I thought I would have some say on who the replacement would be. Instead, I was told who my new assistant was going to be. The bosses were playing chess with their employees, and one person needed to be transferred out (clearance) into my department to allow another person in the other department to be promoted. It is best to be a team player and go along with the realignment, but it didn't make my life any easier.

Decision-Making in Uncertainty (Attack/Defend)

While middle managers operate at a micro-level inside their mature company, companies in a middlegame acceleration or growth stage operate at a macro-level. Both levels are subject to multiple competitive attacks. The initial stage of developing resources and managing risk is transitioned to attacking competitors. If they don't have any competitors, the struggle is to keep it that way. Companies struggle to make and maintain a profit or competitive advantage, and once they have one, they battle to maintain it. In chess, middlegame attacks are more severe than opening salvos and, due to their intensity, often determine the outcome of the game. In chapter 4, Magnus and Vishy attacked each other as early as the second move. But the assaults were superficial and easily defended since the full complement of their workforce was not deployed.

In the middlegame, chess players use three strategies that companies use in their operations:

1. **Attack** your opponent by capturing pieces and enhancing your control of the board. In business, deploy strategies and tactics deigned to gain market share. In both, strike hard and strike fast.

2. **Win** in chess by taking pieces and gaining a material advantage. In business, do it by gaining a dominating market share (capturing customers) before your competition enters the market.

3. **Exchange** in chess by trading off all the forces the opponent has left, thereby reducing your opponent's options to defend their king. In business, you defend your kingdom by raising barriers to entry to your new market. Taking a dominating market share, for example, gives your opponent pause to consider if attacking you is worth the investment. They may have better things to do with their marketing budget than gain a second-tier position in your market.

In *The Attacker's Advantage*, Ram Charan envisages that companies that turn uncertainty into breakthrough opportunities will become winners. "The attacker's advantage is the ability to detect ahead of others, those forces that are radically reshaping your market place, then position your business to make the next move first. ... The more you embrace uncertainty and practice the skills to deal with it, the more self-confidence you will develop and the better prepared you will be to lead."[2]

In chess, uncertainty begins when a new move or position occurs and you have to practice leadership that requires perceptual acuity—that requires you to see opportunity in the new situation, seek a way to take advantage of the opportunity, and transition your way forward by making employees capable of meeting the new opportunity.[3]

In game three of their match, Magnus played 4. d3 against Anand's starting moves and won. In games seven and nine Vishy played 9...Ke8 against Magnus' exact previous moves, and both games ended in a draw. In this, the eleventh game of their twelve-game world championship match, Anand played 9...Bd7 against the same previous moves by Magnus. So this is where the uncertainty of dealing with something new occurred. Did Anand find an improvement over his previous play that would give him a better chance of winning than his 9...Ke8 play?

Since a new situation had been created, a different form of leadership was required in this middlegame, and that is the situational leadership style. Being able to switch from opening-based transformational leadership to middlegame-based situational leadership and forthcoming endgame results-based leadership is what I call contextual leadership. It's leading using the context of the situation as guidance. The actual and potential positions of this game gave both players the opportunity to win or lose.

Attacking Intensifies in the Middlegame

When does a business typically go from the beginning or opening set of strategies to a middlegame or execution phase? One example is when a company is big enough to go public. Since the owners are eager to let the rest of the world in on the company's success, they offer stock to the public. On their initial public offering (IPO) day, lost is the comfort of the self-controlled, private-company environment. The structure of a small number of individual investors where financial information did not have to be released publicly and where a proven successful model is working is foregone. After a company goes public and is traded on an exchange, the middlegame activity of attacking begins in earnest, and a new set of bosses and regulators are introduced into the game.

Facebook Leaves the Opening and Jumps into Middlegame

A company that went from the safety of the opening to the complications of the middlegame is Facebook. For years they remained private. Facebook was led by an illustrious CEO who created a friend sharing information software system on his college campus. He wanted to grow the company, expand into new markets, acquire more users and revenue and going public was the way to achieve that. But the day the company went public new attacks began.

The trouble started on the first day. The initial offering of the stock was riddled with technical problems. Investors were angry and immediately started attacking Facebook because activities didn't happen according to initial public offering (IPO) specifications. Facebook faced various attacks from parties that didn't exist in the opening phase of their company. These middlegame attacks were reflected in their share price and included leadership questions on whether the CEO was capable of leading the company into the next phase. The lawsuits are taking years to resolve from the problems incurred on day one of middlegame public operation. Recently a judge ruled that the claims against Facebook can be consolidated into a class-action suit. The share price is over $100, so anybody who bought and held the stock has certainly made a profit. But once the attacking starts, it can be difficult to stop. The *Wall Street Journal* described Facebook's "botched" public offering as being a "legal morass" citing "about 50" lawsuits, "hundreds" of potential arbitration claims, a huge decrease of 47% that "erased $38 billion" in value, and failures to inform investors about key details relating to reduced earnings and revenue estimates.[4]

While Facebook botched its IPO and suffered the consequences, the company nevertheless retained its number one market-share position in the social media space. It isn't whether you will be attacked or not. The fact is you will be attacked. How you deal with the attack is what shapes you as a leader.

How do companies attack each other during the middlegame? They do it through pricing, by offering a competing product or service, by taking away clients, or through advertising. Companies can attack each other by attempting to acquire their businesses in either a friendly or hostile takeover situation. Corporate raiders can attack a company by requesting seats on their boards. Hedge funds or pension plans that hold positions of company stock can attempt to influence management. Breaking up the company and hiring new management are often the changes the attackers want the company to make. Mr. Ackman was playing those takeover cards with P&G, and Carl Icahn had played the role of shareholder activist with Apple, Dell, US Steel, and TWA, among others.

Defending in the Middlegame

In the zero-sum game of chess and (in some respects) business, if you aren't the attacker, then you are defending. Popularized by Napoleon's military campaigns, attacking became preferred because you are carrying the initiative, your resources are taking advantage of your competitor's potential weaknesses, and you are dictating the outcome of the game. Defending requires very precise reactions to the movements of your opponent. You have to look for threats, understand what the threat means, and then take action to deal with the threats.

In tennis, the player who is on the attack is in control of the point. If you ask most players, they would prefer to be on the attack because they are dictating the course of action. They are driving their opponent off the court with well-placed shots. However, it doesn't mean the defender is lost. The defender can hit a lob shot into the air to break up the momentum. That will buy time to get back into a good position on the court and resume the point with a rally. Maybe the opponent will hit an overhead shot into the net off your lob, and by playing good defense, you may actually win the point.

Introduce Complications

In chess, your appropriately placed pieces on the board reap the benefits of activity. An attack may involve going after a particular piece or directly at the king. A good or bad decision in this phase can determine the outcome of the game as my chapter 3 games against Tyehimba and Zepeda proved. When a chess player or company is losing, a good strategy is to complicate the process. Make the game difficult so that your opponent might not find the right way to proceed and allow you to get back into the game. Even small companies can complicate things for their opponents through tactics like new product offerings or fast turnaround on orders. Small has the advantage of speed.

Companies sue each other over patent infringement ideas to slow down progress and play out the complications in court. An option of the defender is to offer some material like a pawn to stop the attack and allow the position to stabilize. Another strategy to fend off an attack is to trade pieces. Your opponent will find it difficult to continue a chess attack if all his pieces are back in the box. A way to fend off a shareholder activist is to trade off a couple seats on the board of directors. Buying back the activist stock, known as "greenmail," however, is illegal.

Firms defend themselves by buying back their shares and raising the value of all the shareholders, including the activist's shares. Companies may remove an executive that is not performing up to expectations. They may sell off weak divisions to concentrate on core businesses. Another defense is to counterattack—make it a race to see who gets to the other person's king or who can accumulate more material to get the advantage. Political campaigns use attacks and counterattacks among the candidates to differentiate themselves to the voters. If legal action is part of the business attack, companies countersue over their conflict to drag their differences into court where they can seek resolution while buying time to consider future moves as the case makes its way through the court system. In cases like *Apple v. Microsoft*, dealing with the Macintosh look and feel that was replicated in Windows, took years before a final resolution was reached.

Defense Wins

Carl von Clausewitz in his treatise *On War* said the concept of defense is parrying a blow. The object of defense is preservation. Defense is the stronger form of waging war.[5]

In *Marketing Warfare*, Ries and Trout clarify how the superiority of defense wins the game. Two opponents of largely unequal forces can be equalized if the defending side can entrench and make it harder to take a hit during the battle. The defender is betting that eventually the force count will equalize and the defensive force will go on the attack. Throughout military history, defense has proved to be the stronger form of warfare, according to the authors. In the Korean War, America won in the South on defense and lost in the North on offense. England lost in the American Colonies on offense and won at Waterloo on defense. NFL coaches know offense gets the glamour, but defense wins football games. But it doesn't always work this way. Given sufficient force, the attacker will overcome the defender as General Grant did against Lee's defense of Richmond.

A survey of twenty-five leading brands from the year 1923 proves this point. Sixty years later, twenty of those brands were still in first place. In six decades only five out of twenty-five brands lost their leadership position. It's difficult to dethrone a king like Ivory in soap, Campbell in soup, or Coca-Cola in soft drinks. These represent strong marketing positions that can be taken only at great expense and with great skill and energy.[6]

When last we last left them in chapter 4, Magnus and Vishy were still at the chessboard battling away. They never left while we stepped away to analyze how the business they were conducting on the board related to the business in the boardroom. Up to this point both players were using transformational leadership to build a foundation for the middlegame activities to follow. It embodied strategies of centralization, employee development, and risk management. Magnus had his entire team engaged while Vishy was still trying to make that happen. Although the queens had been traded, both players were making it a long-term objective to get their queen to return through a pawn promotion. In order for that to happen, one of them needed to obtain a competitive advantage, and that occurred through situational leadership in the middlegame. Back to the game in progress from the final position in chapter 4.

http://www.365chess.com/game.php?gid=3918815

15.Nd5 g5 16.c4 Kb7

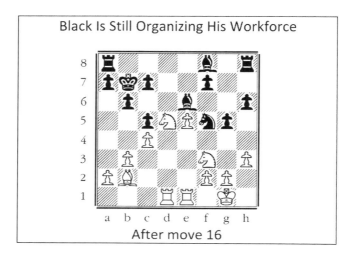

Black Is Still Organizing His Workforce

After move 16

Vishy was getting the remaining members of his team involved. Magnus had transitioned to situational leadership here since he was dealing with a position that had not occurred previously in this match. He seized the opportunity to post his knight on a central square, increasing its worth to the team. Why wasn't he worried about Black's bishop capturing it? Because one of Black's advantages was having the two bishops—if he traded one for the knight, the advantage is lost. If the two bishops can work together with the open nature of the center, Black had a significant opportunity to create a competitive advantage.

Anand's fifteenth move was later criticized because when his g-pawn advanced, it left a hole on f6 that White utilized later in the game. On the pawn's resume, the first objective indicated that leaders need to be careful about advancing pawns because once moved, the squares they leave behind are weakened. Vishy may have been considering an attack against the White king here if his king stays on b7 and he gets his rooks connected over to the kingside of the board. But Magnus had plenty of time to defuse those possibilities.

Looking for Efficiencies

White overprotected his knight with 6. c4 and Black completed his "castling by hand" maneuver, placing his king on b7. As far as efficiency goes, Magnus was able to mitigate the risk to his king on move four, exercising the privilege of castling in one move. Vishy's king took three moves to accomplish the same objective. Yet Black still has a viable position. Management consulting firms are always looking for efficiencies in organizations, so the Magnus method would be considered best practice.

17.Kh2 a5 18.a4 Ne7 19.g4 Ng6

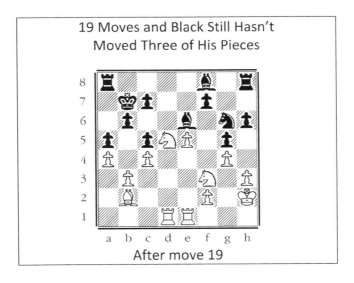

19 Moves and Black Still Hasn't Moved Three of His Pieces

After move 19

A significant series of strategic moves had occurred in the position on the queen's side of the board. This position is like two companies that share a market, with each controlling the space that they want. A McDonald's restaurant will often have a Burger King nearby because both stores are more prosperous as they have each targeted their own market. Gridlock was in place because White and Black blockaded the pawns on the

113

queenside from advancing. If either player advanced their b-pawn, the opponent would capture it and create a protected passed pawn, which is a winning advantage in the endgame.

White got his king off the back rank, waiting to see how Black intended to activate his pieces. This exemplified situational leadership because Magnus was not sure exactly how to proceed in this position. He continued to make moves that generally improved the potential of his employees with the idea of taking advantage of future opportunities. That is much different from Black's actions, which were clearly dictated by getting those rooks on a8 and h8 as well as the bishop on f8 to assume some responsibilities.

Both players advanced their a-pawns into a locked formation. Black repositioned his knight, and Magnus kept it out of f5 by playing his pawn to g4. Vishy realized his knight would no longer arrive on f5 and went to Plan B, moving his knight to g6 with the apparent intention of landing it on f4. These are skilled executives who know how to make the most of their employees.

20.Kg3 Be7 21.Nd2 Rhd8 22.Ne4 Bf8

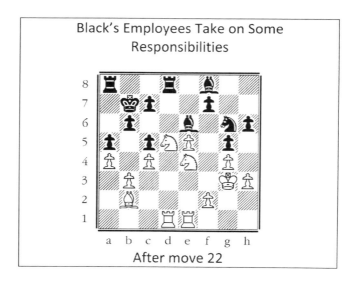

Black's Employees Take on Some Responsibilities

After move 22

Vishy has made serious progress untangling his back rank. The solid reputation of this Berlin Defense formation, established in previous world championship matches, continues to promise his pieces future potential. Magnus advanced his king toward the center, knowing that is a better place for the king with the endgame approaching. It's good strategic play aligned with knowing what the future will require.

Vishy moved his bishop out, allowing his rooks to get connected on the back rank. Magnus obviously noticed a weak square on f6 and reorganized his knight to take a position deep in the opponent's camp. It will take several moves to get there, but once achieved, his knights will be in a good position to protect each other. Black moved his h-rook over to the d-file, finally opposing Magnus' rook and challenging that valuable asset on the open d-file. Magnus moved his knight to e4, eyeing the lucrative destination of f6 and putting Black's position in a bind. With his rooks finally connected, Vishy retreated his bishop, keeping his advantage of the two bishops.

Chess Piece Employee Evaluation Method

A key management responsibility, and a reason I consider the middlegame to be the management phase, is to evaluate their employees. Usually done in the dreaded annual performance review setting, management meets with the employee to discuss what went well and what needed improvement. The review may generate a plan on how the employee can be more effective. After each move, chess players evaluate their employees for effectiveness. Why didn't Magnus snap off the bishop that was on e7? It wasn't free because the knight on g6 protected it. He didn't do it because his knight on d5 was a better employee on his team than the opposing bishop that was locked in behind the pawns on c5 and g5. I regularly see inexperienced players trade off pieces for no particular reason. Good players keep their pieces on the board so that they can use them later to gain an advantage.

Businesses don't enjoy laying people off. They do it so that the company will be in a better position going forward. Years ago companies did everything they could to maintain their workers through good and bad times. Today, as soon as there is a cloud on the horizon, a layoff announces employees need to leave. Airlines have used furloughs with pilots when times are tough. When mandatory retirements take effect, pilots will be in demand, with some predicting a pilot shortage.

After move 15. Nd5, Anand could have eliminated Magnus' knight with his bishop with 15...Bxd5, but he evaluated his bishop and found that, when combined with the other black squared bishop, it was more valuable to his team than the knight, so he didn't make the trade. Business is trending toward using the chess-piece evaluations method by giving employees more frequent feedback and avoiding any surprises during the review. These are positional judgments that business leaders make on a regular basis. Is this division of our company productive from a P&L perspective, or should we sell it and move on? At this writing, General Electric is doing that with their financial division, which for years was the most productive asset in their portfolio.

23. Nef6 b5!! Magnus exercised the principle of "overprotection" by aligning his knights on d5 and f6 together. If Black captures one of the knights, it will be replaced by the other.

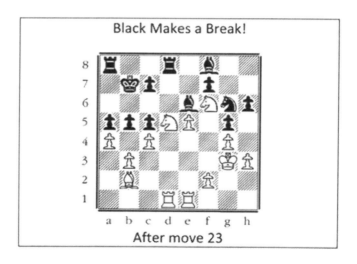

Black Makes a Break!

After move 23

The Principle of Overprotection

Overprotection is a common form of risk management in both chess and business. Companies have multiple datacenters providing backup to each other. If processing is lost at one facility, the second is ready to take up the responsibility. I practiced overprotection as a director of a systems department of twelve people. I was responsible for operating and maintaining more than thirty systems with my direct reports. These were all the systems needed to operate the company, including payroll/HR, general ledger, accounts payable/receivable, fixed assets, electronic data interchange, and purchasing. I designated a lead person on each system and a backup employee that was able to take over if a system failed and the lead person was on vacation, in training, or unavailable to fix the problem.

Overprotection provided clarity to my employees, management, and clients who had a vested interest in their systems. It allowed my team members to work together so that the person on call during the evening production runs had necessary backup. At the time I was managing the department, I wasn't sitting in my office pretending to play chess with my employees. It just came naturally to me as a way of protecting the systems I had to maintain, but it came from my background of playing chess. Several months later, while waiting for a meeting to start in the office of my VP of information technology, I noticed a memo on his desk he had sent out to all the other IT directors. He wanted them to name a lead and a backup for all the systems they were maintaining! My VP must have liked the idea of overprotection; however, he never told me.

Succession planning is a form of overprotection of the CEO who is only a heartbeat away from extinction. In his book *Succession*, Noel Tichy lists twenty-eight CEOs who had unforeseen departures, terminations, or resignations. From 1993 through 2014, the number-one reason for departure was a tie between heart attacks and an improper relationship with a subordinate. And so it goes: 2015 saw the departure of United Airline's CEO for his role with his airline's hub in Newark, New Jersey, and his successor suffered a heart attack requiring a heart transplant shortly thereafter.[7]

Vishy Offers an Investment

Meanwhile, Vishy had made a brilliant move 23...b5!! at the board, forcing Magnus to dig deep into his situational leadership thinking skills to determine what to do here. Black would not have played this move if he didn't have a pawn on c6 since White would have a protected passed pawn heading into an endgame and Black would be lost. But Anand did have a pawn on c6, and that makes all the difference. Anand offered a free pawn, but if Magnus took it, all Anand's pieces would come to life, including the rook on a8 that had yet to move. It is not a good idea to give your opponent's pieces life if you cannot challenge them. In business, don't allow competition to utilize distribution lines or intellectual property that you created. You can obfuscate your actions to confuse the enemy. There's nothing like deploying smoke and mirrors when needed.

Here are the candidate moves involving captures Magnus had to analyze:

- If 24. axb5, a4 25. bxa4, Rxa4 and Black has the pawn on c4 under attack and controls the open a-file.

- If 24. cxb5, c6 25. bxc6+, Kxc6 leaves the pawn on b3 weak and the knight on d5 is attacked three times (B, R, & K) and defended twice (N & R), so it has to move. Plus, Anand's bishops will start to take control of the board.

24.Bc3 bxa4 25.bxa4 Kc6 26.Kf3 Rdb8

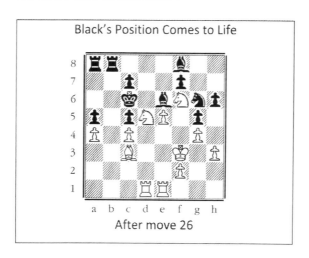

Black's Position Comes to Life

After move 26

118

Magnus saw through the complications and activated his bishop, ignoring the free-pawn offer for the moment. Black exchanged a-pawns. Vishy activated his king to c6. The resilience of his position shows his king is preparing for endgame activity by heading to the center of the board.

Magnus brought his king closer to Memphis (the square e4), and Black grabbed the asset of the open b-file with his rook.

27.Ke4 Rb4!?

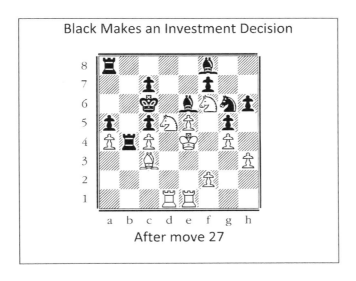

Black Makes an Investment Decision

After move 27

Magnus landed his king in Memphis (e4) ready to support a package delivery anywhere on the board. Black moved his rook to a square where Magnus had a bishop and knight covering it. Wait … did the piece slip out of his hand before it got to its rightful destination? Did he intend to move it to b3? Not at all. Anand called Magnus' bluff with a sacrifice of a $5 piece for a $3 one. If Vishy were a poker player, his move would be an instance of "I'm all in." Knowing he only had this and one more game to produce a victory, he must have felt now was the time. Having caught Magnus by surprise with his 23…b5!! move, could he catch him off guard again?

In my chapter 11 game against Bachler, I overlooked a bishop sacrifice, and I can tell you that your psyche takes a hit when that happens. Your confidence wanes, and you start listening to the inner voice saying, "Okay, I missed that previous move. What am I overlooking now?" It's like the CEO of a large bank who suddenly realizes the firm holds a portfolio of billion-dollar losing positions. The tendency is to exhibit more caution, which consumes valuable time rechecking lines looking for something missing. But in Magnus' case, cold hard calculation is what is needed at the moment, and he is pretty good at that. In business, don't make friends with your mistakes by lingering over them. You have to bounce back quickly or lose any advantage you have over your enemy. You're going to make mistakes, so get used to it and act decisively to make up for it. Good leaders learn from their mistakes, seldom if ever repeating them.

A Sacrifice in Chess Is an Investment in Business

Vishy was exercising the financial judgment that is no different from any trader who has to look at the risk versus reward of making an investment. He was voluntarily giving up more money than he was immediately getting back, but he thinks that the potential reward in the future is worth it. As with any investment, some of them work out, and some of them do not. Vishy was giving up a $5 rook for a $3 bishop or knight. Was the risk worth the reward? If Magnus took his rook, he would be $2 down, but he had a protected passed b-pawn three moves away from becoming a queen. If that pawn costs Magnus a knight or a rook, his investment would be sound, returning his invested capital with a healthy return to top it off. Chess is a great way to teach financial literacy, dealing with all the risks versus rewards of investing. How much did having only two more games in the match make Anand go "all in" on this move? Maybe 27...Rb3, 28. Rb1, Rab8 29. Rxb3, Rxb3 30.Rc1 keeping things balanced and Vishy playing White in the last game was a better strategy?

Getting to Memphis isn't Always Safe

Just like FedEx has to deal with foggy conditions while operating their aircraft in Memphis, having his king in Memphis (e4) at the moment looked completely safe to Magnus. But there was still a dangerous amount of material left on the board, and being exposed to an unexpected check can cause an immediate turn of events. Magnus and Vishy produced a stunning oversight five games earlier when Magnus made an "autopilot" king move, preparing for the upcoming endgame. In game six of their championship match, Magnus had just moved his king to d2 in the following position.

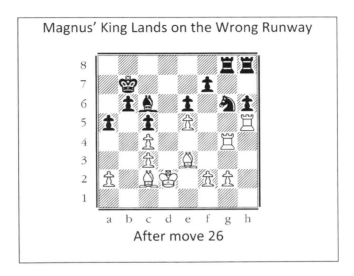

The game can be played from the following link and advanced to move twenty-six:

http://www.365chess.com/game.php?gid=3918073

On move twenty-three, Magnus moved his rook to g4, introducing a huge risk factor in his position. The $5 rook was not protected. That move was a mystery because the fourth rank provides no more access for the rook as every square is covered. It does, however, protect the pawn on c4. On move twenty-six, Magnus, in preparation for the upcoming endgame, played 23.Kd2??

That move could have cost him the game and possibly the entire match with his title. This was only the sixth game, and there was plenty of time for Anand to win even more games. Magnus overlooked the tactic of two "in-between moves" in the position and could have lost two pawns on consecutive moves. Can you see what he overlooked? Imagine having to sit poker-faced in his chair, having to wait for Anand to make his move.

If he had gotten up and started to kick his chair in disgust, Anand would have detected something was amiss, looked harder, and no doubt seen the correct continuation. Instead Vishy followed Magnus' blunder with one of his own, playing 26...a4??

What Did Vishy Miss?

Vishy had a tactical combination and should have played 26...Nxe5! White cannot take the free knight because his rook on g4 was hanging with 27. Rxe5?, Rxg4! His g4 rook was attacked twice, and the best move was to exchange it for the rook on g8 with 28. Rxg8, but then Vishy, before recapturing on g8, had two tactical in-between moves with 29...Nxc4+, requiring a king move by Magnus. If the king advances to d3 with 30. Kd3 to attack the knight, it goes to b2 with check. 30...Nb2+, requiring another White king move. Then Vishy plays 31...Rxg8, recovering his rook and picking up two pawns. If not lost in the position, Magnus would have been on the ropes defending. In a huge twist of fortune, Magnus went on to win that game in thirty-eight moves!

Chess forces you to be vigilant about managing risk. Even the best chess players in the world aren't exempt from the dangers of an exposed king. Like business leaders, they are human and make mistakes. After Vishy played 26...a4?? Magnus slumped over in his chair; Anand saw his body language and what he had missed. Analysts had to go back decades to find out when the last time a double blunder had occurred in a world championship match. Given what he walked into in game six, he must have looked pretty carefully before moving his king to Memphis here in game eleven on move twenty-seven.

28.Bxb4 cxb4? 29.Nh5 Kb7

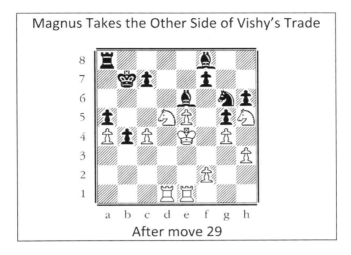

Magnus Takes the Other Side of Vishy's Trade

After move 29

Magnus had to decide between the candidate moves of taking the rook with:

- The bishop
- The knight
- Or leaving the rook on b4

Taking with the knight allowed 28...axb4, forcing the bishop to move, and then 29...Rxa4 and Black is on his way. Instead, he took the rook with his bishop, and Anand played probably his losing move. He recaptured with the c-pawn instead of the a-pawn. This is a natural human reaction of straightening out his doubled c-pawns, but he needed to play for activity. Taking with a-pawn allowed the rook on a8 to enter the game having never moved. Mobility is important in the opening and also in the middlegame.

30.f4 gxf4 31.Nhxf4 Nxf4 32.Nxf4 Bxc4

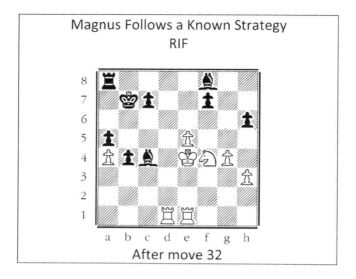

Magnus Follows a Known Strategy
RIF

After move 32

After these moves Anand had cut his capital loss down to $1, netting the pawn on c4. His two bishops had better use of the diagonals, but he still faced an uphill battle in the upcoming endgame. The bishop on c4 is a risk factor for Black since it is not defended, and that plays a role in the outcome of the game. If your advantage is a superior piece (chess) or a superior product (business), keep enhancing the product going forward so that your competition is always a step behind.

Reduction in Force

Having a competitive advantage of material superiority, Magnus followed the known strategy of reducing the chances his opponent could come back by exchanging off material at every opportunity. Once a competitor gets an advantage (usually in the form of material), they use a strategy useful in business called reduction in force (RIF) in order to maintain their advantage. In business, companies reduce their workforce to keep their cost structures viable in the ongoing operating environment. They may be releasing talent that a competitor can employ, but so be it. In chess, when you reduce your forces, at the same time you are reducing the forces of your competition. How cool is that? How do you maintain a material advantage going forward? By trading off material that is no longer necessary to win the game and denying your opponent opportunities to stage a comeback.

Get This Game to the Ninth Inning

Anyone who has managed a baseball team knows a one-run lead is more valuable in the ninth inning than the first. But why? Well, the game is almost over. If you can manage to get three more outs before your opponent scores any runs, you will win. In the first inning you have to get twenty-seven outs, and things can happen along the way that may allow your competition to score a run. They would then be right back in the game—if not taking the lead—by scoring additional runs. So how do you maintain your advantage? Every opposing batter you get out brings you closer to victory. Managers with a bigger lead may play the infield back, giving up a run for a double-play opportunity because two outs can kill a big rally inning of the opponent. But with a one-run lead, they may opt to get the lead runner out to prevent a run from scoring. Chess-playing managers keep the essential things on the board that they need and remove the rest.

Having a material advantage and then trading off queens is a really good strategy. It's the equivalent to getting a lead in a baseball game and then both teams removing the cleanup hitters from the lineup. The team that's losing needs their cleanup hitter on the board so that they can hit a home run and get back in the game. The losing team will have to avoid exchanging queens, keeping it on the board to fight another day. Bullying your opponent's queen by forcing it to retreat may lead to other advantages. Continue to trade off unnecessary pieces, but keep enough material to guarantee that you can still win the game.

Magnus and Vishy will play on, but we will break here because the game has left the middlegame and has entered the endgame, which is the subject of our next chapter.

Looking Back—Moving Forward

- ➢ Embrace uncertainty for an attacking advantage.
- ➢ Meet new positional demands with situational leadership.
- ➢ Attack, win, and exchange for a competitive advantage during the middlegame.
- ➢ Evaluate your employees after every move.
- ➢ Overprotect your assets in business and chess.
- ➢ Invest financially in the future with a sound sacrifice.
- ➢ Reduce your opponent's forces (RIF) in business or chess to maintain the advantage.

The lonely king plays on without his queen, but the yearning is strong to have her return to the game. The opening had some superficial attacks, but in the middlegame these players seriously sought a competitive advantage with their play. Anand spent time just getting his workforce assembled while Magnus maneuvered (reorganized) his knights into a protective alliance. Anand offered a gambit pawn that Magnus refused. But then Anand offered a rook for a bishop, and Magnus jumped on the transaction. Both players advanced their kings while still in the middlegame, knowing that a blunder five games earlier could have changed the outcome of the entire match.

Middlegame situational leadership is giving way to endgame results-based leadership in the next chapter. An exit strategy is in play with the end in sight. Strategies and tactics are still to be played, but when the endgame phase is over, we will know who the next world champion is. Meanwhile, back in Cincinnati, the issue of leadership at P&G was yet to be resolved.

Chapter 6

Endgame:
Expertise Phase - Having
an Exit Strategy

"All's well that ends ..."

In the heat of an August day in Houston in 2001, Chairman of the Board Ken Lay faced an uncertain future following the resignation of his CEO Jeffrey Skilling. Two days after Skilling's resignation—officially for "personal reasons"—Lay took the stage in front of hundreds of his employees. Instead of an honest discussion of his illegal activities and the impending financial disaster the company faced, he explained why he was excited about the future of the company. Enron's stock price traded around $30 per share at the time. In September, the world was distracted from the Enron situation because of the terrorist attacks; in an e-mail to his employees, Lay still stated that Enron was a great buy. He assured them that the company's accounting methods were "legal and totally appropriate."

In October, Enron posted a $618 million loss, and a week later, the SEC opened an investigation into their accounting practices. In December, Enron filed for bankruptcy protection, and employees were told to pack their belongings and vacate the building in thirty minutes. Nearly 62 percent of 15,000 employees' savings plans relied on Enron stock that was purchased at $83 in early 2001 and now traded at $0.12 per share. On that day, the world learned that it was possible for a Fortune 500 company to go directly from the middlegame to immediate resignation and never make it to the endgame.

Avoiding the Endgame

Companies avoid the endgame like a plague. Anything happening in that phase is not good. Like a death in the family, no one (except maybe a competitor) wants to see a once flourishing business wind up in the obituary column. The failure of one "too big to fail" firm like Long Term Capital Management (LTCM) would have wreaked havoc in the financial markets, so the Federal Reserve engineered a bailout from fourteen banks.

One month after the October 1998 bailout, in a letter to Senator D'Amato, Fed Chairman Alan Greenspan "freely admitted that by orchestrating a rescue of Long-Term, the Fed had encouraged future risk takers and perhaps increased the odds of a future disaster. To be sure, some moral hazard, however slight may have been created by the Federal Reserve's involvement."[1] However, he judged that such negatives were outweighed by the risk of serious distortions to market prices had Long-Term been pushed suddenly into bankruptcy.[2]

That was one "too big to fail" firm. What if Washington Mutual, Countrywide Financial, Freddie Mac, Fannie Mae, American International Group (AIG), Bear Sterns, Merrill Lynch, Lehman Brothers, General Motors, and any other Troubled Asset Relief Program (TARP) needy recipient had all been pushed suddenly into bankruptcy in their endgame? The government is still looking for measures to deal with "too big to fail" institutions where an endgame checkmate or resignation must be avoided at all costs. But how do you know you are in a business endgame? Financial analysts run the numbers looking for possible ways the business can continue operating. As quarterly losses continue to mount, fewer options are left to keep the enterprise running. Stores close (Sears, Sports Authority, Blockbuster, Radio Shack), employees are laid off or quit for greener pastures as the rumors circulate, cash on hand is in short supply, bond ratings descend to junk status, payroll becomes a burden, and vendors refuse to supply materials on credit. In the 2008 financial crisis, business headlines declared that "Lehman Brothers is in the Endgame" just days before they filed for bankruptcy.

The Priorities of the Endgame

In the endgame of a company or a chess game, the players have an exit strategy in mind and can visualize the final result. In chess, the endgame will produce a victory, a defeat, or a draw. In business, it will lead to growth by earnings or acquisition, a bankruptcy with liquidation, or a merger. In the final days of the Enron debacle, another Houston-based energy company expressed interest in buying Enron in a stock swap, but the transaction never happened. Once Enron's credit lines were exhausted, bankruptcy and liquidation happened quickly. It's always interesting at the beginning of the year to see financial pundits predict which companies will not be around at year-end. Sometimes they are right, but in this case Enron was never on their radar.

As the leaders prepare for final battle in the endgame, they recognize that the middlegame moves have been made, pieces have been traded, and control of the board has been established. Each leader knows whether his or her role is to defend or attack. By starting with the desired end in mind, the leaders determine the best actions and counteractions to take.

In a chess game, leaders use three strategies to conclude operations that have business implications:

1. **King** is activated. Utilizing all available resources means the king, who has been dormant through the previous phases, takes an active role.

2. **Promote** a pawn. The reduced amount of material means the pawns are important because they represent a potential new queen on the board if they can get promoted.

3. **Checkmate** your opponent. It is important that enough material remains on the board to checkmate the opponent's king or force a resignation.

In chess, a rule of thumb that indicates the endgame is approaching is the queens have been traded. In this game Magnus and Vishy traded queens on move eight, which gave each of them the liberty to march their respective kings to the center early. The endgame is marked by utilizing the king since the threat of checkmate has receded. The king usually has to join the workforce still on the board in order to win the game. In a start-up firm, the CEO is heavily involved in every aspect of the company's business. In chess, there is too much risk to involve the CEO early, and his participation is limited until the risk diminishes. The endgame is where the king can exhibit his true capabilities of attacking, defending, threatening, and capturing like anyone else on the team. If he avoids an incoming check, his alliance with a remaining major piece can spell victory.

Gaining Chess Expertise

As an accumulating value proposition, you gain chess experience by studying, practicing, and playing against stronger players. Players may take up chess for casual encounters or to become serious tournament participants earning a rating. Some people play golf for recreation and pleasure while others compete to lower their handicaps. Our purpose for understanding chess is to apply the experience to business. Studying endgames forms the foundation of correct play while offering guidance for business planning and execution. Endgames are the foundation on which to build your expertise in chess and business.

As your chess game simplifies into endgame positions, you must understand the theory and practice of those positions, or your will lose any winning advantage. World Champion Raul Capablanca, who is famous for his knowledge of the endgame, said, "You must study the endgame before everything else." In business and chess, patterns repeat and, once understood, can be recalled to garner further victories.

The various types of endgames are classified by the pieces left on the board when the endgame begins. For example, a rook and pawn endgame (the most common) is where both sides have their king, a rook, and several pawns left. Since rooks tend to join the game later, it's common for them to be one of the last pieces left on the board. In the endgame, players need to recognize whether the advantage they have will win or not. If not, their opponent needs to make another mistake, or if there is good defense, then no one will win and the result will be a draw. In game theory, this process is called looking ahead and reasoning backward to complete the plan and execute the moves required.

What should you be thinking about in the endgame? In the endgame your recall of winning positions and accurate calculations becomes important. All the information you know from previous games, books you've read, creativity, calculation, tactics, and maneuvers comes into play, even though the position is simplified. You are still the leader of your forces, and whether you win or lose is yet to be determined in the complexity of the endgame. A mistake by either player in the endgame is usually fatal. Mistakes made in the opening and middlegame are recoverable. In the endgame there is little hope of correcting a miscue.

Gaining Business Expertise

In business, company leaders draw upon their previous education and experience, even if their experience came from the "fail fast and fail often" school. Companies that are in a special situation need a leader that has the experience and expertise to accomplish a successful outcome. IBM recruited Gerstner as a turnaround specialist because of his success with American Express and RJR Nabisco. He saw that the culture of the entire company needed to change or it would perish in an endgame. Gaining the necessary experience often comes from on-the-job training, which places fast-tracked leadership candidates into various roles that will give them the critical experiences they require. Knowing how to conclude a won game is why I consider the endgame the expertise phase.

As we left them in chapter 5, Magnus and Vishy were still at the chessboard. We saw them use their transformational leadership skills to build a foundation for middlegame activities. Those strategies involved centralization, employee development, and risk management. In the middlegame, situational leadership took over as they attacked and defended and traded down their positions. In the middlegame, the strategies became attack, win, and exchange pieces, maintaining your advantage. Magnus had slowly been bringing his king toward the center in preparation for the endgame. Vishy, needing a win in these last two games, first offered a gambit pawn. Magnus felt it wasn't worth the trouble and passed. Then Vishy offered one of his rooks. Like a hedge fund trader seeing an opportunity in the markets, Magnus analyzed the offer and pounced on the trade, booking a $2 profit with the transaction. Vishy saw the trade as an opportunity to break his pawn through to a queen, returning his investment with interest, but to make that happen, both sides needed to have their kings play a major role. They needed to promote a pawn, and whoever accomplished that first would win. Back to the game in progress from the final position in chapter 5.

http://www.365chess.com/game.php?gid=3918815

33.Rd7 Ra6

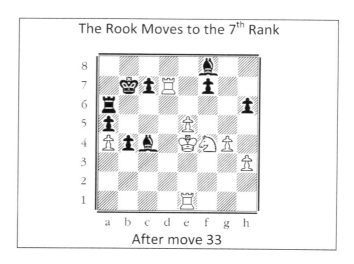

The third objective on the rook's resume stated he likes to hang out on the seventh rank. Magnus' patience brought that objective to life by playing 13. Rad1 and then waiting twenty moves to see his employee at full potential. Here the computer is saying Magnus had (+2.69) worth of advantage. He had only a one-pawn advantage on the board, but the grandmaster-level silicon monster says his advantage was already decisive. This move is powerful because it pins the pawn on c7, which cannot move because the king is behind it, and also puts pressure on the pawn on f7. He can't take it right now because the bishop on c4 guards it, but that may change.

Getting the trespassing rook off d7 is not easy as the following variation shows:

- 33...Kc6 34. Rd4, Ba2 35. Rc1+, Kb7 36. Rd7 with 36...Rc8 37. Nd5, b3 38. Nc3! b2 39. Nxa2, bxc1(Q) 40. Nxc1

Magnus would have cashed in his insurance of extra material. But even though material is back to equality, the weak pawn on f7, White's active king and healthy e5 pawn will be no problem for someone with Magnus' technique to win. Anand saw that the pawn on c7 would soon need another defender and lifted his rook to a6, preparing to slide it to c6.

34.Nd5 Rc6 35.Rxf7 Bc5

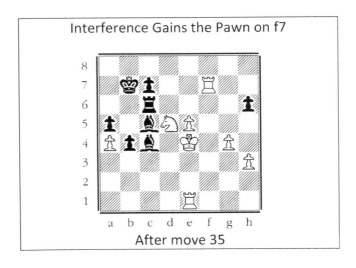

Interference Gains the Pawn on f7

After move 35

By centralizing his knight back to d5, Magnus attacked the c7 pawn twice (R & N), and Black was forced to defend it with his rook and played as expected 34...Rc6. But when the White knight went to d5, it also introduced a tactic into the situation called interference.

Tactical Alert – Interference

In business, interference is when employees cannot do their job because someone is hindering their ability. In the workplace, interference can be a form of harassment. If a company wants an employee to leave, they often make the employee's life miserable. A forced relocation, change in job responsibilities, verbal abuse over mistakes, or changed work hours are often ways to interfere with employees doing their job.

Here the bishop on c4 is no longer defending the f7 pawn because of the interference of the knight on d5. Tactics have a tendency to occur in strategically superior positions, and Magnus took full advantage of his opportunities. After the pawn capture, the rook threatened the free bishop on f8, so Anand moved it to its only safe square on c5. But that isn't a great place to be either. Notice that e7, g7, and d6 (because of the pawn on e5) were all unavailable to the bishop. Black would have suffered a "trapped piece" tactic if it weren't for the c5 square being available. Magnus was putting the squeeze on his opponent and, on the next move, delivered the knockout blow.

36.Rxc7+ (diagram) Rxc7

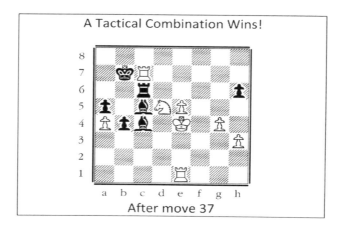

A Tactical Combination Wins!

After move 37

134

Magnus played a move that required calculating at least ten moves ahead or he couldn't play it. A single tactic when available can be powerful. When tactics are linked together over a series of moves in what is called a combination, they will often win the game on the spot. Even in the endgame, the principle of exchanging down forces applies.

The Power of Visualization

I am often asked by non-chess players how many moves you need to think ahead when playing. The answer is that it depends. You have to be able to visually calculate enough moves ahead to make sure the desired situation you are considering playing is favorable to your game, or else you wouldn't play it. Here Magnus appeared to be sacrificing a knight for the pawn on c7, which handed back a substantial portion of his winning material advantage. Why would he do that? Chess players don't think ten moves ahead on every move, or they would become exhausted and miss something, keeping all those moves in their head. They only do that when it's necessary. The more you are in control by forcing your opponent's moves, the easier it is to calculate the branches on the tree you are analyzing.

Of the information the human brain processes, 83 percent comes from the sense of sight, while only 11 percent comes from sound. The brain is much more adept at storing visual images. Because the mind cannot distinguish a real image from an imaginary one, chess helps develop and practice the business skill of visualization. Having the ability to "see" the future in business is no different from imagining your bishop on the square b5 while it actually resides next to the king on the square f1. Business managers utilize the moves they played in similar situations, which helps them visualize a predictable outcome. If a winning combination was played in a similar position, it should work again in the current position.

Here Vishy had to take the rook because if he just walked away from the rook check, he would lose his rook on c6. So Magnus can conclude his rook will be captured, and he will have to capture Black's rook with his knight. Then why didn't he just lose a knight for a pawn with 37...Kxc7? The power of visualization played a critical role here. Iconic leaders like Gates, Grove, and Jobs in the chapter 3 discussion of *Strategy Rules*, or the twenty-five business leaders in *Lasting Leadership* discussed in chapter 1 all displayed a knack for seeing into the future. Just like those iconic business leaders, Magnus saw into the future, and he liked what he saw—no different from a leader that saw a coffee shop on every corner, a PC in every home, or a car in every garage. They see the future and act on it.

37.Nxc7

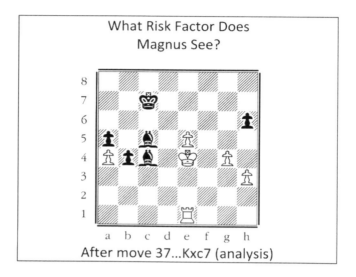

After move 37...Kxc7 (analysis)

Anand's position had the third risk factor discussed in chapter 4, which is one or more unprotected pieces. Magnus noticed that after 37...Kxc7, all Black's pieces were lined up on the open c-file. The unprotected bishops looked like two bowling pins lined up, just waiting for his bowling ball rook to line them up with 38. Rc1. Since the bishops were shielding the king, at least one of them could not move because they were absolutely pinned. He was guaranteed to get one if not both the bishops, so his knight sacrifice was only temporary and sound. But his analysis had to check out the other candidate moves that Anand had available and they were:

- 38. Rc1, b3 39. Rxc4, b2 40. Rxc5+, K(any) 41. Rb5 covering the pawn promotion just in time

- 37...b3, 38. Nd5, b2 39. e6 and the pawn on b2 isn't going to queen

The Devastation of a Tactical Combination

In the first variation, Magnus had to see a total of ten moves ahead to make sure he was playing a winning combination. If he miscalculated and Black promoted his pawn on b1 without it being captured, it would be check and Anand would win the game. In the endgame, the ability to calculate is imperative.

Anand saw these losing alternatives but didn't take the free knight on c7; instead he preferred to centralize his king. Magnus won another pawn and was able to save his knight in the process.

37...Kc6 38.Nb5 Bxb5

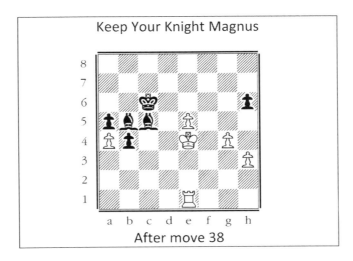

Keep Your Knight Magnus

After move 38

Magnus brought his knight back to a secured square, and Vishy promptly removed it, gaining a pawn back in the process. The endgame strategy of promoting a pawn into a queen was the highest priority. In this game, whoever promotes a pawn first will be the winner. It's off to the races. With their ability to use result-based leadership and analysis, both players already knew what the result of this game would be with best play. Vishy continued to play it out in the hopes that Magnus would make a mistake.

39.axb5+ Kxb5 40.e6 b3

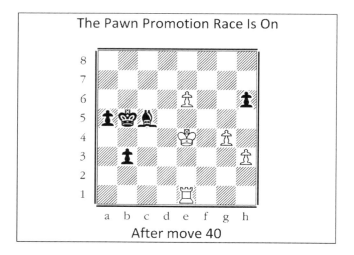

The Pawn Promotion Race Is On

After move 40

Black's connected passed pawns were looking dangerous. This game will come down to a move or two making the difference. Magnus had to play carefully, using his previous experience dealing with a rook versus a bishop ending—not unlike an executive being careful and using the knowledge and experience gained from successfully running a previous company with the current firm—one slip and his hard work could evaporate. The tightrope he is walking here is the need to delegate some critical responsibility. The right person has to be assigned the right job in order to win. If Magnus screws up that task, Anand could still draw or maybe even win this game. You don't get to be a world champion, however, without having the technique necessary to win this position.

41.Kd3 Be7 42.h4 a4

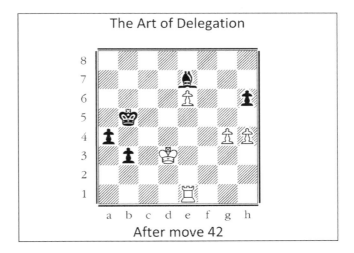

The Art of Delegation

After move 42

One of the hardest jobs of being a leader is delegating or assigning the tasks that need to be done by other employees.

The Art of Delegation

Delegation starts with determining what tasks need to be accomplished. Here the primary task is to stop Black's dangerous pawns. A secondary task is to protect the material on the board and White wants to advance his own pawns to promotion. Since there are only two employees for each player left on the board, flipping a coin is one option, but that leaves it up to luck. Knowing your employee's strengths and weaknesses will, once the tasks are identified, help you to decide which employee had the best skills to accomplish the task. Working together, they can achieve their objective. It's just up to the boss to figure out what role each has to play.

Magnus correctly delegated the job of stopping Black's dangerous pawns to his king. He did it for a specific reason: if he had chosen the rook and the two Black pawns got connected on the third rank, they would beat the rook. The rook cannot stop two connected passed pawns on the third rank. Providing there are no tricky tactics, like pins or checks, two pawns will see one of them promote against a rook. The White king had to be careful of checks from the bishop, but if he stopped the pawns on the white squares, he would be able to establish a blockade and prevent their further advance.

Both players understood this endgame position. The rook kept the pressure on the bishop to blockade the pawn on e6. Magnus took advantage of his centralized king. Like FedEx, he saw that two packages needed to be picked up on the West Coast, so he left Memphis, heading for the pawns. Black stopped the e-pawn and blockaded its advance with his bishop. Seeing that he had stopped the Black pawns, Magnus pushed his kingside pawns in his attempt to promote a pawn. Anand continued to advance his pawns together and played 42...a4.

43.g5 hxg5 44.hxg5 a3 45.Kc3 1–0

The Champion Keeps His Title

After move 45

Magnus forced an exchange of a couple pawns on the kingside. Anand pushed his a-pawn forward, making them look really ominous, but Magnus brought his king over to keep the pawns within reach. Anand realized his gig was up, and resigned. The players shook hands, and this historic match was over. How ironic that Magnus' last move to retain his title was made by his king. Why did Vishy resign? The following variations show why:

- 45...Ka4 to protect his pawns, 46. Re4+ drives the king away.

- 45...Bb4+ is a skewer tactic which in fact wins the rook on e1 but 46. Kxb3, Bxe1 47. e7 and because the Black king isn't close enough, the pawn promotes.
- If 45...b2, White plays 46. g6, Bf6+ 47. Kb3 stopping the pawns.
- If 45...Bxg5 then 46. Re5+ double attacks (forks) the Black king and bishop.

But if instead of 45. Kc3 Magnus had played 45. g6, a2 46. g7?? then b2 would have drawn.

In the final position, Magnus made better use of his king than Vishy. Vishy's misplaced king and overworked bishop were not up to the task of holding the draw. How did Magnus know he needed to practice king centralization? It's what a strategically stronger leader knows to do. It's one of the reasons he is the best at what he does. It's why business executives want to understand what he does so that his insights can help them become better leaders. How did Magnus know his king was tactically safe in undertaking this operation? He didn't notice it five games earlier. He wasn't tactically in the moment then, and he landed his king on the wrong runway, which could have lost him the game and the match. But here, if he kept his king on white squares, Black's bishop wasn't capable of causing him trouble. The situation was "different this time." Contextual business leaders are strategically stronger and tactically sharper when they conduct business on their board.

Meanwhile Back in Cincinnati

Angry Wall Street analysts were attacking Bob McDonald with claims that P&G wasn't delivering results that were in line with competitors Johnson & Johnson, Colgate-Palmolive, Kimberly Clark, and Unilever, all reporting better growth and profit margins. Activist investor William Ackman, with his $1.8 billion of P&G stock, was serving notice of his discontent. But P&G's board said it supported McDonald's turnaround plan and was "monitoring its effectiveness."

In September 2012, McDonald and two members of the board met with Ackman, who charged (among seventy-five pages of complaints) that 25 percent of the CEO's time was being spent serving on other corporate boards. P&G denied the charge. After the meeting, the board gave McDonald a complete vote of confidence. By spring 2013, P&G's results were improving, but the 2 percent sales increase for the quarter disappointed investors, and the confidence of the board of directors was starting to erode.

Even though share prices and financial conditions for the company were improving, eight months after meeting his attacker, Bob McDonald resigned as CEO, saying he did not want to become a distraction to the company. A.J. Lafley was brought back to run P&G. Mr. Ackman's response was he thought it was a good decision by the board and that the only mistake Mr. Lafley had made during his previous tenure was naming a successor. Mr. Lafley started a campaign to streamline the company, and after two years at the helm, P&G promoted internal candidate David Taylor to the chief executive officer job. Defense did not save the day, and Mr. Ackman played his management shake-up cards in the correct order and won. The attacker's advantage checkmated the CEO of Proctor & Gamble. Meanwhile, Mr. Taylor, the new CEO, has vowed that P&G will lift its standards by stating: "We are willing to adapt and evolve and change what is needed to win."[3]

Looking Back—Moving Forward

- ➢ Practice results-based leadership built on a foundation of expertise.
- ➢ Exercise the power of your king, promote a pawn, and checkmate to win.
- ➢ Pursue tactics that appear in strategically superior positions.
- ➢ Live in the moment for tactical opportunities.
- ➢ Devastate your opposition with tactical knockout combinations.
- ➢ Visualize and calculate the future to the point where it looks rewarding.
- ➢ Delegate the right people to the right task.

The opening and middlegame phases were played without a queen. But heading into the endgame, each player made it a priority to get a queen back on the board. Each had an exit strategy ready regarding how this game was going to finish because the end was in sight. Their ability to look forward and reason backward utilized the results-based leadership style. Strategy was important, but tactics made the difference in the result. In retrospect, Anand made a poor financial investment in the middlegame with 27...Rb4!? Magnus took the opposite side of the financial trade and went on to win.

This game was decided by a series of tactical moves called a combination. Tactics contain the power to turn a business or chess game from a failing operation into a victorious competition. Tactics are opportunities that require businesspeople and chess players to be "in the moment" to see, evaluate, and execute. Tactics are played in business to business (B2B), business to customer (B2C), customer to business (C2B), business to employee (B2E), employee to business (E2B), and employee to employee (E2E) situations. Next on our to-do list is examining a sample of these valuable tactical opportunistic moves so that we can make them a permanent part of our professional toolbox.

Chapter 7

The Power of Tactics - Twelve Tactics with Business Applications

"A shot heard around the ..."

Jack Welch had a decision to make. Jamie Dimon had a whale to land. The SEC had a Ponzi scammer to catch. Ford had an employee that needed to leave. Microsoft warned off their competition. Proctor & Gamble had an activist shareholder attack. Ms. Fleischmann, a JPMorgan Chase lawyer, had a business issue to deal with. These situations were resolved by using business tactics that regularly occur during a chess game. Strategy is the choice of actions you can take given the situation. Best practice in business relies on good strategic thinking, which is analyzing the actionable choices. Opportunities occur in situations that potentially could impact the outcome of the situation. Strategy is always present, but the difficult part with tactics is they have to be discovered. They require the leader to "be in the moment" to see and take advantage of the situation.

My one-word definition of tactics is *opportunity*. Due to the placement of our employees in business or our pieces in chess, their interaction creates an opportunity to generate a competitive advantage. In chapter 3, my opponent "trapped" my bishop and won quickly. In chapter 6, Magnus played a tactical combination that helped him keep his world championship title. In order to see and take advantage of a tactical situation, time would be well spent learning the most common chess tactics that relate to a business situation. By no means complete, experience has shown the following twelve tactics are the most common and frequently deployed; this is how they are used in different situations.

The PIN
(When your next move is blocked)

In 1985 Steve Jobs was forced out of Apple in a management shake-up. Twelve years later, with Apple on the verge of bankruptcy, Jobs returned and successfully changed technology and the company forever. Always the company spokesman, Jobs announced the new, creative things happening at Apple. For years, speculation swirled around what would happen to Apple if Jobs were not around to apply his legendary vision. Well, history has happened, and with his passing, a new leader of Apple has emerged. But concerns still persist about how Apple will survive without its visionary leader.

A business is pinned when it has a valuable employee that has no backup; this puts the organization at risk because of the employee's unique knowledge or ability. This is common in information technology where one person maintains a legacy system; if that person moves on, there are consequences to the firm. Trade secrets can be jeopardized if a critical/ pinned employee moves out of the organization.

In a military conflict, troops can get pinned down behind enemy lines during an ambush. They cannot move freely without major casualties and have to wait for reinforcements to arrive to change the status of the battle. In tennis, players are often pinned behind the baseline because their opponents are hitting deep aggressive shots, keeping them behind the court. They can't move forward in the court into a more commanding position.

In chess, a pinned piece is one that cannot move or doesn't want to move. In diagram 1A, can you find the White piece that is pinned? This position comes from a popular Black defense called the Nimzo-Indian. The knight on c3 is absolutely pinned to the king by the Black bishop on b4, and since one can never leave the king in check, the c3 knight must stay put.

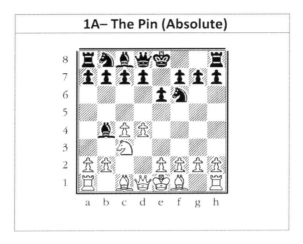

1A– The Pin (Absolute)

Since White's knight is pinned, Black could move his knight to e4 where it could not be captured. That's the enigma of a pinned piece; it's on the board but it doesn't have a full range of movement or function.

Diagram 1B shows the other type of pin, which is known as a relative pin.

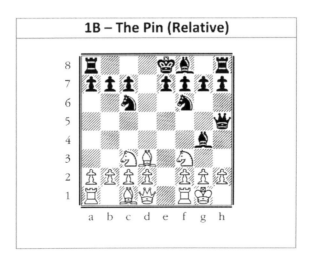

1B – The Pin (Relative)

Can you find the pinned piece in the position? The knight on f3 does not want to leave his post or the queen on d1. A $9 piece would go lost for a $3 bishop—a losing move. However, just because it doesn't want to move doesn't mean it cannot move. We will see this position in chapter 10 when Magnus Carlsen pins Bill Gates' knight to his queen. Bill tried to deal with the pin immediately, but the result was not favorable.

Double Attack
(When you face multiple threats)

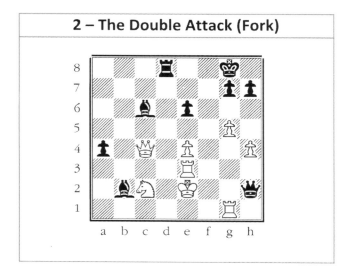

2 – The Double Attack (Fork)

CEO Bob McDonald at Proctor & Gamble had his hands full dealing with multiple attacks. Shareholder activist William Ackman was not happy with his performance and wanted him replaced. At the same time, cost-conscious consumers opted for lower-quality brands, attacking bottom-line profits. Originally able to withstand the attacks, Mr. McDonald eventually succumbed, and the previous CEO came back to run the company. In business, companies can come under attack by two or more opponents simultaneously. A car company can be rejected by consumers yet bailed out by the same taxpayers.

In chess, two pieces attacked at once is a double attack. All pieces can double attack and be double attacked. Diagram 2 shows a queen fork by

Black. The White king is in check, and the rook on g1 is also attacked. The tactic comes about because of the risk factor of having two pieces unguarded at the same time.

Overworked Piece/Employee
(Too much to do)

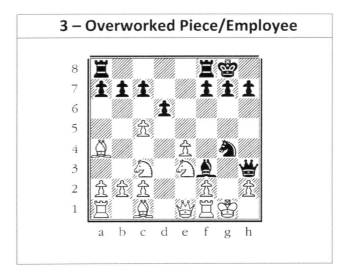

In December 2006, the Securities and Exchange Commission (SEC) received the following complaint from a source identified as a "concerned citizen" regarding Bernie Madoff:

"Your attention is directed to a scandal of major proportion which was executed by the investment firm Bernard L. Madoff. ... Assets well in excess of $10 Billion owned by the late [investor], an ultra-wealthy long-time client of the Madoff firm have been "co-mingled" with funds controlled by the Madoff company with gains thereon retained by Madoff."[1]

In response, a call was made to Madoff's lawyer who reported, "Bernie says he has not managed money for [investor]." Based on this alone, the investigation was closed.[2]

The inspector general's report said the worst mistake was the failure of investigators to follow up and see that Madoff wasn't trading the volume of securities that he claimed. Madoff testified to the Inspector General that when he was asked for his Depository Trust Company account number, he thought, "It was the end game, over." But the agency never followed through.[3]

In her testimony before Congress, Lori A. Richards, SEC's Director, Office of Compliance Inspections and Examinations stated, "The growth in adviser registrants outstripped the staff's ability to examine every firm on a regular basis. Given the number of firms registered with the SEC, the Commission examines only a small portion of the securities business each year. Rather, it is a form of triage, to help match available staff resources to the most pressing risks."[4] This situation had a high price to pay because overworked employees were unable to trust but verify what Madoff was up to.

Giving an employee too much responsibility and not enough time to accomplish the tasks involved is a prevalent situation in today's workforce, one that leaves open the possibility that something won't get accomplished, becoming detrimental to the company. Overworking is not only an employee problem; it can be technical as well. The "denial of service" hacking phenomenon happens when malicious requests interact with a website specifically to overwork the server and bring a company's web server to a halt. It's an overworked piece of equipment. Hackers flood the server with too many bogus information requests, preventing legitimate requests from being handled. With too much traffic to handle, transactions get denied, which generates negative publicity and frustration over the company's inability to handle the problem.

In chess, an overworked piece has too much responsibility. It must stay where it is to defend something and capture somewhere else at the same time. In diagram 3, can you identify the White piece that has too much responsibility? The White knight on e3 has to stay put to prevent Qg2#, yet if he doesn't capture the Black knight on g4, White will play Qxh2#. White can do nothing to prevent checkmate on the next move because he has allowed a valuable piece/employee to become overworked.

Decoy
(Step in the wrong direction)

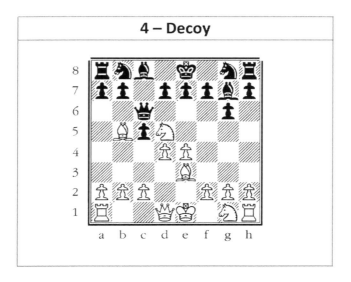

4 – Decoy

As *Computer World* reported, "It's a decoy! Microsoft's present legal saga is amusing, but the company's dance with the Justice Department affects the Internet's past and not its future. With Washington distracted, Microsoft is quietly deploying another of its notorious domination strategies: Swallow up a market." [5]

The purpose of a decoy in business is to have a competitor move into a particular market when you know that is not a good idea. An example might be a bank selling their loan portfolio to another bank right before a huge downturn in the housing market. It's selling someone something for more than you know it's worth. Sometimes companies transfer an employee to a position for which they are unqualified, resulting in a subsequent termination. The Peter Principle is being continually promoted to the point where one is ultimately proven incompetent, having been attracted to a bad position in the company.

In chess, a decoy tactic is an attempt to attract an enemy piece to a bad square. In diagram 4, White has just played the bishop to b5, attacking the queen. Why give a piece away for nothing? It's an attempt to deploy the decoy tactic. If Black captures the bishop, the queen has been decoyed away from guarding c7, so the White knight infiltrates c7 with a fork. It's called a family fork where the king, rook, and queen are all being attacked! This is a perfect example of a combination of two tactics leading to a winning position.

Clearance
(Getting out of the way)

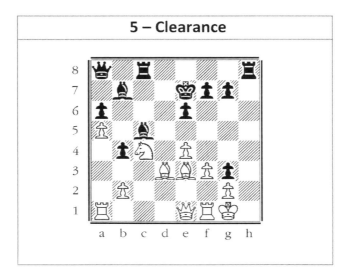

The clearance tactic in business happens when you reorganize or divest a department, function, or line of business. Usually the idea is to reduce the workforce size or reorganize in another way that reduces costs or increases profitability. Clearance is a tactic used when the company plans to increase its use of automation or wants to outsource production. The tactic is often used to give a lower-level employee new responsibilities while eliminating higher-paid staff. The idea is this will help the organization perform better while reducing costs.

An example would be when an advertising agency lays off its art director and gives the art-direction responsibilities to either an outsourced freelancer or to one of its in-house graphic designers. In retail, it's when merchandise needs to be sold to make room for newer models or merchandise. For one of the most impressive uses of clearance in chess, see what Black did on move twenty-four in diagram 5 to force White to resign. He jettisons $10 worth of rooks, clearing the way for the queen to accomplish the task of checkmate. This game proves that material is inconsequential when a higher risk factor of the king is involved. The moves are at this link:

http://www.365chess.com/game.php?gid=1726013

Executives can get "cleared" in large corporations—sometimes in a not-so-subtle way. One day you show up for work in your walnut-paneled CEO suite only to learn that the board has decided you are redundant. The next day, your "outsourced" office is in a warehouse on the wrong side of town. This may sound harsh, but it's what happened to legendary Ford executive Lee Iacocca before he rebuilt his career and reputation at Chrysler.

Skewer
(The fall guy a.k.a. the scapegoat)

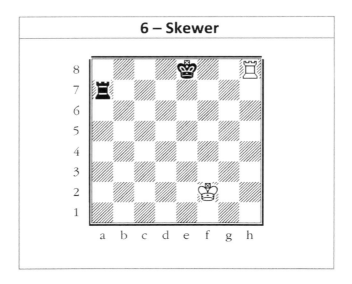

6 – Skewer

In business, when the head of an organization is taking heat for a bad situation, finding a scapegoat is an alternative. Why take the blame when you can step aside and let a direct report burn? During the 2008 financial crisis, Bank of America acquired Merrill Lynch. But shortly after the takeover, Merrill's portfolio tanked and took the BofA stock price with it. Board members and shareholders became agitated with BofA CEO Ken Lewis and ML leader John Thain. These gentlemen were locked in a media dispute about who was to blame for the situation. Ken said he didn't know the portfolio was toxic, and John said he had told BofA management all along. After the media revealed that John Thain had a million-dollar rug in his office while many of his investors were losing their life savings in the crisis, Ken Lewis flew to New York and fired his subordinate John Thain.

If a large bank reports a substantial loss on investments that weren't being monitored, the immediate executive in charge and the perpetrators are released and take the fall for their actions. This "falling on the sword" allows the head person, who is considered too valuable to the organization, to escape any incrimination or consequences. The London whale was providing JPMorgan an expensive lesson in unmanaged risk with positions that involved billions of dollars in losses. Somebody had to be held responsible for this oversight, and Jamie Dimon felt his chief investment officer was the one to go, along with the trader. This situation was discussed in chapter 3 under "Tempest in a Teapot."

In chess, a skewer involves a piece located behind a more valuable piece on a file, rank, or diagonal. When the more valuable piece moves away, the piece behind is lost. In diagram 6, Black's king is in check from the White rook. In a classical endgame skewer, Black moves his king anywhere on the seventh rank, and then White plays Rh7+. The king is forced to move then Rxa7, winning the game. The more valuable king had to give way to the check and allowed the rook behind him to subsequently get captured. Often this tactic is considered the juxtaposition of a pin where the valuable piece is behind the protector. Here the valuable piece is in front and cannot take the hit, so a subordinate takes it when the original target steps aside.

Desperado
(I'm going down and taking you with me)

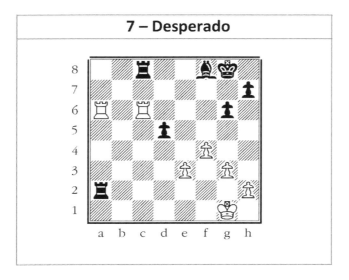

The desperado tactic happens in business when an employee feels they have nothing to lose because they have already lost what they had, and they go after the offenders. The legitimization of whistle-blowing is an example of somebody going desperado. They are being terminated for a falsified condition, and they go to authorities, letting them know what is really happening illegally within the company. It's a disgruntled employee who goes back onto the premises to take the boss with him. A terminated employee files a suit against the company as a last resort. These are acts of desperation that are now—due to legal protection—considered a legitimate form of retaliation.

This tactic was used against me during a payroll system upgrade. Senior executives were miffed that they had to receive their multimillion-dollar bonuses in multiple six-figure deposits because of the size limitation of the special-pay field. The solution was to expand the field by upgrading to a newer release of software that very few companies were using at the time. Even though I considered the project high risk, my client had promised the executives the upgrade. However, if the upgrade didn't go well, my client told me, "If I'm going down, I am taking you with me."

A whistle-blower's evidence prompted one of America's biggest banks to pay out $9 billion to avoid federal prosecution. Alayne Fleischmann was a lawyer with JPMorgan Chase & Co. in 2006 who tried to alert her managers to the bank's policy of reselling subprime mortgages to investors without warning them of the danger. Ms. Fleischmann was let go from the bank in February 2008. The nondisclosure agreement she signed did not prevent her from discussing any criminal wrongdoing. Ms. Fleischmann said she knew that by speaking out, she risked being sued by JPMorgan. She said, "The assumption they make is that I won't blow up my life to do it. But they're wrong about that."[6]

In an interview with *Rolling Stone* magazine, Ms. Fleischman said she could not believe how a private company executive could just pick up the phone and start negotiating with the Department of Justice to settle an active investigation without admitting or denying guilt. Those open lines of communication must have been established during the 2008 financial crisis when JPMorgan Chase & Co. played a critical part in helping the government handle all the failing institutions they were dealing with. Ms. Fleischman may still get her day in court as reports are surfacing that federal prosecutors are still pursuing criminal cases against JPMorgan Chase executives. With time running out on bringing cases from the 2008 financial crisis to court, *The Wall Street Journal* reported: "Prosecutors unearthed a 2007 memo written by a bank employee warning her bosses before the financial crisis hit that they were putting bad loans into securities, warnings that were ignored. That memo helped the Justice Department develop a legal basis for the then-record 2013 settlement."[7]

In chess, desperado happens when a piece is going to be captured. Rather than go away for nothing, the desperate piece takes anything of value with them. I played the tactic against Ms. Zepeda who trapped my bishop in the game described in chapter 3. The position in diagram 7 is from a game I played against Grandmaster Gregory Kaidanov. I noticed that his rook on a6 was overworked, guarding the rook on c6 and a bishop on a2, so I captured the bishop on a2. He was going to be forced to trade a rook. No matter which one he took, his other rook would be captured. He went desperado and got the pawn on g6 for his rook. Rxg6+ was with check. Black captured it with hxg6 then White captured the rook on a2. We went on to draw the game, and if I had one more pawn on the board, it would have made a huge difference and given me a better chance to win.

Sacrifice
(Investing in the future)

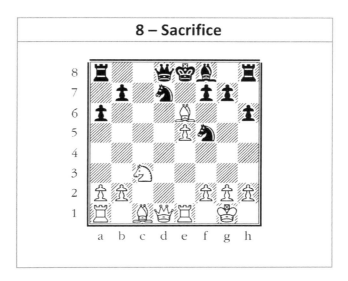

8 – Sacrifice

In September 2013, Microsoft decided to make an investment by buying Nokia's phone business for $7.2 billion. By acquiring the stake, Microsoft intended to compete with Google and Apple in the smartphone business. At the time, CEO Steve Ballmer said it was a great acquisition. In July 2015, Microsoft announced they had written off the Nokia purchase for $7.6 billion in the last quarter, creating only the third unprofitable quarter in the company's history.

A sacrifice in business or chess is an investment. A company might choose to give up the use of cash in the bank in order to build a plant. It might also be a good stakeholder and give away some profits to a worthwhile charity. Usually when they make an investment, the company expects a certain return on the money they are no longer able to use. They invest today's dollars in a project, hoping for a better return in the future.

In chess, a sacrifice happens when a player voluntarily gives up more material now than they get back, hoping to get a better return later. It's a tactic because the opportunity to sacrifice is not always present in the position. There is usually an ulterior motive like exposing the opponent's king or putting them in a weak position. Another reason to sacrifice is to introduce the element of the surprise attack into the contest. A good general knows that attacking an unsuspecting, unprepared opponent can lead to an advantage. In diagram 8, White has just sacrificed a bishop on e6. If the f-pawn takes the bishop, then White will move the queen to h5+ with check. The Black king will be in a precarious position, needing to avoid further checks while potentially losing pieces still on the board. This position is from Bachler vs. Egerton in chapter 11.

In-Between Move
(Getting in the way of progress)

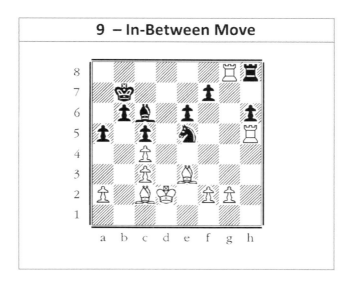

9 – In-Between Move

Business activities often follow a sequential-move type format of a game. A sales cycle, hiring process, or a legal procedure can go back and forth with one expected move after another. Sometimes, however, the next anticipated step doesn't occur. In business, managers most often resort to an in-between move when they find themselves in a weak position.

When you have the upper hand, you push ahead, but if you are in a weak situation, you avoid the decision. A buyer who realizes there isn't enough budget to pay for a purchase may "go dark" by avoiding contact with the bidders after the bids are in. An employee anticipating being fired may beat the supervisor to the punch by quitting, especially if the employee found another job. An in-between move may be as simple as a manager who purposely arranges for an assistant to call them away from a meeting to avoid having to weigh-in on an unpopular decision.

In chess, an in-between move is an unexpected or unanticipated move your opponent plays because your moves were not forced. This tactic is used frequently when an opponent answers a threat with a counterattack. Since the move is not forcing, like a check to the king, alternative moves need to be investigated to make sure they don't contain hidden dangers. In diagram 9 from chapter 6, Magnus had just blundered by moving his king to d2 during game six of his world championship match.

Vishy had a tactical combination available with 26...Nxe5! White could not take the free knight because his rook on g4 was hanging with 27. Rxe5?, Rxg4! His g4 rook was attacked twice, and the best move was to exchange it for the rook on g8 with 28. Rxg8. Vishy had two in-between moves with 29...Nxc4+ 30. Kd3, 30...Nb2+ then 31...Rxg8 recovers his rook. Magnus went on to win this game in thirty-eight moves after Vishy played 26...a4??

Interference
(Harassment)

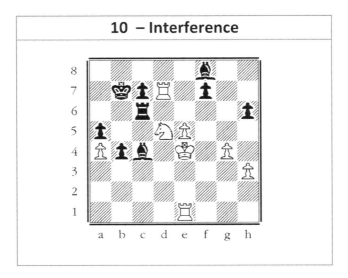

10 – Interference

This business tactic is one of not allowing employees to perform their job in the way they see fit. A department that has a micromanaging director who wants to be involved in the entire decision-making process inhibits productivity. At a more severe level, harassment is where an employee is given unwanted attention that prevents them from doing their work in a nonthreatening environment. A boss or coworker makes an employee miserable and wants them to quit.

Before going desperado, Alayne Fleischmann, the lawyer with JPMorgan, tried to alert her managers about reselling subprime mortgages to investors and met with interference from her management. It used to be that if you wrote a memo, they had to stop because now there's proof that they knew what they were doing. Ms. Fleischman claimed one of her managers wanted to institute a no-e-mail policy to eliminate any paper trail. She said, "If you sent him an e-mail, he would actually come out and yell at you. The whole point of having a compliance and diligence group is to have policies that are set out clearly in writing. So to have exactly the opposite of that – that was very worrisome."[8]

In chess, interference happens when a piece is deliberately placed in a position so that it gets in the way of other pieces that are doing a job. In diagram 10 the knight on d5 interferes with the Black bishop's ability to guard the pawn on f7. In the game, Magnus captured the pawn, forcing the Black bishop to flee to c5, its only safe square.

Under-Promotion
(You'll be next)

In 2001, General Electric CEO Jack Welch had a tough decision to make. Having declared his intentions to retire, he needed to announce who would replace him as CEO. Following the GE tradition of promoting from within, he had three viable candidates from which to choose. Jeffery Immelt became CEO in 2001. So what happened to the two candidates who were "under-promoted" and didn't get the CEO position? With encouragement from Mr. Welch, they went on to become CEOs elsewhere at Boeing, Home Depot, and Chrysler. Their departure was a loss for GE but an honor and a common occurrence in business. When someone doesn't get the top job they were in line for, they leave the firm.

I Experienced Under-Promotion

Under-promotion happened to me when I started my business career. I worked for a facility management company doing heavy technical support of mainframe computers. For four years I maintained a CICS IBM mainframe platform for medical claims processing. I worked for a great boss who sent me to training, gave me good assignments, and took a personal interest in my IT career. We went out socially, and we went fishing on Lake Michigan. He came to our wedding and helped us move into our first house. Why would anybody stop working for such a great manager? When he was promoted, he went outside the company and hired somebody from his past to fill his position. After four years of building up sweat equity, I was under-promoted, which removed my previous support due to a change in reporting. I had a new boss.

I stayed for a few more months but then moved on to another company. Consider this a teaching moment if you are early in your career. Have a strategy in place in case you become under-promoted. Should you stay, move on, or transfer to another position in the company? If you prepare your variations ahead of time, your decision will be easier. One industry that likes under-promotion is the executive search business. They actively seek fresh talent to fill open positions they are recruiting for.

In business, under-promoting happens when a promotion is held back because management prefers another employee. If two people compete for the same job, only one can have it. The loser may be transferred to another position. In some cases, the under-promoted employee may receive a minor upgrade now and a full promotion later when another opening occurs. A "time-in-grade" promotion happens when an employee receives a small bump in salary based on their time with the company and as a reward for their experience. A full promotion may take years of good performance and fills an open position with a new title, more pay, and new responsibilities.

An Olympic Winning Moment
Use the following link to see how this game used under-promotion

http://www.365chess.com/game.php?gid=3825514

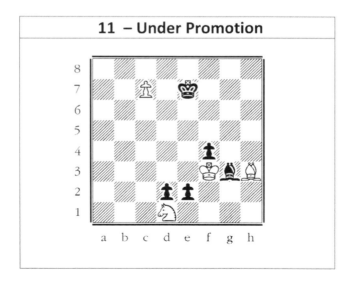

Under-promotion is much rarer in chess than in business because having a queen appear back on the board is usually a winning moment. But in some situations, going for something less is better. It's promoting to something less than a queen for a tactical reason like a fork by using a knight. Under-promotion may prevent a stalemate formation from occurring.

Diagram 11 is from the 2012 World Chess Olympiad held in Istanbul, Turkey. First board player for the USA team was Hikaru Nakamura who was playing White against Vladimir Kramnik, a former world champion from Russia. On his sixty-first move, Kramnik played 61...e2, advancing his pawn with a threat to capture White's knight, which was on d1, and also promoting to a queen with check no less. To see the artistry of this under-promotion, activate the link above and click on Black's sixty-first move to set up the diagram. Through the brilliant use of under-promotion, Nakamura promoted his pawn to a knight with check 63.c8 (N)+, forcing a Black king move followed by Kxe2, capturing the pawn on e2, and he went on to win the game.

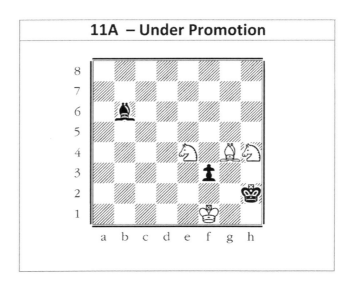

The final winning position warrants its own diagram shown in 11A. With Black to move here, he has few good alternatives. Move the pawn to f2, king to h1, or bishop somewhere. That will be followed up by White moving a knight to f3+ followed by Kh1 and then either Nf2# or Ng3#. Three minor pieces get to the Black king, which has to be driven into the corner first to do the checkmate. Notice that White's king on f1 covered the critical square g2. In business, leaders often have to work with the associates they have available. Here Nakamura had all four of his pieces working together to achieve victory.

If Nakamura had played 62 Kxe2 right away in diagram 11, then 62...f3+ freed up the Black bishop's diagonal to capture the last White pawn on c7, resulting in a draw. By winning this game, the USA team went on to beat the powerful Russian four-man team 2 ½ to 1 ½—a great day in US chess history. The US team finished fifth in the competition of 157 teams. The Russians finished tied for first, but Armenia won the gold medal on the tiebreaker.

Removing the Defender
(Equilibrium lost)

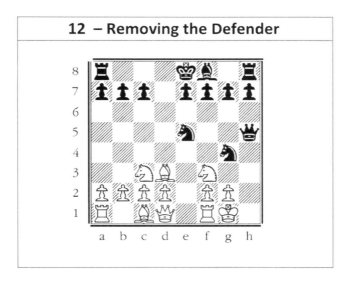

12 – Removing the Defender

In May 2011, Microsoft agreed to acquire Skype, the Internet communications company, for $8.5 billion. "Tony Bates has a great track record as a leader and will strengthen the Microsoft management team. I'm looking forward to Skype's talented global workforce bringing its insights, ideas and experience to Microsoft,"[9] Steve Ballmer said. When the acquisition became effective, Tony Bates, CEO of Skype, reported to CEO Steve Ballmer as the president of the division.

This is Microsoft's standard acquisition process. They take some time to understand and integrate the new business but eventually merge them into an existing business line. After Tony got a new boss, everyone in the Skype organization lost a defender because Microsoft was now calling the shots. Just by coincidence, within a few years after he got under-promoted by not becoming the next CEO of Microsoft, Tony Bates moved on to other opportunities.

In business, when a company is acquired, a new CEO from the acquiring company is usually named to head the acquired entity. The acquiring company has an employee they can trust running the new organization. If the acquired management was left in place, a critical trust factor might be missing. An intellectual capital company is vulnerable to this tactic because it's a knowledge business. If the employees leave, they take their knowledge with them. When high-profile people leave a financial company to start a hedge fund, for example, they often take several people with them to start the new firm. In the old company, those people lost their defender while at the new company their defender is still in place.

Remove-the-defender tactic is used in a military maneuver to cut off supplies and reserves from enemy troops that need support. The maneuver can result in victory over these underdefended fighters. Some conspiracy theorists believe that President Kennedy's assassination was a remove-the-defender tactic because his brother, the attorney general, was prosecuting organized crime during his term. Because Vice President Johnson and Bobby Kennedy were incompatible, if the president were gone, Bobby would leave because the assassin had removed his defender, his brother the president. In fact, Bobby stayed on for several more months after the assassination but did leave his attorney general position in the Johnson administration. This would be a historic example of removing the defender if it could ever be proven.

In chess, at times you may have a piece that must remain on the board to guard another piece or protect a square. If your opponent captures that piece, then the piece it was guarding will no longer be defended.

"Removing the defender" leaves you vulnerable to such an attack. If your opponent removes your defending piece, the piece you were trying to protect will have to face the consequences.

Diagram 12 will appear in chapter 10 when Bill Gates plays Magnus Carlsen. White is threatened with having his knight on f3, a defender of the square h2, removed by Back's knight on e5. If that knight is removed, it is no longer defending h2, and he will be checkmated.

Tactics Applied in Business Situations

Business tactics appear in various situations and are used against different competitors.

A Business to Business (B2B) tactic is Microsoft decoying competitors away from developing other products by announcing new releases way ahead of time. They also decoyed the government from taking action against monopolistic practices they were using.

A Business to Consumer (B2C) tactic is an in-between move, such as when a business decides to offer a coupon but then makes it extremely difficult to redeem the offer. Companies have been fined because they introduce in-between steps consumers must go through to claim their reimbursement. A credit-card company pressured customers into buying credit-monitoring services and has been fined for deceptive credit-card practices. The Consumer Financial Protection Bureau said the company was fined for misleading card customers into buying unnecessary products like payment protection and credit monitoring.

A Consumer to Business (C2B) tactic is an attack when multiple customers boycott (attack) companies that are not operating up to their standards.

The website http://www.ethicalconsumer.org/boycotts/boycottslist.aspx lists numerous companies facing C2B boycott tactics being used against them.

A Business to Employee (B2E) tactic is the use of reorganizations and layoffs. The Iacocca story is a brutal example of this tactic.

An <u>Employee to Business (E2B)</u> tactic is any occurrence of a desperado whistleblower that goes after the company. The Justice Department said it had paid out roughly $1.98 billion in whistleblower awards from 2009 to 2013. Not all is going well for whistleblowers, however; some are receiving retaliation.

> The *Chicago Tribune* reported that whistleblowers in the Department of Veteran Affairs continued to receive retaliation "despite repeated pledges to stop punishing those who speak up" after a scandal over falsified records covering up chronic delays in veterans medical care. [10]

> *The Wall Street Journal* reported that the SEC has been investigating whether companies are "muzzling corporate whistleblowers" especially by forcing non-disclosure agreements or removing financial incentives for participating in programs designed to expose wrongdoings. [11]

An <u>Employee to Employee (E2E)</u> tactic is a desperado employee trying to hinder a coworker. This tactical situation is perhaps the most devastating on the individual level. Employees have to compete for promotions, work assignments, bonuses, etc. against each other, so it is hard to determine when the competition becomes detrimental. The employee-versus-employee situation is the basis of office politics and can destroy promising careers, an example of which happened in my own department.

Office Politics Involves the Use of Chess Tactics

As the VP of an IT systems development department, I had to hire and manage people in large part because of their technical skills. Since these skills were so rare, I had to overlook potential employee character flaws if the employee could maintain a critical system. Most of my IT career involved maintaining HR or payroll systems that contained confidential data. I made it a point during the hiring process to warn potential employees that they had to work with that data. It went with the territory.

My first hire was Tony (names have been changed), a mainframe specialist working on the payroll system. Several months later I hired Tina to work on the same system and provide backup support and other project work.

Within months I hired Bob to work on a system that input data into the payroll system but that didn't require access to HR data.

At my annual employee appreciation dinner in the city, it was getting late, and I thought it admirable when Tony offered to walk Tina home from the restaurant. Weeks went by, and I noticed nothing until I walked into a heated argument between the two in her cubicle one day after work. Unbeknownst to me, they had been seeing each other, but Tina wanted to discontinue that arrangement.

Tina started hanging out with Bob, a military veteran, for protection against Tony's stalking and harassment. Tony realized that his interference tactic wasn't working anymore with Tina. He decided to switch to the desperado tactic against Bob. One day he took the opportunity to pull Bob over to the computer monitor and showed him he was the only employee in my department not to receive a bonus that year. Within minutes Bob was in my office demanding an explanation. "Who told you about that?" I asked, and he replied, "Tony." I told him it was none of his business. He should not have been exposed to the data, and he'd best forget about it. Bob didn't feel that was fair and developed a negative attitude about his work going forward.

Shortly thereafter, Tina came into my office, closed the door, and said, "I have to play a voice mail for you." The phone message revealed Tony in an intoxicated state using the interference tactic to harass her about not getting good assignments in the department and making things difficult for her.

It was time to get HR involved. Within an hour, HR called and asked me to have Tony report to HR immediately. To no one's surprise, Tony never returned from HR.

Weeks later Bob continued to discuss how unhappy he was with his bonus situation and started talking about the guns he had at home. When one of my employees gave me that message, it was time to get HR involved. I called Bob into my office and told him that HR wanted to see him. He didn't ask why or seem perturbed; he simply left immediately. Bob never returned from HR.

We had an armed guard at our elevator floor for two weeks because Bob was a demolitions expert in the military and had complete access to our corporate data center. Statistically, if after two weeks nothing happens, the coast is considered clear, unlike the television interview shooting that occurred years later.

Both of these employees performed their jobs at acceptable levels and were doing the jobs they were hired to do. Yet two promising IT careers were derailed over the use of E2E office political tactics. Tactics are used by real employees, not just by the pieces positioned on a chessboard. Leaders who are strategically stronger and tactically sharper are now aware of the most common tactics and when they are used.

Looking Back—Moving Forward

- ➢ Make or break your company using tactical business opportunities.
- ➢ Name, know, and use the tactics you have in your toolbox.
- ➢ Hunt for tactics in a superior strategic position.
- ➢ Deflect the damage of B2B, B2C, C2B, B2E, E2B and E2E tactical attacks precisely.

In our next chapter, we examine the functional areas with which a business leader needs to be conversant to be successful. The leader must be able to manage projects, evaluate investments, track assets, appreciate and use technology, engineer and build good structures, conduct a campaign, recognize supply and demand, and understand all the rules needed to assume complete responsibility for business on the board. It's a tall order that can challenge even the best businesspeople in the world, but it's next on our to-do list so let's move forward.

Chapter 8

MBA Using Gamification
- First Semester

"Win, Lose, or Draw it's how you play the ..."

When I was promoted to a management position in business, I had a mathematics degree and a communication minor. My on-the-job training was in heavy IBM systems technology paid completely by the employers I worked for because they needed employees with specific technical skills. How did I move ahead without a business degree or formal management training? I had to learn how to play the game. Learning to play the game of business has itself become a big business.

Gamification in business training is a popular way for trainers to make content easier to understand and more meaningful. We grew up playing games, and if anything can be presented in that format, it will resonate. The verb "playing" conjures up what everyone wanted to do after school. Golfers head for the practice range, tennis players hit with the ball machine, and baseball players get into the batting cage. Inexperienced drivers spend time in the simulator before getting out on the road while pilots are in the simulator to rehearse certain situations before they handle them, if ever, in midair. Such simulations and practice are substitutes for real experience. The skills honed during practice, however, carry over to business as well as athletics. Decision-making without consequences makes practice worthwhile. In chess it's called playing. In business it's considered work.

Acquiring Business Education and Experience

Companies grooming future leaders spend heavily on business education, especially to encourage employees to earn their master's degree in business administration (MBA). Several decades of working in corporate America for different Fortune 500 companies was appended with three and a half years of evening classes for me to receive my MBA degree. The MBA formally described and assembled all the pieces needed to see the business puzzle come together, academically at least. Employee development comes in many styles and forms. Formal degree-based education can provide the theory behind business practices. Vendor training on specific types of technology and functional mastery can lead to certifications of project managers and HR professionals. On-the-job training is required to educate inexperienced employees on specific needs and practices of an organization. A consulting firm may spend months bringing a newbie up to speed on their methodologies for auditing, taxes, or system implementations.

Business Essentials

The mechanics of running a business are really not very complicated, when you get down to essentials. You have to make some stuff and sell it to somebody for more than it cost you. That's about all that there's to it, except for a few million details.

John L. McCaffrey,
"What Corporation Presidents Think about at Night".

At best, the MBA degree provides only an overview into all the business disciplines. The accounting content of the program isn't enough to earn a CPA. When I managed a systems department that ran the applications of a holding company, I had to relate to accountants, financial people, engineers, and HR practitioners. I supported the systems they used, and I had to be responsive to their needs. That's where the MBA paid dividends. The biggest benefit of my MBA was that it helped me understand what my clients were accomplishing. Today MBAs are graduating into the best opportunities in over a decade, especially those with a finance or technology emphasis. Those with an MBA often earn double what undergraduates are paid.

The Case for Cases

In his book *Talent is Overrated,* Geoff Colvin says hours of deliberate practice separate great performers from the ordinary. He uses chess as an application of deliberate practice since chess progress can be measured through competition. Chess players get better through studying previous games and positions, which he branded "the chess model." The deliberate move selection process of what you would do in this situation can improve job performance through seeing patterns repeatedly and receiving feedback. The chess model has been used for centuries by chess players. For the last eighty-five years, it's been used in business education as the case method. Championed by the Harvard Business School, the process of defining a problem and generating solutions helps explain why hundreds of business schools use the case method.

The chess model, rebranded as the case method, presents different background material for students to acquaint themselves with the issues of a particular situation. The more cases studied, the more supposed expertise is gained, with students reviewing hundreds of cases during their degree program. The benefits, however, are not just reading the content but acting on the information like a chess player would act upon a certain position with specific moves and dealing with the consequences. Chess games become unique and, if recorded, can be inspected for winning and losing moves, not unlike actions that companies make in business. During intense periods of the MBA program, I did three to four case-study presentations a week while working my full-time management job and supporting a family.

The Case against Cases

Although the case method has its advocates, there are those who do not see the value of the method. One drawback to reading so many cases is how to remember all the content reviewed or completed. As time passes, so do the details or even the memory of previous case analysis done in business school. This is not so with the chess case method. Chess study continues to add value where previous information is updated with a game or study that has more recent content. I have been playing the Sicilian Defense for decades. When I return to chess competition, it's like Celine Dion singing in the background, "It's all coming back to me now," as previous games and analysis get pulled from long-term memory. My chapter 3 strategic mistake occurred in 1996; the tactical mistake was twelve years later in 2008, yet the first five moves were the same, with the second game going a different direction on the next move.

In their insightful expose, *Management, It's Not What You Think*, Henry Mintzberg, et al., harpoon some of the most classic thoughts on business management training and the negative effects it generates. "The only thing a chief executive sits atop is an organization chart. And all that silly document does is demonstrate how mesmerized we are with the abstraction called management. The next time you look at one of these charts, cover the name of the organization and try to figure out what it actually does for a living."[1]

Mintzberg believes: "It's time to close down conventional MBA programs. We should be developing real managers, not pretending to create them in the classroom. It's plain silly to take people who have never been managers, many of whom have neither worked full-time for more than a few years, and pretend to be turning them into managers in a classroom. The whole exercise is too detached from context. We need to stop dumping management theories and cases on people who have no basis even to judge the relevance."[2]

In line with what Jack Welch wanted to create at GE with his corporate training, Mintzberg believes, "Managing is learned on the job, enhanced by a variety of experiences and challenges."[3]

Others believe that Harvard Business School has not kept pace with the times in teaching management during the technology era. HBS's strict adherence to the case-study methods focuses on business dilemmas from years or decades past, rather than the current forces shaping the business of technology, which includes issues with which the graduates are expected to be well versed. HBS trains people to be CEOs, CMOs—every sort of C except the CTO or the CIO role. Harvard says they are working on the situation although they admit, compared to MIT and Stanford, they have less tech in the air.[4]

Depicted below is a functional company organization chart. In deference to Professor Mintzberg, this company manufactures chess players who go on to become leaders because they know how to make these departments work together.

Organization Chart for Business on the Board

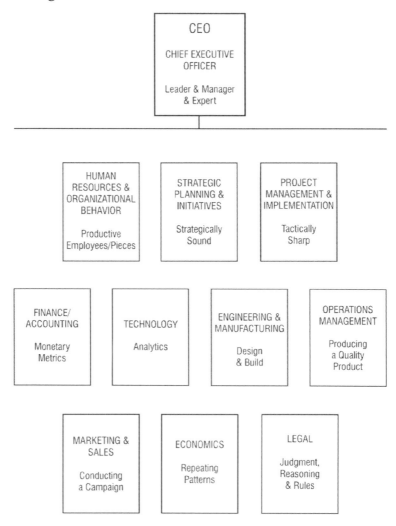

Like each unique chess game, no two businesses are exactly alike, but each one has common similarities. The employees in the organization are the pieces on the chessboard. Some of the pieces have human characteristics and have evolved in description and functionality during the centuries. The corporate hierarchy existed in the kingdom with the king ruling the enterprise. A picture is worth a thousand words, but this organization chart needs to be broken down to see what value each function adds to the company.

Human Resources & Organizational Behavior

Human capital accomplishes the work of the organization. HR helps create an organization and maintains the policies that govern the behavior of the company along with how the enterprise is organized, who is going to work there, and how they are going to be compensated. In chess, we have inherited sixteen employees with six different skills sets ready to go to work. The leader of the chess workforce incorporates the role of the chief HR officer (CHRO). HR decisions are made at high levels with significant impact to the outcome of the game. Strategically focused on improving the team's performance, the CHRO works with other "C-suite" individuals to develop and execute plans on how employee performance will win the game of business. How this organization chart box relates to chess was discussed in chapter 2, HR & Organizational Behavior.

Strategic Planning & Initiatives

The Strategic Planning department is charged with determining what projects will add the most value and what the priority should be for accomplishing each project. Alternatives are available, and deciding whether to attack the competition and what will constitute a successful outcome needs to be determined. Strategies like playing for a certain sector of the market, establishing a location, getting proper resources aligned to carry out the campaign, and keeping the opponent from inflicting damage to our enterprise all need to be evaluated. Strategies, including mergers and acquisitions that businesses and chess players use, leadership strategies, and management and expertise phase strategies were discussed in previous chapters. The decisions regarding which projects to do are based on financial decisions using metrics covered under Finance and Accounting in this chapter and implemented in chapter 11.

Project Management and Implementation

Larger companies utilize a department responsible for implementing projects. The project management office (PMO) manages the project, acquires resources from within the company, allocates a budget, and sets a timeline in a project plan to accomplish their deliverables. Once the required and selected projects have been determined, the PMO maps out the order of activities and tactics to employ, including the timing for best results. Chess projects proceed one step at a time since, in this sequential board game, we have to wait to see what our opponents are doing. In business, project tasks can be parallel, but some are contingent on tasks to complete before other tasks can start.

Projects require separate management. Every business venture, every chess game, every job search is a project and requires specific resources in order to be successful. So what is a project? According to Eric Verzuh, author of *The Fast Forward MBA in Project Management,* "Projects are all the work that's done one time, and ongoing operations represent the work we perform over and over."[5]

Two characteristics of projects are:

- Every project has a beginning and an end. Official kickoff meetings notify participants of their involvement. In chess, it's when the tournament director announces "start your clocks" for the round. Everyone has to know when a project is complete. In chess, it's over when the players post their scores on the official results sheet.

- Every project is unique, and every chess game produces a unique set of moves. The outcome could produce a building, a software system, or a document on employee hiring policies. Chess games, like a piece of art, are unique and end. The project of a world championship chess match could go on for months. The Carlsen and Anand match was mercifully limited to twelve games, so the players knew where the end was before it began.

Completing a game of chess is the same as managing a project. It has a specific start date, goes through cycles or phases, requires resources to compete, and ends with a checkmate, resignation, or draw. Each game becomes unique and follows a series of steps (moves) that initiate the project, design, and construct formations, while implementing strategies and tactics to win the game.

In my career, I managed hundreds of projects. They ranged from moving people from one floor in a building to another building entirely. We moved mainframe computers inside a data center and moved entire data centers. The projects involved training groups on using their systems and maintaining the software they were using. Thousands of employees were paid through the numerous payroll conversion projects I managed.

Chess-game projects follow a critical path (CPM) of activities needed to start the game off on a solid foundation. Good chess players develop one piece before another so that the two pieces do not interfere or block each other. Interference prevents two pieces from accomplishing anything constructive for the team. If a task is on the critical path, it must be completed when required, or other tasks on the project can be delayed.

In the opening, a short-term project deliverable is to mitigate the risk to the business by moving the king into a castle. Castling is a good example of a project because you do it only once a game. Castling should be on the critical path of any chess game. At the beginning of the game, the king is in the middle of the back rank, so certain tasks have to be accomplished before the castle can be occupied. All the squares between the rook and the king need to be vacant, so the following tasks need to be accomplished.

Project Plan for Castling the King Short (0-0)

Task #	Explanation of the Work Item – Work Breakdown Structure (WBS)
1	Move the knight on g1 to f3 toward the center of the board.
2	Move the e-pawn or g-pawn up to allow the bishop to move.
3	Move the bishop to c4 or g2, depending on the previous move.
4	Move the king over two squares and the rook around the king.

By breaking the goal down into the tasks necessary for completion, we can monitor the progress being made toward the objective.

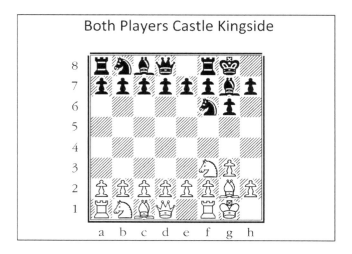

The castling work breakdown structure (WBS) introduces the concept of contingent tasks. Task 1 could have been accomplished any time before Task 4. However, Task 3 could be done only after Task 2 was completed, so a Gantt chart would only show that task starting after Task 2 was completed. If the e and g pawns were glued to the board and could not move, the king would never castle, at least on the kingside.

Once a project is completed, it is turned over to operations to run and maintain on a set schedule. In my career, payroll conversion projects were all different, but in the end the objective was to put the new employees on the payroll system to get them paid.

Finance and Accounting

Finance and accounting are essential functions in any business. These disciplines are responsible for tracking company assets and deciding how the company wants to allocate their assets and resources. They work with human resources to establish a compensation system where the employees are determined to have relative value for the company and get paid accordingly. Business writer, Colin Barrow, defines accounting as "… the process of recording and analyzing transactions that involve events that can be assigned a monetary value."[6] Finance uses accounting information for acquiring and allocating the resources that a company needs with the intent of getting the best return on those resources.

Business accounting generally makes the news when it is improperly conducted. Enron imploded into bankruptcy because of their "creative" accounting practices. Toshiba appears to be a more current example of "cooking the books." Herbalife and Boeing are two companies facing scrutiny over their accounting practices. Even Warren Buffet believes some companies are playing loose and fast with the generally accepted accounting principles (GAAP). Headlines aside, our business game of chess allocates 100 percent of our working capital to our employees. HR determined the value of our employees based on their work capability. How the players go about using their human capital determines whether they win or lose the game. If they don't create enough value from their workface to win, they could break even (draw) or even lose if they don't use their resources wisely.

Where did funds for our human capital come from? Not unlike Monopoly®, in this particular business game they were granted to us to use. It compares in kind to a portfolio manager who is given a certain amount of working capital or money from a pension fund or a 401(k) and told to invest the proceeds wisely. In order to tell whether our portfolio managers are doing an acceptable job with our money, we need certain metrics to analyze their performance.

In chess, one of the first things a player will do to assess a game is to count the pieces to see who is ahead. Understanding accounting is critical for anyone wanting to succeed at chess.

Financial and Managerial Accounting

The two types of accounting deal with tracking the firm's external reporting or internal asset evaluation. The balance sheet and the income statements drive the reporting for the company's long-term position and current period use of assets. The four primary financial statements—the balance sheet, income statement, statement of retained earnings, and statement of cash flows—must adhere to strict GAAP rules that provide an accurate picture of an enterprise's financial position.

Managerial accounting tracks, measures, and analyzes the firm's financial information. That information is used to strategize about future undertakings to bring the organization success. The chief financial officer (CFO) is in charge of the entire financial operation, and thus is responsible for financial organization and planning. A chess player acts as their own CFO, determining what moves to make that will lead to success and tracking what capital has been expensed and any profit that has been returned in that effort.

Cost accounting is used to determine the costs of products, processes, or projects. If we pursue an attack against our opponent, we will most likely incur costs in the form of exchanged or lost pawns or pieces in order to conduct that campaign. The important concept is that the value of our pieces is relative. A pawn on its original square does not have the value of one on the seventh rank threatening to promote. If it makes it through to promotion, it may cost our opponent a piece to keep our new queen off the board.

In chess, when pieces are exchanged, the value of the asset is removed from the books. But the objective is to obtain fair value or, better yet, a profit due to the exchange of material on the board. After each exchanging move, there should be the mental equivalent of a general-ledger transaction on the books that debits working capital and credits cash for the piece. For example, if we give up a bishop worth $3 and get a rook worth $5 (called "winning the exchange" in chess), we would debit working capital $3 and credit cash $5. If we did a closing of the books after that move, our income statement would show a profit of $2. The long-term balance sheet that is maintained throughout the game would be projecting a healthy outlook for the firm because assets outweigh liabilities and profits are increasing. Because of the zero-sum nature of chess, our opponent's books would show the opposite side of the transaction, including a loss on the income statement and negative balance sheet.

Chess Margins Are Thin

In business, margin is the difference between profit and breakeven. That is what a for-profit business seeks: sell something for more than its cost and keep the profit as retained earnings. In chess, the margins between winning and losing are very slim. A $1 deficit is a cause for concern if there is no compensation like a lead in development or exposed king to show for the transaction. If you are $2 down, you are on the edge of defeat (i.e., bankruptcy) if you don't have adequate compensation for the loss. When they are $3 down against a good player, most opponents resign because they know that the loss is generally unrecoverable. That's what occurred in the following position. Black had just played his bishop to d6.

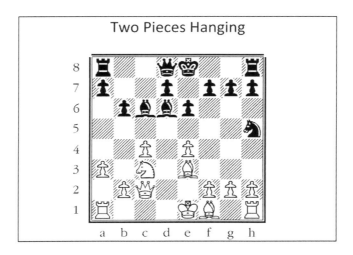

The auditors would report that a $3 knight and $1 pawn have been traded, so both players have breakeven book value transactions in the position. Black, however, had a huge risk factor in the position with an unprotected knight on h5. It wasn't a problem at the time because if White attacked it, the Black knight could move back to safety. However, Black introduced a second risk factor by moving a bishop to d6, which left a second piece unprotected. We know from our risk factor discussion in chapter 4 that having one or more unprotected pieces can allow our opponent to obtain a competitive advantage.

And White does exactly that. Can you find the move that White played? The move involves a double-attack tactic. Is there a move that attacks the knight on h5 and the bishop on d6 at the same time? There is 12. Qd1!! wins a piece. Both pieces cannot be protected at the same time, so Black suffered a $3 loss and chose to resign the game.

A game between two of my high school players, you might think? Try again. White was Grandmaster Larry Christiansen from the USA and Black was Grandmaster Anatoly Karpov, world champion from Russia. Yes, Karpov blundered and dropped a piece on move twelve. This was played in the second round of the strongest of grandmaster tournaments Wijk aan Zee in 1993. After the game, it's rumored that the affable Mr. Christiansen asked Anatoly if he wanted to go over the game, to which he replied, "Nyet."

The game is available at the following link:

http://www.365chess.com/game.php?gid=1762913

A bad day at the office for Mr. Karpov. But several months later he learned from his mistake and played 11...Qb8 first before moving the Bd6, protecting the square d6 before occupying it. In chapter 11, my opponent sacrificed, or invested, a $3 bishop for a $1 pawn for the compensation of my exposed king during the game. Here the world champion got nothing for his loss, and he shut down the enterprise—at least for the day.

Financial Metrics for Evaluating Business Projects or Candidate Moves in Chess

Some of the best decision-making tools available for business involve financial analysis. After "running the numbers" on the benefits and costs of a project or transaction, the results will determine if making that product or offering that service generates a profit. Chess players rarely use these formulas since they may not be aware of them and calculating them in your head could lead to mistakes. They would come to the conclusion that a sacrifice makes sense because they have compensation for the material. An exposed king, for example, would be worth more than a piece if it led to larger material gain or even checkmate. Good chess players do not give away their assets if they expect to win. Once when I was going over a game of mine with Grandmaster Gregory Kaidanov, I suggested using these metrics to him when considering candidate moves. He laughed off the idea with a resounding, "No." Like a financial analyst inspecting investment opportunities, he uses them when he considers his moves, he just doesn't know it.

Cost-benefit analysis. It costs time or material to do a set of moves in chess or transactions in business, such as buy and sell. To determine whether those actions were profitable, the benefits need to be compared to the cost. If we had an opportunity to take a queen from our opponent and had to give up only a rook, the benefit would outweigh the cost: $9 in for $5 out, resulting in a profit of $4.

Return on Investment (ROI). After a move or business transaction, what kind of financial return can we expect when the transaction is over? Getting ahead in our business game means we need to get more than we give up, making a profit. It's the cost-benefit expressed as a percentage. So if we give up our queen and a few moves later get our queen back plus a bishop, we earned 3/9 of profit, or 33 percent return on our investment.

Payback period is a classic metric for making good decisions based on time. How long must we wait—days, months, years—for our business investment to be returned? (In chess, we would ask, how many moves do we have to wait?) A longer period of time increases the risk because we may have overlooked an opponent's resourceful chess move. A thirty-year bond is longer than a five-year bond. Our money is at risk longer, so a thirty-year bond should have a higher rate of interest as compensation for the added risk. If we sacrifice, or invest, our $9 queen in a series of moves, do we have to wait four, five, or six moves to get our money back? If we don't get it back, it wasn't a wise decision, and we were better off doing something else.

Breakeven analysis is a metric that helps us know, after we have expended a certain amount of money, how much we have to get back in order to come out even. If we give away a rook to an opponent and get a bishop and pawn for it, we need another pawn to get to our $5 break-even point. If a company develops a widget that costs $1,000 to build and sells each widget for $2, they need to sell 500 widgets before they break even.

How long do we have to wait until we get our money back? What if we don't get our money back? We will have to recognize a loss; investments can lose money and often do although it's not the preferred outcome. However, because there always is risk and nothing is guaranteed, recognizing that a break-even point, payback period, ROI, and cost/benefit can fluctuate is an important consideration.

Applying Financial/Accounting Metrics
to Our Business Game

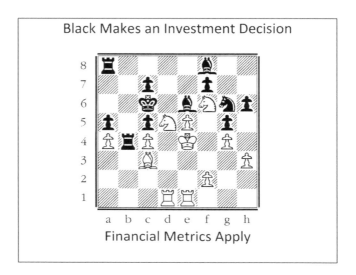

In chapter 5, GM Anand chose to sacrifice his rook in an attempt to generate counter play. Mr. Carlsen took the exchange and went on to win. Anand had to play from calculation and intuition here, but financial metrics might have helped him make a better decision. The metrics we have discussed, however, have to be simple for practical use in playing chess so that you can make calculations in your head and over the board. Net present value (NPV) and internal rate of return (IRR) are valuable metrics, but without having a calculator available to determine their values, it's beyond normal calculating ability. Fortunately, these valuable financial tools are readily available to support your business decision-making.

In chapter 11, these metrics will determine if a sacrifice my opponent played was "best play" sound or a mistake. Accounting and financial responsibilities are not shared but remain the sole domain of the players at the board.

Technology

Businesses and chess players use analytics to make information out of data. In a recent survey of chief information officers (CIO), a major consulting firm found that when asked which technologies will have significant impact on their business within two years, CIOs named analytics and business intelligence number one. Especially in those industries like manufacturing and construction with sizeable customer databases and intricate value chains, 77 percent selected analytics. Not far behind were digital, cloud, cybersecurity, and legacy/core modernization of existing systems as disruptors to their businesses.[7]

In our "Getting off to a Good Start" video, we used analytics to determine which two moves grandmasters use to start a chess game, which was based on gaining mobility for the pieces. All significant chess games from major tournaments are available electronically and can now be drilled down from a vast amount of data into meaningful information, all through the use of technology.

Information technology and social media have changed business and chess profoundly. Has this position ever been reached before? Who played it? What occurred next? Who won and lost? Was there an important improvement in the theory of handling this position? All of that is now available at the click of mouse.

Most chess games are won by having a material advantage (profit) that was gained through experience or insight. Having an advantage allows the leader flexibility in deciding which pieces to keep or exchange, thereby increasing chances for victory. Having an advantage is like having an insurance policy that can be "cashed in," allowing you to keep the direction of the game going in your favor. In chess, we can offer our opponent a gambit, which takes time and resources to maintain, putting a strain on other parts of the team. Many times players decline extra material or return it when they think it fits into their best strategy. When making a decision in the workplace, take into consideration what worked in the past, what didn't work, and what are considered best practices in your field.

Chess technology mirrors business technology and consists of engines, databases, websites, software, books, and periodicals. Engines are chess-playing programs that generate analysis using sophisticated programming to find the best move in a position. Those are the software models that businesses use to drill down into data, slicing and dicing their way into profitable scenarios. A large bank or insurance company could use such an engine/model to determine their value at risk (VaR).

Databases are large collections of chess games entered, classified, and sometimes annotated. Many of the databases are now online, which allows study of an opponent's preferences. The databases come with query and analysis modes where games can be selected by opening preference or position. Companies use databases to manage customers (CRM), maintain inventory, supply HR directories, and operate profitably. The legal department uses databases to review cases, judicial decisions, and prior litigation.

Chess websites allow people to play chess online, take training, or buy equipment to improve their abilities. Companies use their website as their customer-facing platform. Contact information, goods and services offered, as well as testimonials find prominent places on company websites. Chess software is available for strategic and tactical training as well as engines that play against an opponent. There are more chess books written than all other games combined, so there are plenty of publications available.

A List of Chess Technology Resources
That Have Business Applications

Engines	Website
Fritz	http://www.chessbase.com
Rybka	http://www.Rybkachess.com
Stockfish	http://Stockfishchess.org
Databases of Games	
Chessbase	http://www.chessbase.com
365chess.com	http://www.365chess.com
Chesstempo.com	http://www.chesstempo.com
Playing Websites	
Chess.com	http://www.chess.com
Internet Chess Club	http://www.chessclub.com
Playchess by Chessbase	http://en.playchess.com
Software & Books	
US Chess Federation	http://www.USCFSales.com
Chess House	http://www.chesshouse.com/
The Chess Store	https://thechessstore.com/
Periodicals	
Chess Life	https://new.uschess.org/home/
New in Chess	http://www.newinchess.com
British Chess Magazine	http://www.britishchessmagazine.co.uk/

Chess technology will be used in chapters 10 and 11 to determine whether the moves played were the best. Previous chapters have relied upon databases with graphical user interfaces (GUI) on the Internet to review games of mine and others. Business leaders often have a dashboard of important information present on their computers which allows them to monitor their company's vital signs in real-time.

Engineering and Manufacturing

Chess players and businesspeople use the power of engineering and manufacturing. The work of engineers and manufacturers is dedicated to making the properties of matter and sources of power in nature useful to humans in structures, machines, and products.[8] Fortresses, bridges, pyramids, and the utility of a chain are examples of structures and a device that have stood the test of time for the advantage of the owner.

In chess, the environment or original setup is anything but useful to the pieces on the board as 75 percent of the employee pieces cannot move. The most valuable piece is landlocked in the center of the board, and if he stays there, trouble is just around the corner. The space is limited to sixty-four squares, but some squares are more important than others.

Players have to engineer useful structures from what is available in the environment. It's not enough to know about these structures; you have to manufacture them at the board during the game. Insightful minds can build bridges, form and play from within a pyramid, reinforce chains, and construct fortresses, all of which keep our opponents from breaching our enterprise, allowing us to win the game.

The Functionality of the Pyramid

The pyramids of Egypt awe by their implausibility more than by their scale. Most were built between 2700 and 2100 BC by a civilization that labored without benefit of the wheel, the pulley, or a metal tougher than copper. More than the sum of its 2.3 million blocks averaging 2.5 tons each, the Great Pyramid of Giza soared 481 feet and still guards many secrets of its construction. Building for the ages upon 13.1 acres was not sufficient for the Egyptians. Preoccupied with their pharaoh's afterlife, they aimed for eternity.[9]

Structural formations like bridges, fortresses, and pyramids are found all over the world and can be replicated all over the chessboard as well. These configurations have been tested through hundreds of years of serious tournament play and are still the best formations for your employees/pieces to utilize today. Knowing these formations and incorporating them into your play will help you succeed at business and chess. These strong structures are manufactured through the moves being made during the game.

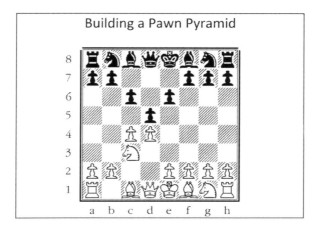

Building a Pawn Pyramid

The first useful formation is a functional two-dimensional pyramid with pawns that guard each other. Because pawns capture diagonally, when a pawn has another pawn supporting it from behind, the leading pawn is protected. A pyramid can appear in the middle of the board or when building the castle fortress for the king. In this example, the pawn on d5 is protected twice by c6 and e6 and is a stable formation for Black. This position is known as the Slav Defense against the Queen's Gambit.

The fianchetto (Italian for flanking) formation of playing the bishop into the pyramid was used when the pawn could not move two squares on its original move. Moving a central pawn only one square meant a bishop's movement was going to be obstructed by its own pawns.

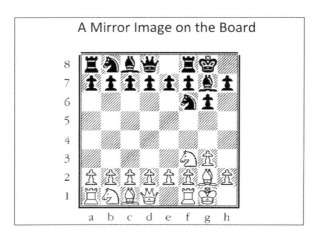

A Mirror Image on the Board

In India, where chess originated, pawns could only move up one square, which makes it difficult to get both bishops into the game. Their strategy was to fianchetto the bishop; these formations are easy to remember since they have the word *Indian* in their title. King's Indian, Queens Indian, Bogo-Indian, Nimzo-Indian are all pawn formations that shield the king and allow pieces to take positions of strength using only one square of movement by a pawn. The king resides in a castle formation, which resembles a pyramid.

The Engineering Marvel of the Panama Canal

The Panama Canal is an example of engineering that made the world easier to navigate. Building the canal was originally undertaken by the French, who, fresh off their experience of building the Suez Canal, felt the much shorter canal in Central America wasn't much of a challenge. Their strategies were correct, but they failed tactically in dealing with the situation. They thought once the two ocean bodies were connected that would allow the flow of waters between the oceans. However, the differences in tides made that impossible. They were not prepared to deal with the intense jungle and perpetual rains that made construction difficult. They fell victim to the smallest of enemies, the mosquitoes, that plagued their efforts with malaria, forcing the French to abandon the project.

The US became involved under President Theodore Roosevelt with his gunboat diplomacy and undertook the canal building, piggybacking on the efforts of the French. The US drained the swamps, eliminating the possibility of infectious disease. They used more dynamite than in both World Wars in removing a mountain along the way. Fresh from building a cross-country railroad, the US used railroad technology to remove the vast tons of rock created in building the canal. They harnessed the use of gravity for the water in the canals and dammed Lake Gatun to hold the naturally occurring rains for the fresh water in the locks.

After seventy years of trying, the canal was finally expanded in 2015 to allow larger container ships to navigate between the oceans, saving more than sixteen days of time and fuel to make it from the Pacific to the Atlantic. There are still tactical opportunities happening today at the canal. At the end of the locks, where the canal doors are being opened, sit numerous birds on the side of the canal. What are they waiting for? When the freshwater locks are opened up to the saltwater ocean, the freshwater fish cannot tolerate the salt water and start jumping out of the water—and the birds are sitting there, waiting for their lunch to arrive. Strategy rules, but tactics prevail.

Engineers and chess players make use of levers, bridges, fortresses, chains, etc. to make progress toward taming their environment. One of the best examples of the use of a pawn chain occurred in the following position. White has used a pawn chain to implement the divide and conquer strategy against Black.

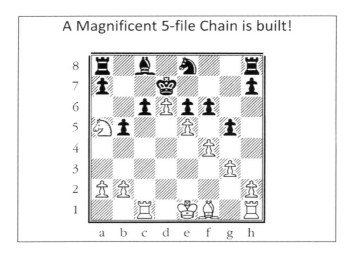

A Magnificent 5-file Chain is built!

White's pawns divide Black into two camps, one on each side of the board. It was only a matter of moves before White was able to win the game. Black is almost in Zugzwang, not having any good moves available.

Engineers can utilize chess to keep their problem-solving skills sharp. The leader that understands engineering capability can create a competitive advantage.

Looking Back—Moving Forward

➤ Ongoing business education is an investment.

➤ Understand how the functional business disciplines interact.

➤ Chess can be used as a guide to understand and practice financial literacy.

➤ Generating, analyzing, and knowing what to do with analytics is essential to staying competitive.

➤ Engineering with a better design leads to manufacturing with lasting structures.

This chapter completed a semester of core subjects covered in a typical MBA program. Each of these disciplines has to be understood and utilized to excel at chess and consequently to be useful in leading a business. In business, these disciplines can be entire divisions or departments; in chess, you're a sole proprietor in charge of everything. The next chapter completes the second semester of core MBA courses.

Chapter 9

MBA Using Gamification
- Second Semester

"If at First you Don't succeed, Try ..."

A master's degree in business administration (MBA) prepares you to use core business concepts and disciplines necessary to win the competitive battles you will face during your career. Business school is your advanced infantry training (AIT) while chess is the war-game arena used to practice the strategies and tactics needed to win in business. In business as well as chess, you cannot shortcut the education process.

During my MBA program, graduate business education underwent a marketing and scheduling change from eighteen-week semesters to twelve-week quarter classes. In order to accelerate the time it took to achieve an advanced degree, universities tailored their MBA programs to accommodate a mobile job-hopping workforce. Under the semester system, it took me three and a half years, taking one or two classes per semester, to graduate. Competing schools on quarters graduated their students in eighteen months—short and sweet, but a fine wine takes time.

Cornell Tech offers a one-year MBA degree for students with a technical background. For me, night classes were the only way to continue to work on a career and have a life. In retrospect, I am glad it took that long to achieve the degree because six more weeks in a semester program allowed for a better in-depth dive into the subject content. Once you achieve the degree, what you retain and apply to your career makes the difference.

To complete your business education, follow the military education model by attending the equivalent of War College in the Pentagon. For business leaders who have earned their MBA, the business equivalent of a War College is to work with a mentor who is more experienced than you. And since chess is your war-games arena, seek out a chess mentor to keep you engaged in the strategies and tactics taught in *Business on the Board*.

With our first semester (chapter 8) in the books, it's time to dig into the second semester of courses.

Operations Management

I sensed something was wrong the moment I stepped outside the limousine. I had just arrived at O'Hare International Airport in Chicago for my flight to Orange County, California. I did two things before that trip that were not my usual practice. First, I usually fly out the night before an important business meeting; second, I printed my boarding pass at home. My flight was to leave at 9:00 a.m. and arrive at 11:00 a.m. in plenty of time for a noon meeting near the airport. I was meeting my book publisher to work out the details of publishing this book.

The first oddity was there were a number of people milling around the curbside check-in area, probably getting some fresh air. But once inside, I saw a terminal packed with people who were spilling out the door waiting to check in for their flights. *Wow*, I thought, *United is really doing well for a midweek early morning departure time; just look at all the customers*. I should have recognized these goings on as a wake-up call about my soon-to-dissipate travel plans. In my innocence, I only thought about how I didn't have to stand in lines because I was using carry-on luggage and had my boarding pass with me. Off I went to the security checkpoint and walked right up to a waiting TSA official who looked glad to see someone in his line. I breezed right through that usual bottleneck. I headed off to my gate listed on the departure board. While approaching the gate, I noticed none of the electronic overhead gate destination signs were working. *They must be saving electricity*, I thought. I arrived with plenty of time before departure and took a seat just in time to hear the gate attendant's announcement.

"Ladies and gentlemen, as you can see, we have no computer systems operating at this time. We cannot issue gate assignments, seats, or boarding passes. Due to FAA regulations all United flights arriving and departing at O'Hare are on a mandated ground stop. We will keep you posted on further updates." The operations of one of the world's largest airlines halted because of an upgrade to their computer servers. I assumed it was a minor malfunction that wouldn't take long.

Time passed. People who were supposed to be on the previous flight that had not departed were filling my gate area, and each of the other gates was starting to hold two or three flights' worth of people who weren't going anywhere. 8:00 a.m. ... 9:00 a.m. ... 10:00 a.m. ... 11:00 a.m. ... Time wore on, and after three gate changes, complete with handwritten boarding passes for the lucky ones, we were finally in the friendly skies. I made the meeting at two thirty, which actually wasn't bad. The compensation of free TV for the delay had me watching Wimbledon, making the four-hour flight seem shorter.

This outage demonstrated the power and vulnerability of operations to an organization. A computer server affected the lives of thousands of people who were in the market for transportation services. The textbook definition of operations management is "...the management of the direct resources required to produce the goods and services provided by the organization."[1]

Operations management balances and applies optimizations on time, resources, and cost in a process. Just like marketing has its four Ps, an operation has five Ps that involve the production of the firm: people, plants, parts, processes, and planning with systems.[2]

In business, the people represent the workforce; in chess, it's the pieces. In operations, the plant is the facility; in chess, that takes place on the chessboard. The parts are the materials or services that are utilized; in chess, it's the capabilities of each piece. Processes utilize assembly lines or services; in chess, it's the respective moves that are processed. Planning is perfecting a process or using information to operate. Chess players use information retained from previous play or study that helps them build and execute a successful game plan.

Operations and Chess Relate

The following diagram illustrates how a work-in-process (WIP) chess position mimics operating a company. During the game, White had just played 3. Bd3.

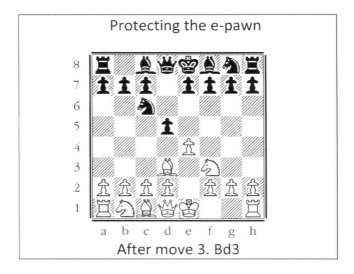

Protecting the e-pawn

After move 3. Bd3

Concerned about losing his e-pawn, which was threatened with capture by the black pawn on d5, he had several choices on how to defend the e-pawn—or he could just trade it off and not worry about it. The move was to guard it with the white square bishop, which accomplished the task of guarding the pawn but is about as destructive as United's server problem for future operations. By blocking the d-pawn, the bishop on c1 is barricaded on the back rank for the foreseeable future. If that bishop never moves, the rook on a1 will remain paralyzed and ineffective. The b1 knight has instant mobility due to his jumping skill and needs to be developed.

Operations involve logistics and Just-in-Time applications, which are covered in chapter 11. This misplaced piece on d3 will cause future loss of productivity for the other White forces. It is something a good chess player or operations manager would never voluntarily do since it affects the operations of the rest of the team. This position (revisited in chapter 10) in part contributed to a quick loss for the White operations team. I saw people getting in each other's way in the terminal as the flights were stacking up, unable to move to a better destination. The piece that needed to move was the airplane, but it was stuck in gate D3.

Marketing and Sales

Marketing communicates the value of a product or service to potential customers for the purpose of promoting a sale. Modern marketing is more programs driven than campaign driven. Data acquisition and interpretation, search engine optimization (SEO), and myriad non-campaign things drive today's marketing. The focus is on making it easier for the customer to find you than finding the customer through traditional cold-calling and advertising techniques.

Executed in the form of a campaign, business marketing creates awareness of your product or service while informing clients and competition of your intentions. "Campaign" is an old-school academic term that isn't much used by marketers except for the specific aspect of marketing involving a promotional campaign. Maybe chess is showing its age in terms of campaigns. But every time an election nears, the television overflows with commercials, voice mail fills up, the mailbox clogs with fliers, and signs litter the highways, all of which are part of an integrated campaign to get elected to office.

On the topic of age, played for over 1,500 years, chess is a war-emulation game that became favored by kings and queens. Today, customers play a form of chess on one side of the board, seeking to satisfy a want or a need. Companies playing on the other side of the board evaluate the customer's needs and offer a solution. Both parties exchange things of value in order to achieve their objectives. In business, it's a win-win proposition. Chess is a zero-sum game of one winner and one loser. When customers feel like they are losing the business game by not getting enough for their money, they pick up and start a game with another company. It's a contest over money.

Echoing Karl von Clausewitz in *Marketing Warfare*, Al Ries and Jack Trout believe marketing isn't just a competition between companies and customers—it's company versus company in outright warfare.[3] Companies conduct marketing analysis to determine whether the product or service they are offering has a market. Will a customer want to play our game? Who is going to buy our product or service? How much buying capacity do they have? Is this product or service something they want or something they need?

It's a Game of Targets

Targeting your market is critical when conducting a successful business campaign. Segmenting your target market consists of defining who is most likely to use your service. Sales techniques encourage customers to purchase your good or service. The push-versus-pull marketing strategy debate has been ongoing for years. Marketing online is about engagement, which is a pull tactic designed to make it easy for the customer to find you. You could argue that this is selling online and it is, but it is usually performed in the marketing department. Companies don't usually deploy the sales team for online marketing.

Steps in the Marketing Process

Marketing professor Philip Kotler says, "Marketers have a mindset, just as lawyers, accountants, bankers, engineers, and scientists have their mindsets. Marketers see the marketing management process as consisting of five basic steps."[4]

Professor Kotler's five steps in the marketing process include:

1. Market research
2. Segmentation, targeting, and branding
3. Marketing mix (product, price, place, and promotion)

4. Deployment

5. Evaluation and improvement

Market Research

Chess players have a mindset that parallels the marketing process based upon the opening, middle, and endgame strategies. According to Philip Kotler, "Research is the starting point for marketing. Without research, a company enters a market like a blind man."[5] Chess players conduct research by studying chess books, analyzing with software, taking lessons, and playing online or in tournaments to see if their moves are competitive. Playing chess without researching appropriate strategies produces "I don't know what I'm doing" moves and a lost position. Chess players, like marketers doing competitor analysis, research their opponent's moves with online databases, looking for exploitable weaknesses in their play.

Segmentation, Targeting and Branding

Once a market is revealed, marketers segment their customers based on their specific needs or wants. Chess players segment their knowledge around openings and defenses they know and prefer to play. They might adapt their style of play depending on whether they need to beat an opponent to win a prize. Identifying a market segment enables a company to target specific customers who are likely to do business with them. Chess players target markets when they play by identifying what they want to attack. Typical targets are the king, an unprotected piece, or a weak pawn structure in their opponent's position. Companies position their products so that customer benefits exceed what their competitors are offering. Chess players position their pieces in a way that will provide them a superior return. One poorly placed piece can often be the deciding factor during a game.

Marketing Mix

After the marketing strategy is set, the tactical use of the "Marketing Mix" determines which of the four Ps (product, price, position, or promotion) will be used with the offering. In business, that is the product itself, the price to be charged for the product, how the product will be distributed through channels, and what promotions will be used to communicate the product to the customer. The chess marketing mix consists of pieces (products we have to offer), values (prices to be paid for the exchange of our pieces), lines (channels of open diagonals, ranks, or files for pieces to distribute their powers), and effective programs (promotions).

Deployment

Deployment means making the moves necessary to bring the product to market successfully. A market-centric website backed by SEO will drive engagement with customers and lead them through the buying process. Traditional sales activities, including a salesforce focused on business development rather than traditional "cold-calling" will help customers make offline buying decisions. Distributors who have their own customer base can be engaged to further build sales. Chess players implement their offering by making the moves in the game that bring the team the best chances of being successful. All the pieces should have a role in making the team the most effective force possible. If the game resembles a marketing campaign, then the results are easily monitored for their effectiveness as opposed to random moves that don't seem to have any purpose. In chess, we use the phrase "planlessness punished" for moves that don't have a purpose.

Evaluation and Improvement

Evaluation and improvement is the last step where financial and marketing metrics are applied to determine whether the product is generating the profits expected. Reviewing, auditing, and evaluating the overall marketing effort are required to keep the program on track. Chess players have complete control over the moves that they make but are influenced by the moves of their opponents. Strategies, tactical opportunities, and accounting metrics are evaluated, often after each move, to determine if the game is under control and taking the intended course of action.

The Power of a Campaign

Successful chess often requires a marketing style campaign, seeking answers to many of the same questions a business must resolve. The ultimate objective in chess is the opponent's king. Attacking the king without resolve signals the end of the competition. But if the king is secure, alternative targets like expanded market share (space), competitive weaknesses (misplaced pieces), and nonstrategic alignments (overcommitting time or resources to the detriment of the team) become the objectives. These smaller, incremental advantages eventually combine to yield the ultimate objective of checkmating the opponent's king.

Existing targets are not always present in a chess game; they are created by forcing your opponent to make vulnerable concessions in their position. Those targets later become the seeds of their defeat. This position is from one of my games and illustrates the power of a campaign. White and Black have castled on opposite sides of the board and have begun an attack on each other's king. The pawns are pushing forward, intending to create weaknesses in the opponent's camp, which can be attacked by the pieces. The rush to get to the other king is the highest priority, and other concerns like sacrificing material are secondary considerations.

Boeing recently announced the need to cut 4,500 jobs during a period of record orders for their planes. Cost cutting comes at "a time when price carries more weight than ever in sales campaigns." The CEO explained the move as "playing offense in a competitive marketplace." Management felt that, "If our costs are high, it gives us less pricing flexibility, and customers will be forced by the own competitive pressures to take their business elsewhere."[6]

Marketing and sales efforts require a disciplined approach to be successful. Identifying and taking advantage of targets are essential CMO skills. In business, marketing and sales may be delegated to an entire team of specialists. In chess the entire program to bring about success must be generated and implemented by one person, in their head, under restricted time allocations.

Economics

In 2008 during a speech in Singapore, Harvard economics professor Ken Rogoff made an astonishing prediction. After reviewing his work, he predicted that a major bank was about to fail. "We're not just going to see mid-sized banks go under in the next few months, we're going to see a whopper, we're going to see a big one – one of the big investment banks or big banks."[7] The next day his remark was front-page news all over the world. Less than a month later Lehman Brothers collapsed. The professor had looked at the flow of funds and did not see how the capital markets could continue without a failing institution. Little did he know that a host of big banks were about to fail and that, without government intervention, the global financial system would have collapsed. Analysts were abuzz, seeking answers to the question, how did he know that?

The textbook explanation of economics states, "Economics is the study of how people choose to use their scarce resources in order to satisfy their nearly unlimited economic wants. Scarcity exists whenever there are insufficient resources to satisfy these wants."[8] Everyone, whether they realize it or not, participates in economic decision-making with decisions as trivial as whether they dine out or take in the latest movie.

Chess has been played recreationally and competitively for centuries. A game with few barriers to entry other than a chessboard and a set of pieces, it can be used to model a microeconomic environment of two competitors (an economic duopoly) battling for supremacy of their kingdom using decision-making and looking for patterns that repeat and give advantage. Both parties exchange things of value in order to achieve their objectives. It's a battle over resources.

For a variety of reasons, often one of distribution, economies can suffer from a scarcity of resources available to meet the wants and needs of its people. People decide how the resources they have are going to be used. Chess players decide how the pieces they have are going to be used. Once the resources are exhausted through exchanges, they are gone for the duration. Chess players exhaust the resources they were allocated as the game proceeds.

Chess is a Closed Economy

Economics is a social science based on how humans relate and behave within an economy. Chess is a social science (if you are playing against another person and not your computer) that uses pieces to relate to each other in a game structure. Economic decisions involve trade-offs, and there are costs associated with the choices people make. Chess players are involved in trade-offs of their pieces and realize there is a cost or value component to those pieces.

People make a number of economic decisions over their lifetime. Chess players make a number of important decisions during the course of their game. The decisions they make will reflect the quality of the life they lead. On the chessboard the quality of their decisions will directly affect the outcome of the contest.

Economic Decision Making

Everyone participates in economic decision - making through the choices they make over the resources they control.

Chess decision-making results in a slight movement of a piece, but the effort required in rendering that decision could be as intense as landing a plane, needing a birdie to stay in a golf match, or serving match point down in tennis. The wrong decision could have a disastrous effect on the overall outcome.

Micro-versus Macroeconomics

Similar to how a chess game is divided into phases to allow a better understanding of the subject, economics is separated into internal and external considerations. Investopedia.com describes economics in this way:

> The field of economics is broken down into two distinct areas of study: microeconomics and macroeconomics. Microeconomics looks at the smaller picture and focuses more on basic theories of supply and demand and how individual businesses decide how much of something to produce and how much to charge for it. Macroeconomics looks at the big picture. It focuses on the national economy as a whole and provides a basic knowledge of how things work in the business world. ... Thus, for an overall perspective of how the entire economy works, you need to have an understanding of economics at both the micro and macro levels.[9]

Economics and Chess Relate through Game Theory

Economists use a branch of mathematics called game theory. According to Scott Stevens, author of *Games People Play*, "Simply put, game theory is the study of strategic interactive decision making among rational individuals. Any time people are making decisions that affect others or in response to the actions or even the expected actions of other, they're playing a game."[10]

Thirty-two years before his prediction about a major bank that would fail, Harvard professor Rogoff had another occupation. He was a chess grandmaster (GM) good enough to qualify for the tournament that was to determine a potential candidate to play for the world chess championship title. American grandmaster Ken Rogoff was exercising his understanding of economic principles on a chessboard. In this game he was playing against a former world champion, Russian player Mikhail Tal.

The following position occurred after White's move thirteen. The game can be played from the following link:

http://www.365chess.com/game.php?gid=2459318

Tactical Alert – A Relative Pin

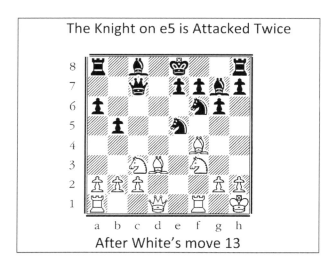

The Knight on e5 is Attacked Twice

After White's move 13

The first six moves were the same as my game against Tyehimba in chapter 3. In this game GM Rogoff fianchettoed his bishop to g7; I chose to activate mine at e7. Tactical opportunities appeared in the position, and when a tactic is present, strategic ideas take a seat and wait their turn. The auditor's report shows that White has five pawns and Black has six, so GM Rogoff is up a pawn. GM Tal has a history of sacrificing or investing his material to create difficult positions, allowing his opponent to go wrong amongst the complications. Here he has pulled it off again.

In this position, Black was threatened with the loss of the knight on e5 by either the White bishop or knight capturing it. The queen was the only defender and would be too valuable to recapture and hence the game would be lost. Black could not move the knight out of trouble because his valuable queen would have been captured by the bishop on f4. He had a problem. He needed to use more economic resources to supply an adequate defense to the knight and retreated **13...Nfd7** increasing the supply of defenders from one to three.

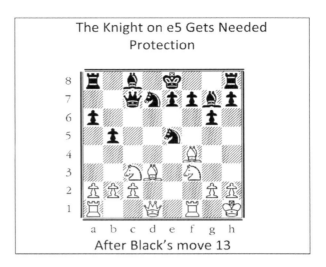

The Knight on e5 Gets Needed Protection

After Black's move 13

Since the knight is attacked only twice and defended three times, Black for the moment has "overprotected" the knight, which could allow his queen to move away from the pin, giving the knight its mobility back.

The Importance of Patience

With this move this position is the only one in the mega-database, so these two GMs are making history. The opinion here is that Black is getting the advantage. GM Tal with his next move of 14.Qe2 increased the demand of his attackers by one to match the Black supply of defenders to three apiece.

Black's pieces are forced to stay in the same formation. If one of them moves away and no longer defends the knight, the equilibrium will be broken and Black will lose the knight. Having patience and skill, GM Rogoff was forced to allow the pin to continue while GM Tal ramped up the pressure on the pinned knight. A productive strategy in chess is to continue to attack a pinned piece. In archery it's easier to hit a fixed target.

In business, continuing to hammer at a competitor's fixed weakness could produce similar advantages. If Company B has higher fixed costs than Company A, eventually that has to be reflected in their prices and profit margins, and cost-conscious clients may opt for lower-priced goods from Company A. Here a $3 knight is fixed because of the pin. It is operating at less than full functionality and has decreased value to GM Rogoff's team.

Supply and Demand Equilibrium

Chess is a self-contained microeconomic contest played on a sixty-four-square board with $42 of capital invested in the form of eight pieces and eight pawns for each player. Once those pieces are eliminated through exchanges, that's all there is. It's not in the rules to open up a new bag of pieces and start populating the board with fresh employees. In basketball, if a player fouls out, their productivity is over.

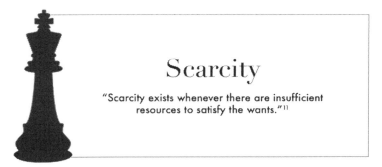

Scarcity

"Scarcity exists whenever there are insufficient resources to satisfy the wants."[11]

There is a limit to the resources available to each chess player as they attempt with unlimited abandon to checkmate their opponent. With the ebb and flow of piece movements, the economy expands and contracts as pieces grow in relation to their responsibilities and diminish as they are exchanged off the board. Chess positions require a supply and demand of resources in order to reach and maintain a balance or equilibrium.

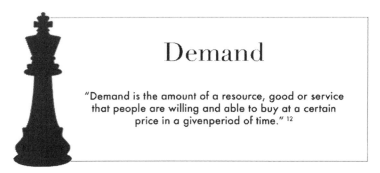

Demand

"Demand is the amount of a resource, good or service that people are willing and able to buy at a certain price in a givenperiod of time."[12]

In this position White is demanding Black supply resources to save his knight. Chess players need to make a profit on the pieces they exchange (or at least break even with their trades), or winning becomes less likely. If Black doesn't have the resources or chooses not to deploy them as necessary, then, like a firm that goes out of business, his chess game will soon be out of business.

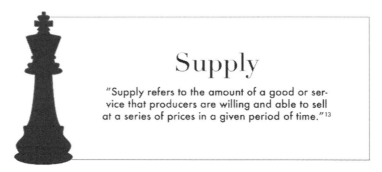

Supply

"Supply refers to the amount of a good or service that producers are willing and able to sell at a series of prices in a given period of time."[13]

14.Qe2 Bb7

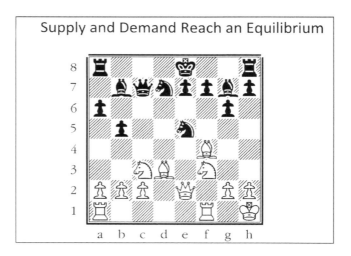

Supply and Demand Reach an Equilibrium

In this position the $3 knight on e5 is compromised because it has limited mobility. It shelters the $9 queen on c7 from the White bishop on f4. The tactic, a relative pin, was covered in chapter 7. The longer the pin continues, the harder it will be for Black to equalize and attack the ex-world champion. He has a pawn advantage, however, and GM Rogoff must feel that a pawn is worth some trouble.

With equilibrium in place, Black calmly develops his last minor piece, getting ready to castle in either direction. The absence of any White pawns in the center lowers the risk to the knight on e5 because there is no way to attack it with a piece of lower value.

Demand of the White Attackers of Ne5	Supply of the Black Defenders of Ne5
1. the Knight on f3	1. the Queen on c7
2. the Bishop on f4	2 the Knight on d7
3 the Queen on e2	3. the Bishop on g7

With supply and demand in balance, if players decide to exchange pieces, the material lost will be in-kind with neither player suffering any loss of working capital in relation to their opponent. The chess economic conditions will diminish because there are fewer resources available to accomplish the task of winning. Black has been able to keep his supply of defenders in line with the demand of White's attackers. But what if White were able to add more attackers?

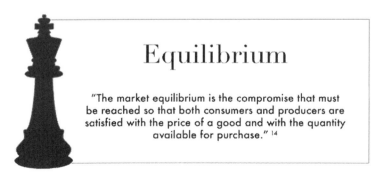

Equilibrium

"The market equilibrium is the compromise that must be reached so that both consumers and producers are satisfied with the price of a good and with the quantity available for purchase." [14]

Breaking the Equilibrium

What if White could drive off a Black defender or add another attacker of the knight on e5? The equilibrium would be broken in his favor, and his one pawn investment could win the game. What would GM Rogoff have done if GM Tal had continued to pile on the pressure and played 15. Rae1 attacking the knight on e5 a fourth time? White is demanding that Black supply yet another defender. But his resources are limited. Does he have another defender? Yes, he does. It would be an ugly pawn move, but defending his knight with the pawn on f7 by moving it to f6 maintains the equilibrium. The bishop on g7 guards it with an X-ray and has compromised mobility, but sometimes in chess or business you have to take unpopular action.

15.Be4 Bxe4 White senses that the bishop on b7 aiming at his king on h1 is too good of a piece for Black and decides to liquidate it. *Fritz* evaluates the position as dead even.

16.Qxe4 0–0 17. Nxe5 Nxe5 18. Nd5 Qd6 GM Rogoff addressed the risk to his king and protected the rook on a8 by castling kingside. It did nothing to address the annoying pin to his knight, but as compensation he continued to hold onto his extra pawn. GM Tal exchanged knights and moved his knight to the center, attacking Black's queen who stayed perched on the diagonal, defending the knight on e5.

19.Rad1 f6! 20. Bxe5 Qxe5 GM Tal moved his a-rook to the d-file, threatening a tactical discovered attack against GM Rogoff's queen on d6. The American decided to turn his knight on e5 from a liability (it cannot move and requires further protection) into an asset (outpost in the center that doesn't require the queen's protection) and protected it with a pawn. Now the knight can sit there as long as necessary and the pieces defending it can move away, getting the queen out of the pin. GM Tal, sensing the knight is now an asset for Black, immediately liquidates it. The remaining moves are available on the online database. The game exchanged down to an eventual draw but in the process exemplified another economic principle, the Nash equilibrium, which is discussed later.

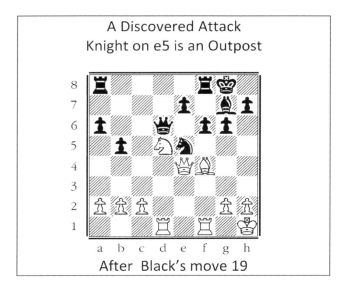

A Discovered Attack
Knight on e5 is an Outpost

After Black's move 19

During the game, GM Rogoff had to maintain a sense of calm and patience. He was being attacked by one of the greatest of Russia's world-champion grandmasters and had to see his way through the complications in order to succeed, albeit with a draw against a much higher-rated opponent.

Remain Calm

One of the skills Professor Rogoff attributes to his years of playing professional chess is the ability to remain calm in a business situation. "I think having played chess was very helpful in my work. I can also say, much later in my career, when I became Chief Economist at the International Monetary Fund, I again found chess useful. I would say particularly in negotiations, where at least chess taught me to think about what the other person's thinking in a disciplined way and to stay very calm."[15]

Professor Rogoff also stated, "Another important skill you learn in chess is that we all make mistakes. And if you panic after you made a mistake you're doomed. Chess teaches you to stay calm in difficult situations. I've certainly faced many challenging situations in my career as an economist, particularly over the last decade, where I think that has been very useful. ... If you make a mistake during a lecture, if you stay calm you can think of how to recover from it. In chess that is very important, both within a game and say within a tournament."[16]

A Game Theory Moment

Dr. Rogoff had the following observation about how nations handle their debts. "I do a lot of work on financial crisis and countries defaulting and that too involves game theory. Because when countries default on their debt, it's almost never because they can't repay it, it's because they don't feel like it and it's a strategic interaction."[17]

When doing a rollback analysis of the moves in a chess game, players might have multiple strategies to follow. This is known as a strategy profile. In this endgame one player may try hard to invade their opponent's position with their king. If the king can become an attacking force, then the few remaining pawns on the board can be at risk. Or their strategy might be "let's just defend our position and not allow our opponent to gain any advantage and split the point with a draw." If neither player can benefit from changing their strategy profile, it's known as a Nash equilibrium. According to game theorist Scott Stevens, "A Nash equilibrium is one in which no player can get a better expected payoff by unilaterally changing his or her strategy. Nash equilibrium is the foundation of the solutions found in almost all non-cooperative game theory."[18]

The trick, of course, is to know when you have arrived at a Nash equilibrium. That's where your experience and skills as a manager come into play, the same as it would in chess.

Legal

In chess, we have the phrase: "The threat is stronger than the execution." Even though you have threatened your opponent with an attack, that doesn't mean you have to immediately take advantage of it. Whether you do or not, your threat is still there. You may be able to capture a pawn on your next move without a responding capture from your opponent. Waiting on this attack could allow you to build a much bigger threat and requires a few moves to position yourself for the attack.

Three scenarios can happen when your opponent threatens you in chess or business.

1. You can *underestimate* the threat by not seeing it, ignoring it, or evaluating it as nothing to fear. Your opponent reaps the rewards of the threat if that occurs.

2. You can *nail* the threat by understanding it and taking appropriate action to diminish any damage. That might be taking evasive action that gets your queen out of danger, or advancing a pawn near the castle to prevent a checkmate.

3. You can *overestimate* the threat by thinking the situation is the worst, when you actually have a potential resource available. In this case your move makes the position worse than if you had just ignored the threat.

When your opponent underestimates or overestimates the potential danger from your threat, the resulting moves can cause their position to deteriorate. The acquired skill of evaluating a threat is called judgment. Judgment is useful and can be practiced with chess. It's a critical skill in business, particularly in the legal profession. Very few professions have full-time judges.

Companies threaten competitors when they make moves in the marketplace that change the game, such as lowering prices or introducing new products or solutions. Depending on how they perceive the threat, competitors may respond appropriately, underreact, or overreact. Moving into a competitor's geographic market, initiating a hostile takeover, calling a critical witness during a legal proceeding, or challenging the ownership of intellectual property are all threats. But what if a company overreacts to the threat and gets out of a market too quickly or overinvests in defensive moves with little chance of earning a good ROI?

A Financial Under-Reaction

In the financial crisis of 2008, JPMorgan Chase & Co. (JPM) at first was interested, and then said no, but after considerable input from the Federal Reserve agreed to acquire the investment bank Bear Stearns. Bear

Stearns was in financial trouble because of the subprime mortgage crisis and repo holdings between trading partners. Former Federal Reserve Chairman Ben Bernanke provided the following explanation of why Bear Stearns could not be allowed to fail.

"Bear had nearly 400 subsidiaries, and its activities touched almost every other major financial firm. It had 5,000 trading counter parties and 750,000 open derivatives contracts. The problem of how to handle troubled financial institutions like Bear has been labeled as too big to fail. ... Bear was big, but not that big compared to the largest commercial banks. Actually it was too interconnected to fail."[19]

What's Been Played Before?

Like a good chess player who is looking over previously played games, the Federal Reserve chairman tried to use precedents to seek possible solutions. Two games came to his mind. The first game was investment bank Drexel Burnham Lambert's failure, which happened because of a junk-bond scandal. The Fed decided correctly that DBL's failure would not endanger the financial system, so they let them fail. The second game was the unwinding of Long-Term Capital Management (described in chapter 3), a strategy engineered by the New York Federal Reserve. But funding a timely, private-sector solution for Bear was not feasible in this crisis. Their clock was ticking, and if they didn't move soon, (in chess parlance) their flag was about to fall. There were no previous chess games in the database for this position, so the chairman had to use situational leadership to get out of this crisis.

Initially, Jamie Dimon, the CEO of JPMorgan & Chase Co., wanted to pay around $2 a share for Bear. Shareholders of Bear Stearns were irate that the company could go for so little, whereupon Dimon iterated, "There is a difference between buying a house and buying a house that is on fire." He obviously didn't want to overreact to the situation and get burned. The firms eventually agreed to $10 per share as a reasonable figure.

In his book *The Courage to Act*, Benjamin Bernanke explained what changed Dimon's mind about acquiring Bear. Even though JPM had a balance sheet of $1.6 trillion, which was four times larger than Bear's, and they could have handled the acquisition, he didn't want to take on the deal without reassurance that his firm would not suffer any consequences. Any reasonable CEO would pass on the deal. After the Fed agreed to a $30 billion loan, JPM put up $1 billion to finalize the deal.

When it came to determining the share price of the acquisition, the Fed wanted to avoid moral hazard (an insurance concept of bailing out private companies from bad investments) and punish Bear's owners for mismanaging the firm. The Fed and JPM were concerned, however, that Bear's shareholders might reject the $2-per-share deal and let the firm fail. After all, their shares were down from $172.69 per share just fourteen months earlier. If Bear shareholders rejected the deal, it would have thrown the global financial system into chaos. By 2015, the loan was repaid, generated $765 million in interest, and had $1.7 billion in profits for the Fed and tax payers.[20]

The loan temporarily quieted the financial market, but as described in *The Courage to Act*, the Lehman bankruptcy was the failure that opened the flood gates to a crisis not seen since the Great Depression of the '30s. The government did not want Lehman to fail, but their assets were so poor they couldn't be used as collateral for a loan, and they couldn't find a buyer; bankruptcy was the only option.

A Financial Overreaction

An overreaction in a financial situation may be when a company overpays for an acquisition because a competing firm has bid up the asking price, and the winning firm did not receive fair value for the assets. What if a company threatened with a takeover sells a valuable asset the potential acquirer wants in the deal? If that makes the takeover go away, what shape is the company in now that they sold off one of their prized divisions? What if they buy off the hedge fund manager and make their threats go away? Is their cash on hand at risk after buying them out? Did they take on too much leverage to take the company private and keep the raiders at bay?

ABN-Amro Is in Play

Before the financial crisis of 2008 was in full-blown mania, a London-based hedge fund acquired an equity position in the Dutch bank ABN-Amro based on their evaluation that the firm was undervalued. They planned on breaking up ABN-Amro to unleash the fair-market value of the bank's assets. Once the bank was in play, several groups put together takeover offers. RBS, Santander, and Banco Real won the bidding war, but only after ABN-Amro sold one of the crown jewels, LaSalle Bank in Chicago, to Bank of America in North Carolina. The consortium was livid that the assets they wanted were no longer part of the deal and sued ABN-Amro for not having shareholder approval to sell LaSalle. The Dutch Supreme Court ultimately decided that approval wasn't necessary.

The bottom line is all three companies that acquired a piece of ABN-Amro overpaid for the assets they received and required assistance from their governments to allow them to remain solvent during the financial crisis. Many believe this egregious overreaction to acquiring the bank is what in part triggered the global financial crisis. The threat of a competitor getting to ABN-Amro first caused a severe overreaction in financial terms for the acquirers.

Guilty of Overreacting in Court

What if feared trial witnesses have nothing to say or have credibility damage that can be used against them during a cross-examination? Perhaps there was nothing to worry about. Might these threatened parties have not overreacted to their situation and made it worse?

In a court case near Chicago, a man was on trial for the murder of his wife. It was originally ruled an accident. The man confided to his next wife that he did indeed murder his previous wife. And guess what? That wife has disappeared.

With the defendant's encouragement, his lawyer wanted to call a lawyer who represented the missing wife as a witness. The missing wife's lawyer testified that she asked him if they used the fact that he admitted killing his ex-wife in their bathtub, could they get a better settlement against him in their divorce. Her lawyer told her not to even bring that up since she could be criminally charged for concealing a homicide. The reason the defendant wanted that witness to testify was to substantiate the fact that his missing wife had a motive for wanting to divorce him and run off with another man.

Though the missing wife hasn't been found, the defendant was found guilty of murdering his first wife. The reason jurors convicted him was that they believed this "testimony from the grave." Did the defense lawyer who called the lawyer/witness overreact in trying to help his client? His co-counsel and the judge could not believe that they would have called this witness because of the damage it did to their client. The threat was their client may be found guilty of murder. By overreacting to the situation and calling a hostile witness, they made their situation worse, ultimately guaranteeing a conviction for their client.

In a more notorious case of making your position worse, the prosecutors in the O.J. Simpson murder trial originally had enough DNA evidence linking Simpson to the crime scene. They were not planning to have Simpson put on a bloody glove found at the crime scene, which had more DNA linking Simpson and the victim. But at the insistence of defense attorney Johnnie Cochran, they allowed O.J. to try on the pair of leather gloves, weakening their case. The glove had been frozen and refrozen and no longer fit, which led to the defendant's attorney infamous quip, "If it doesn't fit, you must acquit."[21]

Legal Process and Chess Relate

Two of these cases involved the legal system to resolve the situation. In my research with members of the legal profession, they explained the following correlations between chess playing and the legal system.

Both chess and the law have a strategy of putting the strongest argument forward in their case. In chess, that would be making a significant opening move and in a legal proceeding the strongest charges that can be brought.

Both chess and the legal process are sequential. Each side has their opportunity to present and make their best moves based on what their opposition is doing.

Lawyers and chess players map out the strategies and tactics they intend to use when either prosecuting or defending their case.

The law and chess games are based on historic cases and previous judgments. After a series of moves has been played, a verdict is reached about their viability. If the position is positive for White, Black has to find an improvement, or the line is abandoned. Lawyers want certain testimony entered in the trial because it can strengthen their case while the opposition wants it excluded because it weakens the position of their client.

Lawyers and chess players have to be able to cope with choosing an answer to a question that has no provable right or wrong answer by considering and weighing a number of factors. The "likelihood of confusion" test for trademark infringement requires the consideration of a number of factors including the degree of similarity of a defendant's mark to a plaintiff's mark, the level of sophistication of relevant consumers in their respective markets, the degree of overlap in their respective markets or channels of trade, and the similarity of the goods or services offered. In evaluating a position, chess players consider factors such as king safety, material, pawn structures, piece activity/quality, and control of space or particular squares on the chessboard. Given all of these considerations, the player may have to make an unprovable judgment call based on intuition or experience as to who has the overall advantage, either in the current position on the board or a position that the player is envisioning a few moves ahead.[22]

Chess requires quick thinking about moves that need to be played just like an attorney uses when raising an objection to a question. Sometimes they are forcing the judge to make an immediate ruling that can be overturned on appeal, giving their client a second chance to a trial.

Chess can help lawyers anticipate the answers to their questions in court. I once played against an attorney who brought his case work with him to the board during our game at the National Open. I was surprised that he thought he could play and beat me while he was doing his legal work. He lost. Afterwards he told me that playing chess helps him anticipate the answers of potential jurors he questions. If a skilled lawyer always knows the answer to the question before he asks it, then like any other skill, it needs to be practiced. Just like a series of opening chess moves you have played before can draw good and bad responses, the sequential nature of questioning a juror can be as lethal as a powerful series of pieces interacting on a chessboard, even if the other player (prospective juror) is a total stranger picked at random.

Just in Passing

Just as a lawyer has to be well versed in case law, in chess, it pays to know all the rules. One rule that continues to confound players is the *en passant*—French for "in passing"—rule of pawn captures. It's best explained with examples that occurred twice in my game against Grandmaster Alexander Baburin.

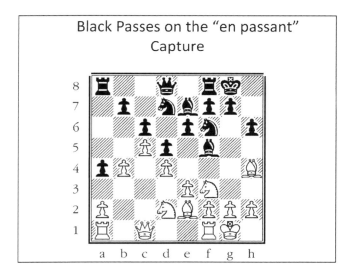

Black Passes on the "en passant" Capture

In this position I had just pushed my b-pawn up two squares from b2 to b4, and Black was eligible to make a pawn capture that has mystified new players since the move was introduced around the year 1500. When the rule changed to allow the double pawn move, it was possible for one pawn to pass right by another without being captured. Hence the en passant rule was created to disallow that anomaly.

Since GM Baburin's a-pawn is on my side of the board and he wasn't given a chance to capture me on this move, he could have done it en passant. But he passed, and his opportunity was over.

En Passant

When my pawn went directly to b4, Black's pawn on a4 didn't get a chance to capture it as it went by. For this move only, he could have captured the pawn en passant as if it had advanced only one square to b3. He takes the White pawn off the board and puts his a-pawn on b3. But if he doesn't take it on this move, it cannot be captured en passant later. It's now or never. This capture in particular seems to mystify many who think they understand it.

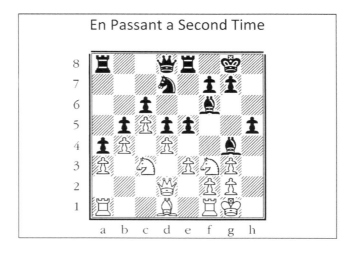

En Passant a Second Time

It's en passant déjà vu

Seven moves after GM Baburin chose not to capture en passant, he presented me with the opportunity to capture his pawn by playing 21... b5 from his b7 square. In this position I did capture his pawn with my pawn that was on c5, leaving him with a weak pawn on a4.

The en passant pawn capture is a rare occurrence in a game, and having two opportunities in the same game is highly unlikely. When the en passant capture is available, most times it is taken because the advancing player is trying to keep the position closed. If it were to their advantage to open up the position, they would move the pawn up only one square. This would guarantee a pawn exchange opening up the position to their advantage.

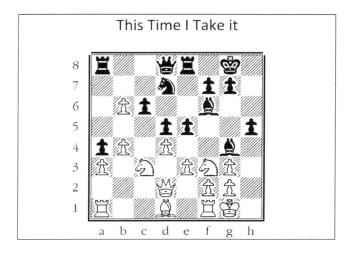

This Time I Take it

In this game, GM Baburin eventually offered me a draw, which at first I didn't want because I assumed he thought I was better. On second thought, however, I took him up on his offer, and the game ended peacefully.

The practice of law is involved with setting and knowing the rules of the game. Some legal customs are passed from one generation to the next but are subject to change as case law evolves. But not knowing about touch-move, en passant, stalemate, resigning, proper piece setup, castling, check, checkmate, promoting a pawn, and draws can get players involved in nasty disputes.

Chess players need to know the rules because they don't have the ability to seek legal advice during their game. The tournament director serves as the arbitrator if a dispute about a rule does occur at the board. Sometimes the tournament director needs to be physically present to see an infraction, like when both players are in serious time trouble and are playing like "clock-banging monkeys" to finish their moves. If there are no witnesses, it can be one player's word versus the other. I've been there, and it isn't pretty.

Looking Back—Moving Forward

> ➢ Operate at maximum capacity, making each employee or chess piece add value.
> ➢ Integrate the required resources into a campaign to bring down the opposition.
> ➢ Economic patterns repeat in business and chess.
> ➢ Situational supply, demand, and equilibriums can determine winning or losing.
> ➢ Judgment should be practiced like any other skill.

In the next two chapters, we will see how the business functional areas relate on a chessboard. Business disciplines have to work together to support a well-run operation. The glare of a television studio encounter was no place for the richest man on Earth to face the best chess player on the planet. But they played, and it's a business education moment for us and is next up on our to-do list.

Chapter 10

The Rich Baby Boomer versus the Powerful Millennial Fast Thinking versus Slow Thinking

"Haste makes ..."

What happens when the richest man in the world decides to take on the best chess player in the world in a game of speed chess? It happened in a television studio and is a popular video available on YouTube. The game ended quickly because Magnus Carlsen agreed to play his moves in thirty seconds, and Bill Gates had a whopping two minutes to complete his moves. Thirty seconds was a lifetime for Magnus to play a chess game, especially against an amateur. Two minutes for someone like Bill Gates who was out of practice didn't allow time for him to properly evaluate the threats he faced.

Few people have done more to advance the use of technology than Bill Gates and Microsoft. The company's name is derived from writing software for microcomputers. The company's Windows® operating system makes all the applications run on the Windows environment, including chess programs. Chess engines, databases, websites, software, books, and manuals were covered under "Technology" in chapter 8.

This game was part of a publicity tour Magnus conducted after winning the chess world championship in 2013. His tour included games against Google engineers, the Facebook CEO, and the retired cofounder of Microsoft, among others. Designed to generate interest in chess, this miniature game gave us an opportunity not only to see what happened, but more importantly, to observe how the two players went about their moves.

Bill Gates has played chess before because his play was grounded on good strategic moves. Playing mechanically, he built a position that should have withstood the devious moves of his opponent. Given a little more time to work through the challenges he faced, he could have won the contest. Unfortunately, his two-minute clock was ticking.

Thinking Takes Time

A bad decision always leads to a good story.

Magnus' chess career from his precocious days of beating all the competition to winning the 2013 World Chess Championship had been well documented. I reviewed the last game of his 2014 world championship match in chapters 4 through 7. He had played numerous opponents at the same time without even looking at the board in an event known as a blindfold exhibition. He befuddled mere mortals of the game with his prodigious memory. *60 Minutes* highlighted his achievements in a segment called the "Mozart of Chess."

In this encounter he gave Bill Gates a "different look" during the game by transposing moves and not letting Bill play a familiar position. He obviously wanted Bill Gates to make slow-thinking, time-consuming moves to neutralize his 4-1 time advantage for the game. Luckily for Magnus, it worked. He succeeded in creating a checkmate trap that Bill didn't see. The intensity of the encounter was revealed on video. While it's not easy to see what moves were made, watching the body language of the two players speaks volumes. Mumbling nervously, a confused Bill Gates was not sure what to do. This was exactly what Magnus wanted to achieve.

Bill Gates was a good sport for playing against Magnus. He appeared embarrassed by being beaten so quickly as the world watched. Gates became the richest man in the world with astute critical strategic and tactical thinking. Along the way, Microsoft has advanced personal and business computing around the globe.

Thinking, Fast and Slow

In his bestselling book *Thinking, Fast and Slow*, Daniel Kahneman addresses at length the difference between the two types of thinking and their applications. Fast thinking is all the reflex, reactionary decisions we know and make. For example, if you were asked to find the product of seven times six, the answer would be immediate. If you were given the problem of seventeen times twenty-six, however, you would have to stop and think of a strategy for resolving that question. That's the difference between fast and slow thinking.

In chess, we use fast and slow thinking all the time. If a position exists that we have seen before and we know how to proceed, we rip off the move and prepare for the next one. However, if our opponent gives us something that we have not seen or reviewed recently, we may have to slow down and take a look at the new situation. Along the lines of "trust but verify," our intuition tells us to make sure we haven't overlooked something. Encounters like this demonstrate how lack of time for slow thinking (called time pressure) can cause us to make errors (called blunders) at the worst time.

Magnus is the world champion. He plays chess against the best players in the world all the time, and he beats them. There isn't much, if anything, that he has not seen on the board. He can recognize a winning position and recall the strategy necessary for winning the game immediately.

As a youth, Bill Gates loved to play games; to him, chess is an amusement. He is amenable to subjecting himself to the risk of losing a chess game with the only damage being to his ego. It's not much different from playing in a pro-celebrity tennis event at Indian Wells, California. He is comfortable in his own skin and willing to be exposed as a weak chess player while the world watches over his shoulder.

Although brief, this game involved tactics based on the placement of the pieces. When these tactical opportunities avail themselves during the course of a business career or a chess contest, be alert to where and when they happen. In this game Magnus created a tactical minefield around Bill Gates' king. Bill did not recognize the combination of moves he faced even though there was a refutation. Rushed for time, he missed the correct move and became Magnus' foil. Our previous games showed tactics prevail and, if played correctly, can deliver victory on the spot.

The ex-CEO took it on the chin from the twenty-four-year-old world champion, but he handled the defeat well, commenting, "That was quick," with a big smile at the end. Start this case by watching the encounter on YouTube at the following link:

https://www.youtube.com/watch?v=84NwnSltHFo

It's time to analyze the spectacle we just saw with an introspective look at how the richest man in the world thinks when he is up against the strongest chess player in the world. Their body language discloses more of the story than their moves.

Click on the following link to see the moves of this game.
http://www.chessgames.com/perl/chessgame?gid=1744566

Bill Gates - Magnus Carlsen
Television Exhibition 23.01.2014

The initial indication that Bill Gates was in unfamiliar territory occurred when the moderator suggested that the game begin. Bill made his move and then sat back without hitting his chess clock. You can see that

Magnus was fiddling with the pieces, trying to figure out what he could do on his move, but he should have been doing that while his clock was running. To start out on even terms, Magnus magnanimously started his own clock, losing a precious second.

1.e4 Nc6

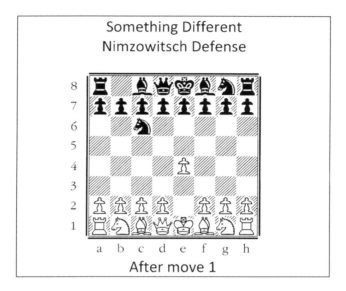

Bill Gates played one of the two best opening moves with his king-pawn, indicating he had some fundamental training on chess. If he had moved a rook pawn up, that would have been another story. This move came from his long-term memory acquired from his previous chess-playing days. The drawback was he had created a risk factor by committing a pawn to the center of the board, and it was not defended. Magnus was more versed in how to handle that pawn move than Bill Gates.

Magnus knocking over the pieces may suggest that he was intimidated in the presence of a superstar business executive. With a little coaching, Gates would have been able to use his status to psychological advantage, especially if he appeared tough, confident, and a fast mover. I would have recommended a move like 1. Nf3, keeping the position closed and possibly flanking the bishop and getting castled as soon as possible. Magnus had only thirty seconds to play his whole game, and if Bill managed to get this contest to thirty moves or more in an endgame, he had an excellent chance of winning on time, especially if Magnus kept knocking over the pieces during the contest. If the game takes thirty-five moves, Magnus has to make his moves in less than a second apiece.

Invoking strategic centralization, Bill grabbed a center square with his king pawn, increasing his mobility count from two to five. If he can quickly develop his employees, Bill may give Magnus a game after all. Magnus' objective was to use White's pawn for a target later. The world champion's response was playable but not popular.

Opening History

In business and chess, you can beat your competition if you know the landscape better than the other person. How well do you know your industry and your company? How well do you know how the people you work with will respond to change? By gaining the advantage of time through quick, well-conceived action, you significantly increase your ability to succeed against slow-moving (and slow-decision-making) competition.

For Magnus, time was of the essence. If Bill Gates could hold him off for about thirty moves, he stood an excellent chance of winning based on the clock. By opening with a classic pawn move (1.e4 Nc6), Magnus must have realized that Gates could well have enough chess knowledge to hold on long enough to win. Magnus knew his game so well; he instantly went into a rarely used but effective Black defense. The Nimzowitsch Defense has been around since the nineteenth century. While chess masters recognize that it is a solid defense, they almost never choose it because they feel it cramps your ability to move. The most likely reason Magnus chose it here was he knew the defense so well he could still make rapid moves while slowing down Gates's ability to decide on the next move, making him consume valuable clock time. If Magnus had selected a more traditional defense, Gates may well have recognized it and known how to proceed without having to think about each move.

In business, if you have experience in a certain area, you can move much faster the second, third, or fourth time you do it. For example, if you have previously launched a new product, you don't have to spend quite as much time planning the launch activities. Instead, you can roll out your product quickly because you already know the steps, and you know your market. If you don't have the necessary experience, make sure someone on your team does.

Analytics Using Technology

How rare is the Nimzowitsch Defense? Consider that 5.4 million games are recorded in the 2013 ChessBase mega-database, of which 20,247 reached this position. Just over 0.3 percent of the database games had this position, which indicates the lack of interest for Black's move.

Since Magnus' move could be a response to either d4 or e4 from White on the first move, the statistics indicate that not many grandmasters consider this defense "industrial strength." Magnus more than likely would never have used it against Anand in either of his 2013 or 2014 world championship matches. Magnus's sole purpose in using it against Gates was to create an unbalanced situation from move one. Magnus's plan was to get Bill Gates started with slow thinking quickly.

2.Nf3 d5

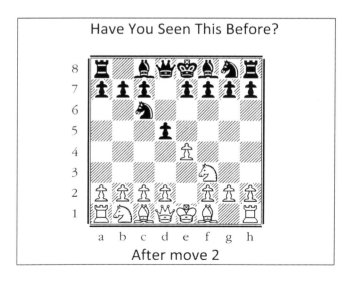

Have You Seen This Before?

After move 2

Bill followed up with a solid move of his king knight, moving it to its best central square and getting one of his employees between the rook and the king out of the way. Having been involved in numerous employee deployments at Microsoft, we can assume he knew that the people in the organization need to be deployed to their best location to realize the optimal return on their investment.

Magnus, on the other hand, instead of creating a position Bill was familiar with by moving his king pawn up two squares with a double king-pawn opening, played a move that immediately had to be analyzed because there were two pawns attacking each other. The video showed Bill having a hard time deciding what to do. A sign of a leader is the ability to understand how to direct the actions of others for strategic purposes. Perhaps Bill would have liked some help right here, but phoning a friend was not one of his lifelines.

In the mega-database this position occurs 1,163 times, which is .02 percent. Table 1 shows White wins 6 percent more games, but since this is based on weaker players, there isn't much stock in the results.

Position	# of games	Results % W-D-B
2...d5	1,163	42-22-36

Table 1

With this move, Magnus left the beaten path and dragged Bill Gates along with him. The theory of this opening is now more of a Center Counter Defense where White plays e4 and Black responds d5 on the first move. Moving the knights first confuses the situation. Magnus is up to some chicanery.

3.Bd3 Nf6

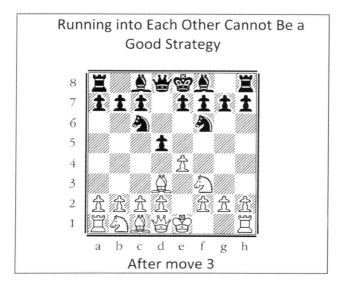

Running into Each Other Cannot Be a
Good Strategy

After move 3

Seeing his king pawn attacked by Magnus' queen pawn, Bill had a decision to make:

- Defend
- Trade
- Advance

The candidate moves he should have considered were: 3. exd5 or 3. e5. Instead he made his first strategic mistake in the placement of his employees by defending it. A manager doesn't want employees duplicating efforts or working against each other's objectives, resulting in a loss of productivity. A coach doesn't want football players running into each other, and it's not productive chess either.

Mobility Is Key

Lost productivity can be felt across the entire team when one player impedes any progress by the others. If a football play drawn up in the playbook goes awry, players think they have one responsibility, and unbeknownst to them, that becomes detrimental to the actual play outcome. The "butt fumble" is an infamous play between the New York

Jets and New England Patriots. Jets quarterback Mark Sanchez collided with the backside of his teammate on a busted play. As a result, he fumbled the ball. The Patriots recovered the ball and returned it for a touchdown. To see the play, follow this link:

https://www.youtube.com/watch?v=moJKMI4Yzck

The bottom line (no pun intended) in business, football, or chess is you don't want your players running into each other. After the move 3.Bd3, the d-pawn ran into the bishop on d3. The bishop on c1 ran into the d-pawn on d2. The rook on a1 ran into the bishop on c1. Much of Bill's team was paralyzed by one piece moving into the wrong position. The poor choice of defending his e4 pawn with the bishop caused a lack of mobility. Attempting to rectify a broken football play caused Mark Sanchez to run into something bigger than a chess piece.

Tactical Alert – Pawn Fork

Magnus Was Threatening to Win the Game with a Pawn Fork

(analysis)

By bringing his king knight to its best square, Magnus had introduced the first tactic into the position. He was threatening to take the pawn on e4 with his pawn on d5 to create a pawn fork with a winning position. This was another drawback to having misplaced the bishop on d3. Gates made the best move here and traded off the pawns, removing the threat.

In his tenure as CEO of Microsoft, Bill Gates made numerous hiring and placement decisions of his employees. In *One Thing You Need to Know...*, Marcus Buckingham says, "Bill Gate's true genius, the genius that differentiates him from the masses, lies in his ability to find just the right partner at just the right time. This genius might not always be conscious but review his career and you will find that he is a serial partner-finder."[1] From Ken Hood Evans to Paul Allen to Steve Ballmer, he has always found the right partner. Mr. Buckingham continues "Effective partnering is the quiet secret of the successful."[2] Unfortunately against Magnus, his success with real partners isn't rubbing off on his wooden partners.

4.exd5 Qxd5

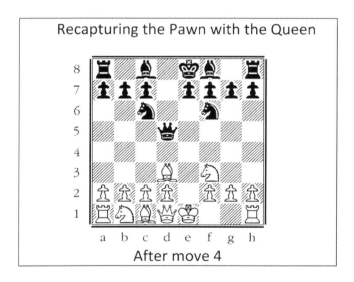

Recapturing the Pawn with the Queen

After move 4

Having analyzed the threat correctly and not wanting to fall for the pawn fork, Bill traded off the pawn and forced Magnus to recapture in order to remain even in the material assets. Magnus decided to capture the pawn with the queen. The drawback was the queen was in the center of board and subject to attack. Bill Gates' next move convinced me that he had played chess in his day. His move was automatic for chess players and is the downside of the Center-Counter defense with White picking up a free move by attacking the queen. Do you see what move to play that causes the queen to have to vacate the center of the board? *Fritz* would have recaptured with the knight, keeping the queen out of trouble for the moment.

Picking Up a Free Move

5.Nc3 Qh5

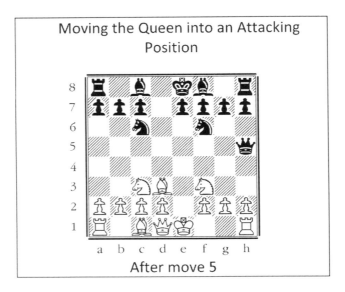

Moving the Queen into an Attacking Position

After move 5

Good move on Bill's part. These are the kind of automatic moves that experienced players make, and you can tell from the video that he knew what was going on by how quickly he played the move. He had probably seen the Center Counter defense before and was quick to play a good strategic, developing move with his knight while at the same time forcing Magnus to get his queen out of "Dodge."

The place where Magnus moved his queen should have signaled to Gates that his opponent was planning for a quick attack since the queen usually goes to a5, back to d8 or even to d6 in the best defensive lines. However, with the bishop on d3 paralyzing half his opponent's team, Magnus decided to go for the quick kill. The mega-database doesn't have any position with the Black queen on h5 but has twelve games with the queen back on d8. None of the games have been played by strong players since they know better and stay away from these slash-and-burn type positions. The players exchanged a pawn, so the game was even at this point. *Fritz* liked moving the queen to c5 with a dead-even game. Transformational leadership still needed to happen with the rest of the employees, but since this position had never occurred before, situational leadership was the style of the moment.

Tactical Alert – A Pin

6.0–0 Bg4

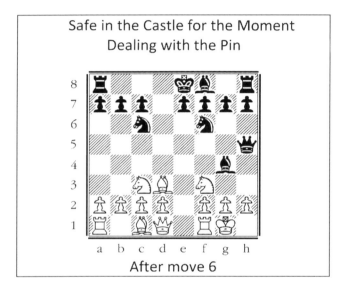

Safe in the Castle for the Moment
Dealing with the Pin

After move 6

After the queen went to h5, *Fritz* would have liked to see the bishop come back to e2 with a veiled threat on the queen. It also reversed the damage caused earlier by Gates' move 3.Bd3. Now he can advance his d-pawn and involve the rest of the employees in the game. In business, quick recognition of a mistake is tolerable if it's identified early and rectified. Bill Gates, however, played a strong, strategic move managing the risk to his king and castled.

Businesses conduct competitor analysis to determine their course of action, which Microsoft did with monopolistic tendencies at times. With Black's queen on h5, he might have been wiser to hold off castling. Bill sensed he is castling into Magnus' attack by lamenting about his situation. But after an "oh shoot" comment, he proceeded to castle. Magnus activated his bishop and pinned the knight to the queen. He was preparing the queenside castling move, bringing the rook into the attack if necessary.

A Combination Is a Small Project

Tactics are even more powerful when they are used together to form a combination, like a small project that companies do to remain competitive. The combination has a defined beginning and end, and its results can be measured. Certain resources are allocated to the moves, and it results in a significant—often winning—advantage.

With the White knight on f3 pinned to the queen on d1, Magnus created a position that could win him the game quickly. Bill Gates played a logical move trying to break the pin, called "putting the question to the bishop," and attacked it by moving his h-pawn up one square. It's not likely Magnus would keep his bishop there. If captured, it would give Bill a winning material advantage.

7. h3 introduced a weakened pawn formation into White's position, something we discussed in chapter 4. The move weakened the castle by moving a pawn that was sheltering his king. Magnus looked at the threat and ignored it. He made a move that sets up a trap with a forced continuation of moves. However, his move was a losing blunder, and if Bill Gates had seen the refutation, he would have been well on his way to victory. *Fritz* again would have preferred the bishop going back to e2 to break the pin and give the knight on f3 some support. With 11 h3 he gave Magnus a miniscule advantage.

7.h3 Ne5??

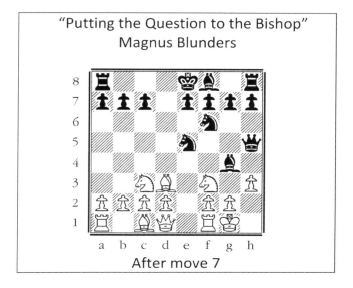

"Putting the Question to the Bishop"
Magnus Blunders

After move 7

After leaving his bishop en prise (eligible for capture), *Fritz* showed Bill Gates to be up (+-2.81) almost $3, which was clearly winning.

I'll Take the Money

True to his business demeanor, Bill Gates was interested in making money. By taking the bishop, he opened up his h-file and exposed his king to an attack with the two knights and queen hanging around his castle. But he just made a $2 profit. What's wrong with that? He was playing the best chess player in the world who doesn't give his pieces away without reason. Possibly 8. Be2, maintaining the threat and allowing 9. d4, getting his other pieces to play in a transformational leadership moment was better? With a little more time, Bill Gates might have understood his problem and found the winning move.

Reality was that Magnus blundered on his last move, and there was nothing wrong with taking the money. Magnus created a very tactical situation that required "being in the moment" by seeing what was threatened and taking action against it. Unfortunately, Bill Gates didn't have time to be in the moment and relied on past business behavior of making more money. He even followed that behavior on the last move of the game.

8.hxg4 Nfxg4

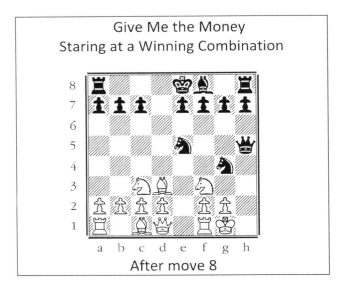

Give Me the Money
Staring at a Winning Combination

After move 8

The game had reached a critical point. Everything in White's position was held by a thread. Magnus wanted to pull off his game-winning combination in the next two moves. The auditors showed Bill Gates with a winning material margin if he could make his way through the complications.

Economic Equilibrium

Economics, as we discussed in chapter 9, is concerned with supply and demand and their effect on behavior. Here we have an economic situation on the square h2 where the demand of the attackers (Q on h5 & N on g4) is equal to the supply of the defenders (N on f3 & K on g1). If Magnus tries to enter the castle with Qh2??, then Bill would play Nxh2, Nxh2 and Kxh2, coming out a queen ahead. So at this point, Magnus could not make any progress with his attack. However, he was threatening to unbalance the equilibrium by taking out the knight on f3—with check no less. He would then have two attackers, and White would have only his king covering the h2 square.

Tactical Alert – Removing the Defender

In chess, if your king is under attack, called check, it must be defended immediately in one of three ways as shown in table 2. If one of these three options is not available, the king is not only in check, he is in checkmate and the game is over.

Block	Block the check by interposing a piece
Move	Move the king away from the check
Capture	Capture the piece that is checking you

Table 2

If the White knight on f3 were not present, Magnus could have brought his queen to h2 and it would have been checkmate since his knight on g4 protected the queen. But the knight was there, so for the moment he couldn't do that. But Magnus threatened to use a "remove the defender" tactic of exchanging his knight on e5 for the White knight on f3. His move would have been with check, so either the pawn on g2 or the queen would have to capture the knight on f3. But in either case Magnus could bring his queen to h2 and win on the spot.

How could Bill Gates have saved his hide in this situation?

This crazy blitz-game time control worked to Magnus' advantage. It would have been nice to have some slow-thinking time to find a solution if there was one to the combination he was facing. Can you determine what Gates' problem was in this position?

With the h-file open, it was like having a door blown off his castle; Magnus was ready to use that to his advantage. Bill Gates' problem wasn't as severe as the government threat to break Microsoft up because of monopoly practices, or as involved as the Apple litigation over the use of icons with the Windows operating system. He was up to those tasks. If he had not been so out of chess practice, he could have found the move here. He had to see that the knight on f3 was critical to his position, but it was going to disappear on the next move.

Microsoft Uses "Remove the Defender"

Bill Gates knows the "removing the defender" tactic in business because Microsoft uses it on practically every acquisition. The way it works is Microsoft has the head of the newly acquired company report directly to the CEO of Microsoft. This allows the CEO to get a handle on the acquired business while effectively reducing the acquired executive's decision-making ability.

This happened in 2011 when Microsoft acquired Skype for $8.5 billion, its largest acquisition ever. Skype became a division within Microsoft, with Skype's former CEO Tony Bates reporting to Microsoft CEO Steve Ballmer as the president of the division. The effect of this move was to remove Bates as a defender of his team since Microsoft took over calling the shots. Skype's executive team had to establish good relationships with Microsoft or risk being removed.

Considered a potential CEO of Microsoft, Bates left the company after being tactically "under-promoted" following the decision by the company to appoint Satya Nadella to succeed Steve Ballmer. Bill Gates didn't understand the dynamics of the "removing the defender" tactic on the chessboard, or he would have never made his next move.

Give the King Some Breathing Room

In the scenario where Magnus is able to remove the defending knight on f3, if Magnus' queen gets to h2 with a check to the White king, the option of blocking will not work because the queen is right next to the king. The option of capturing the queen is not available because if he did, he would be moving into check from the knight on g4. So the only available option is to move the king away from the check on h2. Bill's king didn't have any place to move after the check on h2. He could have provided an escape square by moving the rook from f1 to e1. If he had, *Fritz* said he would have had a (+-3.29) over $3 worth of winning material advantage.

After the knight on f3 was captured, the White queen could recapture, and on the Qh2+ move, Gates could slide his king over to f1. If Magnus played his queen to h1+ and then the king heads out of the castle, he could have survived the attack. His castle is on fire, but he would have escaped through a side exit. Magnus would have been hard-pressed to find winning moves with the limited amount of time available. As it was, he used eight of his seconds to play eleven moves and lost time by knocking over the pieces and having to set them up on his time. Oh, how the world would have sat up and taken notice if Bill Gates had defeated the world chess champion at his own game.

Bill Gates Makes Money Everywhere, Including on the Chessboard

Over his previous moves, Bill Gates had taken a lead in the monetary value for captured pieces. He placed himself in the same position he has been in most of his business life—how to deal with all the money he has. His next chess move proved that earning more isn't always the solution. Putting his wealth in trust and giving it away to charitable causes is his current passion. He is also encouraging other ultra-wealthy people to consider giving away their fortunes in the same manner. If his investments work out, then more money will be available to fight disease and improve educational opportunities.

Just because Gates is rich doesn't mean he is foolish with his money. In yet another instance of Mr. Buckingham's observation that Bill Gates is a serial partner-finder, enter partner Michael Larson. For more than twenty years Bill Gates has used Cascade Investment LLC in Kirkland, Washington, a suburb of Seattle, to handle his financial affairs. In an unmarked building, Mr. Larson and his secretive associates handle the financial affairs of Bill Gates. Under their discretionary control, Cascade has turned $5 billion into more than $80 billion, which helps Mr. Gates sleep at night. Cascade, which controls most of Bill Gates' personal fortune, also directs over $40 billion in the Bill & Melinda Gates Foundation.

With around 100 employees, Cascade is less than one-tenth the size of the Gates Foundation. To keep potential sellers from discovering the Gates connection, Cascade employees sign confidentiality agreements and forgo social media technology like Facebook, Twitter, Instagram, and LinkedIn. Outbound work e-mail to nonbusiness-related partners is also taboo.

While having done well with Mr. Larson, Mr. Gates might have been just as well off buying an annuity or keeping his Microsoft stock, which would be worth $150 billion. Yet Mr. Larson had Gates positioned in real estate, stocks, and private equity. For Bill Gates at least, diversifying his investments is a defensive strategy rather than offensive. Bill traded a potentially higher return for a safer return. Possibly an even more practical return was his $18 million investment in a horse farm near San Diego acquired from Jenny Craig for his daughter to practice her horse-riding skills.

Don't Go for More Money

Instead of recognizing his real problem as a lack of mobility with his king, Bill Gates decided to go after more money and made the worst move possible. In the video, after the move, Magnus looked like he was asking Bill if he really wanted to play that. Bill voluntarily removed the knight from f3 thinking he was capturing another piece to move farther ahead in the race for money. Instead, the game was over. He voluntarily removed the defender of h2 on his own.

Like a CEO that is only interested in short-term profits and not long-term viability, Gates looked only one move ahead, appearing to use the strategy of trading off opponent pieces to his advantage. In general, this strategy works, but in this case, the strategy didn't account for the resources needed for his survival. It's okay to make some high-risk investments, but you also need to secure your future with safer, long-term investments.

Later, Magnus expressed disappointment in his play that he went for a trap against his opponent. It didn't allow Bill Gates to demonstrate his middle and endgame technique. Lost were the revelations about how he thinks in critical moments in chess or business. A trait that Warren Buffet believes both Bill Gates and Steve Jobs had that led to their success was the ability to stay focused on the task at hand and not get distracted.

In this case the task at hand got away from him. With one minute and twenty seconds still left on his clock, Bill Gates played:

9.Nxe5?? Qh2# 0–1

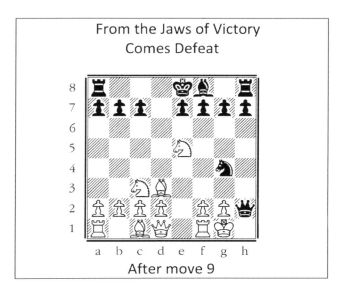

From the Jaws of Victory
Comes Defeat

After move 9

Table 3 has a potential winning continuation of moves.

9. Re1	e6
10. Be4	0-0-0
11. d4	Bd6
12. Qe2	Nxf3+
13. Qxf3	c6
14. Qh3	Bh2+
15. Kf1	Qxh3
16. gxh3	Nf6
17. Be3	Nxe4

Table 3

If Bill Gates had played the moves in table 3 and Magnus had played on, being down in material while behind on the clock by two minutes to thirty seconds, those conditions would have given Magnus a challenge. Bill Gates had to have spent little if any time getting ready for this encounter. The irony was that his strong strategic play should have been rewarded with a better result than a nine-move defeat. As a parallel in real life, Bill Gates has way more money than his opponent; unfortunately, there is a higher purpose than just accumulating more money during a chess game.

The Auditor's Report

White has an overwhelming material advantage. Magnus is down the equivalent of a $5 rook. He has two pawns for $2, and Gates has two minor pieces and a pawn for $7. This audit verified that material does not matter when the ultimate threat of checkmate is in play. Magnus set a trap, and Bill Gates, without thinking, made a poor decision but a good story.

White – 7 Black – 2

As the auditor report shows, material is relative and doesn't mean anything if the ultimate risk to the king is not addressed every day at the office or at every move on the board. Magnus won because he made Bill Gates use slow thinking when he had time for only fast thinking. Bill Gates was a good sport for doing this exhibition because, as anyone who is familiar with him knows, Bill Gates doesn't like to lose at anything.

Looking Back—Moving Forward

- ➤ Think fast and slow as the business or chess situation requires.
- ➤ Frame the situation with analytics using technology.
- ➤ Pounce on tactical opportunities being sharp and "in the moment."
- ➤ Devastate an opponent with a tactical combination.
- ➤ Balance attackers and defenders in an equilibrium.

- ➢ Dig down to the level needed to address the real problem of a situation.
- ➢ Block, move, or capture your way out of check.
- ➢ Force your opponent to make fast decisions that generate opportunities for you.
- ➢ Win with single-minded focus.

In our next and concluding chapter, we observe many of the business functional areas utilized on a chessboard. Business functions have to work together to support a well-run operation. The emotional roller-coaster ride encountered while competing against a master-level chess opponent relates to the daily ups and downs faced in the business world. It's next on our to-do list, and we're just in time for the game to start.

Chapter 11

Operating on the Edge - Logistics: Just-in-Time World

"It's now or ..."

"Your flight is delayed" are words any passenger dreads hearing when attempting to make a connecting flight. Flight delays are a repercussion of just-in-time scheduling. Airlines need planes in certain cities at certain times to route passengers to their destination. If weather and safety concerns interfere, the passengers' just-in-time schedules are abandoned.

School buses pick up students just in time for their first class. Arrive an hour early and the school has yet to open. Arrive an hour late and the students will have missed the first class. Dismissal time is easy to predict. Watch for a line of cars forming around the school just in time to pick up their precious cargo. A wait in the parking lot is the reward for arriving too early. Arriving too late generates a disgruntled student.

Train commuters also abide to a just-in-time schedule. If a passenger arrives at the train station too early, they wait along the tracks, thinking about boarding. If they show up late, they are doomed to catch the next train and will likely miss their start time at work. Income taxes are due on April 15. Paying taxes early surrenders your money before you have to. If due a refund, filing earlier is better. However, filing before the IRS can process returns is too soon.

Henry Ford knew that he needed supplies to arrive just in time to keep his assembly lines operating at peak efficiency. If they arrived too early, there may not be room to store them. If they arrived too late, production had already been shut down.

A key component in the logistics of material management is maintaining adequate stock so that it's available when required. This alleviates warehousing and the lost capital invested in storing those goods. JIT involves not only transporting an item from point A to point B, but ensuring that the item arrives just before it's needed. Time is of the essence!

Chess Is a Just-in-Time (JIT) Activity

Just-in-time (JIT) is defined as a "pull (demand) driven inventory system in which materials, parts, sub-assemblies, and support items are delivered just when needed and neither sooner nor later."[1] We live in a world that favors punctuality and precision. In the business world, when people and information are not in the right place at the right time, performance suffers.

JIT practices occur in chess. Complete your moves within the time allocated on your clock. Each move is an opportunity and should have a productive purpose. Analyzing a chess position helps you recognize when threats require immediate attention. Ignoring them will only make things worse. It accentuates when space, ranks, files, or diagonals need to be opened up as a resource, allowing the pieces to perform better as a team. Sometimes things can wait. Sometimes they have to happen immediately in order to take advantage of an opportunity. A fine sense of judgment is required to tell the difference.

This business case exhibits the value of applying JIT concepts by making a resource available just before it is needed. My opponent made an unexpected bishop sacrifice, and I was subjected to the highest risk factor in chess, a king exposed to attacks in the middle of the board. Move after move I found the resources needed to survive the attack when an inflection point enabled me to stop defending and switch to attacking. This chess case illustrates the importance of staying focused. Remaining calm in high-pressure situations is often the key to success. If you panic or allow high-pressure stress to unnerve you, you set yourself up for defeat. Fortunately, it's easier to stay calm and focused in chess than it is in the real world, and practicing "at the board" builds a player's confidence for high-stakes career decisions.

32:1 Odds

As the players hustled into the tournament room searching for their opponent, across the board from me sat a strong player with a significantly higher rating of 2210. At the time, I had a solid club-level Class A ranking. Separated by an expert-class level of ratings 2000-2199, my opponent was heavily favored to win. Our ratings were 347 points apart. If two player's ratings differ by more than 350 points, the rating system assumes the odds are 32:1 in favor of the stronger player.

This game was the last round of the same two-day tournament that started with my first-round match against master-level opponent Mr. Tyehimba. My analytical skills were not up to par in the earlier game; I made a strategic mistake and lost. With the benefit of two days' practice, my skills were sharper. Even though I made another strategic mistake, this game ended differently. My opponent and I played once before in the early 1970s when we were both in high school. Even though I won the 1971 match, twenty-five years later, he was now ranked among the best chess players in the United States.

Coach vs. Coach

Both of us were coaching our sons' school chess clubs. Our sons had played against each other several times at state competitions, and I was paired against his son in a previous round in this tournament. Out for revenge, there was more at stake than a few rating points.

How this game made it into the chess databases remains a mystery. However, this contest is one of my games on the ChessBase® "mega-database." Somebody must have judged it to be a quality contest, and it was included and is now replicated on the Internet. This game is right there with all the world champions' games. Does it belong there? Isn't everyone entitled to fifteen minutes of fame? The database game is not annotated, so the story behind the moves only happens here. There were moments when I was equal, then slightly worse, on the edge of losing, lost, better, and then, finally, victorious. Not unlike a business sales cycle, chess games often follow a trajectory in which travail precedes triumph.

Click on the following link to have the game Bachler vs. Egerton appear on your screen.

http://www.365chess.com/game.php?gid=1326271

Bachler, K - Egerton, J [B12]
Oak Park Master Challenge (5), 23.06.1996

White and Black both opened the game with pawn moves. A king pawn opening indicated that my opponent preferred a quicker attack because his kingside pieces would be developed and his king would soon be castled. His mobility count went from two to five; mine increased from two to three.

1.e4 c6

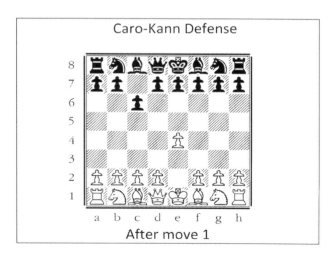

I varied from my usual Sicilian Defense, which I played against Tyehimba in the first round of this tournament and against Zepeda in 2008. Those games were analyzed in chapter 3. Here, I played the Caro-Kann defense against my opponent.

Why Caro-Kann?

Nick DeFirmian, author of *Modern Chess Openings*, described the history of the Caro-Kann: "Implemented by Polerio in 1590 this defense was little understood and scarcely played until H. Caro of Berlin and M. Kann of Vienna analyzed it seriously in the 1890's. "[2] The Caro-Kann works well against overly aggressive opponents, especially when they do not see the danger. It looks weak to the uninitiated, but usually results in better pawn positioning and a stronger endgame. The downside for Black is White gains more maneuverability during the opening. But White has to figure out what to do with the extra mobility, which can eat valuable clock time.

...c6 the Caro-Kann Defense is the fourth-most-popular response to 1 e4. It trails behind 1...c5 (Sicilian), 1...e5 (Double K-Pawn), and 1... e6 (French). It was used by World Champion Anatoly Karpov, so it has a solid reputation as a slow-building defense that takes time to develop into something intense.

While my son had played this defense extensively, I was familiar with it only on a conceptual level. Playing an opening you are not familiar with is never a wise strategy when playing against a master-level player.

2.d4 d5 3.e5 Bf5

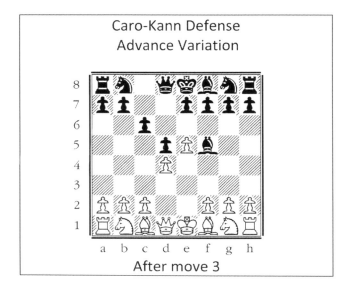

Caro-Kann Defense
Advance Variation

After move 3

White's e4-pawn is under attack from Black. White cannot ignore the threat, or he loses a pawn on the next move. There are several ways to defend it and a couple to get it out of danger. Of the more than 4,500 games in the *Fritz* opening book database on the Caro-Kann, White played the second-most-popular continuation.

Move	# of games
3 Nc3	1.5K
3 e5	1.2K
3 Nd2	.9K
3 exd5	.8K

This is the advance variation since White pushed his e-pawn past d5 and we can no longer exchange on e4 or d5. These moves determine which employees/pieces are more valuable than others. When the center gets closed up, the bishops have fewer diagonals to operate on, and their values go down. The knights, however, enjoy positions blockaded with pawns, and their values go up. Deciding which employees to keep and which to lay off comes from on-the-job experience of playing this opening and knowing your business plan.

Black activated the bishop before pushing e6, which would have reduced its value to the team. The bishop on f5 is similar to a halfback in a football game that was able to sneak through an opening in his line before his linemen got pushed back by defenders who were trying to close the opening. It is an active bishop out ahead of its pawns, as opposed to a bad bishop caught behind the pawns, or a good bishop where pawns do not block any movements.

4.Nf3 e6 5.Be2 Nd7 6.0–0 c5

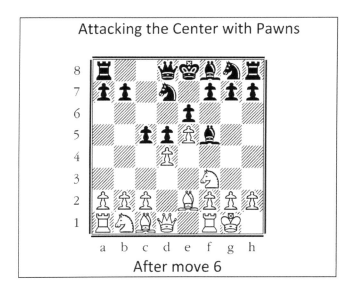

Attacking the Center with Pawns

After move 6

White developed his knight, and Black protected the bishop on f5, allowing the other bishop into the game. From a business perspective, beginning a game of chess is like starting up a new venture. For any new business venture, it is important to target a certain market, develop your resources, and mitigate your risks. Following these principles helps improve the chances that the enterprise will become more successful. Both players made two more standard developing moves, clearing out the bishop before castling and bringing a knight toward the center. From the footprint proficiency chart in chapter 2, the knight's maximum influence value is eight. However, because the c6 square is not available, the Black knight goes to the next best square with a proficiency value of six. With White having used two minutes to my six to make his moves, both of us were playing moves from recall and not moves that required time-consuming calculation.

White mitigated the risk to his king by castling, and Black started an attack on the base of the White pawn chain. If the d-pawn disappeared, then the pawn on e5 would take some effort to avoid being captured. It's standard chess procedure to attack a pawn chain at its base. In business, opponents identify the weakness in a competitor and use that as a point of attack. Black should be concerned that his recent moves were not getting the king ready to castle.

Black's last pawn move appears to be a loss of time since it could have gone to c5 immediately. However, White had spent two moves on his king pawn e4 then e5, so the time loss had not yet become toxic. Black was neglecting development, and his king was still three moves from castling. With the center closed, the need to shelter the king didn't seem important.

Analytics Using Technology

We were still in the book here, and of the 148 games that *Fritz* had in his opening database with this position, he liked:

Move	# of games
6... Bg6	63
6... Ne7	52
6... h6	28
6... a6	3
6... c5	2

The more popular moves had better results for Black. My move was at the bottom of what had been played. Things might still transpose, but 6... c5 would not be considered the best practice here. Using a chess-playing grandmaster-level computer is like having a powerful consultant at your beck and call in business. Their insight can help business leaders steer their companies into a better position.

ChessBase provides a comprehensive record of this position with actual game-based results, and it indicated that White had performed much better than Black. The position reached after six moves in the previous diagram has occurred 319 times in the database and White has tried five different moves on the seventh with the following results:

Position	# of games	Results W-D-B
7 Be3	130	71-36-23
7 c3	113	46-30-37
7 c4	73	47-12-14
7 Re1	2	0-0-2
7 dxc5	1	1-0-0

The ratio was more than 3:1 favorable for White or 38 percent better on 7 Be3. Black does much better after 7 c3 and much worse after 7 c4. There are only two instances of the rook move to e1. One of them occurred in this game, and both ended in a loss for White.

White did not follow the best opening theory, and we reached a point where our game left the database. Making history, we were on our own. A few more resources needed to be developed, and then the situational leadership style would take over from transformational. Engines like *Fritz* can help calculate new trends, but nothing in chess history was going to help either player gain an advantage. In business, a case study can take you only so far before the uniqueness of your situation causes you to move into uncharted territory. Knowledge and experience as a manager are the best guides to success, coupled with an in-house team of consultants.

7.Re1 h6 8.c4 Ne7 9.Nc3

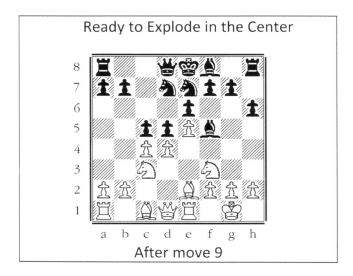

White made another developing move, followed by Black moving another pawn. The idea was preventive: to keep a White piece off the g5 square (prophylaxis) and give the bishop a retreat square on h7, if White attacked it or it needed to move.

The center pawns were attacking each other, and various captures and exchanges were under consideration. This is where a strong player uses their experience to guide them into the optimum position. It's like a CEO who launched various start-up ventures using the knowledge gained from previous ventures on the next one (fail fast, fail often).

Nothing had been captured yet, and the accountants have not had any transactions to book. The middlegame strategy of attacking was next up on the agenda, but Black hadn't completed his opening yet. Black's knight overprotected the bishop on f5 but blocked in the f8-bishop, so castling was still three moves away. *Fritz* evaluated the position as (+/- .82), which meant White was slightly less than a pawn ahead in the current position, even though material was even and the auditors had nothing but zeros to report.

9 ...cxd4 10.Nxd4 dxc4 11.Bxc4 a6 12.Nxf5 Nxf5

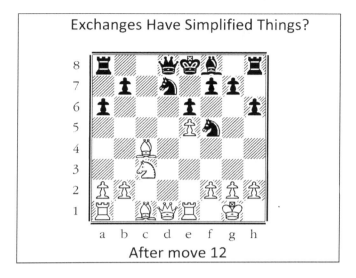

Exchanges Have Simplified Things?

After move 12

Black started exchanging pawns in the center in an attempt to free up lines and allow his last pieces to enter the game. White missed a promising continuation here with [10 Nb5, Ng6 11 Nfxd4, Ndxe4 12 f4, Nxc4 13 Nxf5, Bc5+ 14 Kh1, 0-0 15 Nfd4] where White had a piece for two pawns and a (+/- 1.01) advantage according to the computer. My experience had shown that the player who started exchanging first came out with a worse position. 9...Nc6 completing development may have been better. In business, being the first to start exchanges in a media war may serve to escalate a negative situation. The William Ackman attack on Herbalife's method of business has generated an exchange of numerous volleys with the outcome being resolved by Herbalife agreeing to pay $200 million to consumers and change its business practices as a part of the settlement with the FTC, while avoiding the pyramid scheme designation. The situation harkens back to the playground dispute resolution method of "he started it."

Unfamiliar Territory

Mr. Bachler continued to pound out his moves, having used only nine minutes to make ten moves. My lack of experience with this opening showed as I had used up thirty-eight minutes after making these pawn exchanges. White recaptured the pawn, activating his bishop, and Black prevented a piece from getting to b5 by moving up the rook pawn 11... a6—again invoking prophylaxis, a preventive countermeasure to a threat before it caused a future problem. Many of White's winning continuations involved putting a knight on b5. He had several chances to do it previously, but now it would cost him a piece.

This series of exchanges freed up space and eliminated the cramped position in Black's camp. With an "all quiet on the western front" mentality, I planned to get my bishop out to c5 and then castle to achieve a solid porcupine-like defense with good prospects. It appeared that our rooks were going to fight over the open c and d files with an uncertain outcome. But that wasn't the case.

Instead, a cannon shot blasted right into the heart of my position. The volley tested the premise that a surprise attack has a better chance of success. In one move, the game opened up, and Black had to face the consequences. After these moves, *Fritz* had calculated White's position as greater than (+-1.41), so technically I was down over a lost pawn even though the auditors said it was even. White had better development, which explained why the computer gave him the advantage. In business, never underestimate the element of surprise. When planning your next move, consider alternatives that may help you win by surprising your competition.

Tactical Alert - Sacrifice

13.Bxe6!

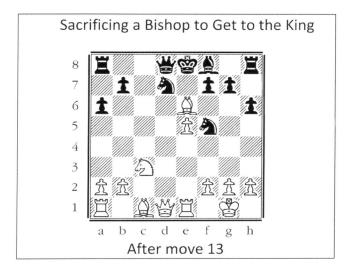

Sacrificing a Bishop to Get to the King

After move 13

In his classic treatise *On War*, Carl Von Clausewitz wrote: "Take the enemy by surprise. ... Surprise therefore becomes the means to gain superiority, but because of its psychological effect it should also be considered as an independent element. ... The two factors that produce surprise are secrecy and speed. Basically surprise is a tactical device, simply because in tactics time and space are limited in scale. ... Major success in a surprise action therefore does not depend on the energy, forcefulness, and resolution of the commander: it must be favored by other circumstance."[3]

The element of surprise in chess can be devastating because the move you could not foresee was lurking in the position. It was apparent to your opponent, so why didn't you see the move coming? Clausewitz says two factors that produce surprise are secrecy and speed; however, there are no secrets on the chessboard, and speed is not a factor because a player can make only one move at a time. So unlike a blitzkrieg attack at sunrise, in chess, the enemy may come from your side of the board for allowing the position to occur. Sacrificing a bishop for only a pawn in order to keep the king in the center was not on my radar. If I didn't take the bishop, I would have to either protect my knight on f5 or move it. If the late semiconductor pioneer and serial entrepreneur Andres Stephen "Andy" Grove were looking for an example of a business inflection point in a chess game, this move would have been one.

Suffering a Body Blow

Masking equanimity after suffering a body blow is tough for a boxer. This mental blow struck me just as hard at the chessboard. I'd become a victim of a surprise attack having overlooked this sacrifice. A heart-rate monitor would have shown my nervous tension off the charts. As the point of the sacrifice slowly sunk in, my habit of writing down the time taken for the moves suddenly stopped. When you overlook such a shocking move, your psyche gets rattled and doubts about your ability to anticipate your opponent's moves escalate. In business, analyzing trends is a critical component of successful planning. Nevertheless, one can only minimize the likelihood of a surprise; they can never completely eliminate it.

Making an Investment

A sacrifice in chess is the equivalent to an investment in business. One party voluntarily decides to give up more capital, money, or pieces than they get back in the expectation that they will receive a future return. However, a skilled chess player considers the investment like any financially savvy person might because they believe they will see a better return on their money in the future. It is not certain whether this investment will prove financially correct. In chess, we use the phrase "Is it sound?" to question whether or not a sacrifice should be successful. That's exactly what investors ask: "Will I get my money back?" Sacrifices are just like investments: some work out; some do not.

In financial investing there is always risk. If you are willing to take a greater risk, the reward should be that much higher. Investors know the higher the risk, the higher the potential reward. A thirty-year bond pays more interest than a five-year bond. Waiting twenty-five more years to get your money back is riskier. One of the risks working to the investor's advantage in chess is that your opponent might not find the best defensive moves when playing out the position, thus enhancing the attacker's position or return on the investment (ROI).

Chess players like to determine with "best play" whether a sacrifice is sound or not. As we saw in chapter 9, World Champion Mikhail Tal loved to sacrifice against his opponents and won many games by creating complicated positions where his opponent did not choose the right responses. With the use of computer analytics, many of his sacrifices have been proven to be statistically unsound. In this case, White had Black's king on the run for the rest of the game. Use your financial analysis tools to figure out if you think this investment/sacrifice is worth it. What moves should White play to justify his sacrifice?

13...fxe6 14.Qh5+ Ke7

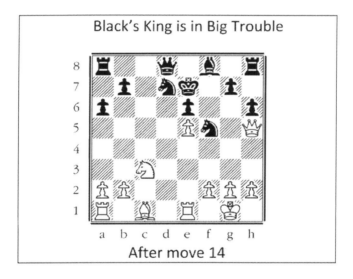

Human > Computer

Ironically, *Fritz* did not suggest the sacrifice as its move, preferring 13 Qc2 instead with a (+- .22) nominal advantage for White. Although, when the sacrifice was plugged in as the move that was played, *Fritz* immediately liked it. Even though White is down $2 in material, *Fritz* evaluated the position as (+- 1.04) in White's favor as if slightly more than a pawn ahead. That meant the computer thought White's sacrifice was sound or that at least he had compensation for the lost material. Good executives know that while the advice of their consultants is valuable, the mantra of "trust but verify" should be applied in business and chess.

Black had fallen victim to a flank attack from the queen. The only viable alternative was to move the king up to avoid the check. There will not be any celebrating in the castle tonight. Here one type of asset (material) was exchanged at less than book value to bring about the ultimate risk factor from chapter 4, king exposure to attacks. White gave up more material than he got back, and it remained to be seen if the sacrifice was sound. Meanwhile, woe to Black's deplorable king position.

15.b3 Qa5!

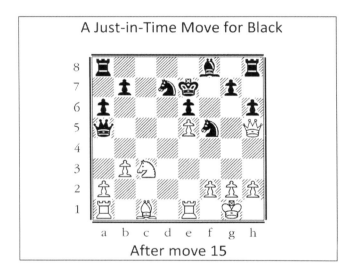

A Just-in-Time Move for Black

After move 15

Computer > Human

In this instance, erroneous human thinking was clarified by a computer. *Fritz* pointed out that White missed the best continuation here with [15. Nd5+ exd5 16.Qxf5, Qa5 17 Be3, Rc8 18 b4, Qb5 19.e6, Nf6 20.Bc5+, Rxc5 21 bxc5, Qa5] and Black must resign. White may have dismissed this knight sacrifice because it traded an active piece while none of his other pieces were involved. It makes perfect sense, from both a managerial and chess-player's perspective, to involve more employees. It is difficult to call this teamwork if the queen was the only piece attacking. Once the c1-bishop was activated, the back rank squares of a1 through e1 become available for White's rooks, all very logical, but wrong.

Unbelievably, 15. b3 threatening Ba3+ started to give me hope. Playing *Fritz's* move could have kept the attack rolling, a move my opponent found a little too late. Timing is critical for just-in-time to succeed in business or chess. It's natural that White wanted to introduce more forces into his attack. This natural move threatens check, and since the Black king had no flight square, the game would soon be lost. As humans we've been trained that if we want to continue an attack, then bring more reinforcements into play. If you want to defend an attack, trade off some of the attacking pieces. Trading knights in this position to keep the attack going is something only a computer would find because it is not bound by our faulty maxims.

The JIT practice of creating a necessary resource when it's needed appears with this move. Black's king had no available square to occupy. If Black allowed 16 Ba3+ then 16...Nc5 blocking the check was the only move, 17 Bxc5+, Kd7, 18 Rd1+ skewers the king to the queen sitting behind him, and it's over. After 15. b3, *Fritz* gave Black a slight numerical advantage, but the weakness of the Black king more than compensated for the material inequality. The position was evaluated at (-+ .42) or just under half a point advantage for Black. The last audit report hadn't changed, but now Black's trend line started to become bullish as his position and chances continue to improve.

Black needed to prevent the bishop from getting to a3. 15...Qa5 is the epitome of JIT applied to chess. Black delegated his queen to play critical defense just in time to deny the White bishop access to a3. This move also provided Black with a resource he needed, a square safe from enemy checking attacks on d8.

As the surprise attack receded, my heart rate and blood pressure returned to normal. I went back to recording the time used for our moves. It took me nearly ten minutes to find the JIT move, which had prevented the bishop from getting to a3. White had used only twenty minutes of game time. So far, I had used fifty-one minutes. In business, an aggressive JIT delivery program can be the difference in making the sale or losing out to a competitor. How quickly can you beat your competition?

16.b4 Qxb4

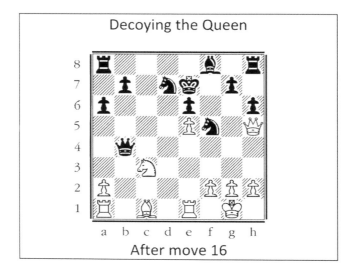

Decoying the Queen

After move 16

Tactical Alert – Decoy

If White had played 16 Bb2, then Black would have gained a slight advantage. White is offering a free pawn. Should I take it? If I don't, then I must move my queen. I decided to take it for three reasons:

1. It's another pawn in my bucket.
2. I am attacking his free knight on c3.
3. My queen accesses the fourth rank.

White was attempting to decoy my queen onto a bad square b4 with some powerful threats, but he had given me access to the fourth rank. My queen could continue to cover White's threats with powerful defensive moves. The computer had Black ahead by about a pawn here (-+ .71) even though Black was actually three pawns ahead. *Fritz* calculated White had compensation for the sacrifice, and his investment had potential to pay off.

17.Bd2 Qh4 18.Nd5+

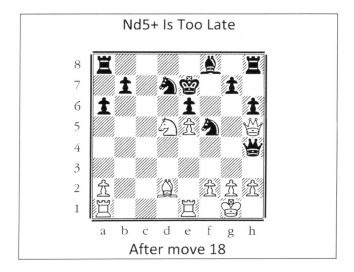

Nd5+ Is Too Late

After move 18

Tactical Alert – Discovered Attack

White threatened a powerful discovered attack on my queen with the move 18 Nd5+, exd5 19 Bxb4+ winning the queen.

Combining strategy with tactics, just in time Black's queen evaded the bishop's tactical threat and attempted a trade of queens. Strategically, one of the best ways to break the back of an attacker is by trading off some of the attacker's pieces. White cannot afford to allow major assets to leave the board after everything he had sacrificed. Exchanging commodities in order to survive an attack works as well in chess as it does in business, where maintaining a competitive advantage can offset the competition.

White found the knight move he should have played on move fifteen. If he discovered it earlier, I would have been forced to take his knight. In this instance, my king occupied a safe square. By not capturing the knight, I provided shelter to my king. By occupying a position in the center of the board, however, my king was still playing Frisbee on a highway.

After this move, *Fritz* says Black was winning (by -+1.75 points). On the board, however, I was attempting to dodge checkmate threats and bring the fight to my opponent. I got the sense that the White attack was slowing down, which gave me hope that I just might survive this onslaught.

18...Kd8 19.Qf7 Bc5

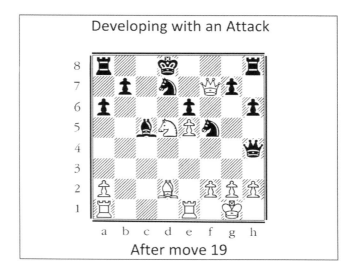

Developing with an Attack

After move 19

The king used the d8 square, which the queen previously liberated. Without the ability to move, the Black king was still in trouble.

Defense to Offense

White correctly kept the queens on the board and slid his queen onto a menacing square near my king. Safe from a direct threat, I developed one of my moribund employees, as the Black bishop shifted into to attack mode.

When the implementation of opening strategies, like employee development and risk management are delayed or eliminated, going headlong into the middlegame is undesirable. Black was unravelling the back rank and putting pressure on the f2 square in White's castled position. The bishop was developed with an attack. Among his alternatives Black threatened,

20...Qxf2+ 21 Kh1, Ng3+ (see next diagram) with a discovered attack winning the queen on f7. After 22 hxg3, Qxf7 the threat of 23...Qh5# was lethal.

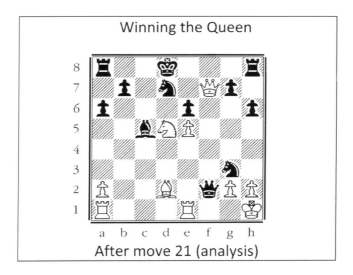

Winning the Queen

After move 21 (analysis)

There was also the helpmate with Bxf2+, Kh1??, Ng3#. In any case, *Fritz* had Black here by (- +3.58) points, a winning advantage. It's easy to see that in the afterglow of the game with a powerful computer, but with my awkward king there was still trouble to plow through like dealing with pesky checks.

In *The Military Maxims of Napoleon*, Maxim 29 is: "The transition from the defensive to the offensive is one of the most delicate operations in war."[4]

Annotator David Chandler reflects on that maxim: "History shows that this observation is true indeed. Here the requirements of military art call for careful calculation and a sense of timing if success is to be achieved. What is possible at one moment may not be feasible at the next: opportunity is a fleeting matter, and it requires a good commander to recognize it and seize it."[5]

The Importance of the Initiative

Momentum is a desirable condition in business and chess. In chess, the player with momentum is said to have the initiative. They are dictating what will happen in the immediate future. In business, companies have numerous ways to maintain their momentum. They can continue to enhance their product line with value-adding features their customers want, which keeps competitors playing defense. After my last bishop move, I have managed to parry the White threats and am generating game-winning threats of my own. Since the threats are severe enough to win me the game, my opponent has to stop his immediate plans and switch to defending mode.

The server has the initiative in tennis, setting up what is going to happen next. The player who is in control of the point dictates what is happening during the rally. Both tennis and chess are sequential. Opponents take turns hitting their shots, and each player's move depends on the one before it. This position demonstrates the importance of the initiative.

20.Ba5+ b6 21.g3

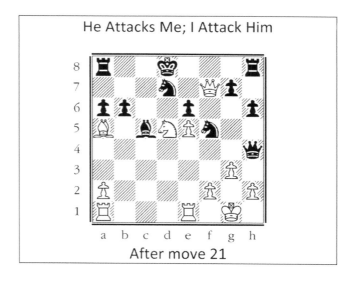

He Attacks Me; I Attack Him

After move 21

White played a forcing check move on Black's king, delaying any action on dealing with Black's threats on f2. Blocking the check was Black's best alternative. White had managed to put another piece in danger of being captured; his knight on d5 was in danger as well.

Unbeknownst to me at the board, *Fritz* had the position evaluated as (-+ 6.08) here, so if Black avoided checkmate, he had a won game. White needed to keep the Black queen out of f2, and by pushing up the pawn to g3, he attacked it as well. I already had plans to start shredding the pawns around the castle where White's king lives.

21...Bxf2+

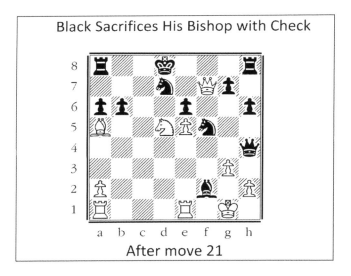

Black Sacrifices His Bishop with Check

After move 21

Castling with the king only mitigates his risk; it doesn't eliminate it. Keeping the initiative, I start to strip away the pawn shelter around White's king by sacrificing my bishop with check, postponing any action with my queen. Sacrificing a bishop to expose the enemy king was a recurrent theme in this game and was something on White's mind eight moves earlier. It was (-+ 9.98) for Black now.

22.Kg2 Bxg3

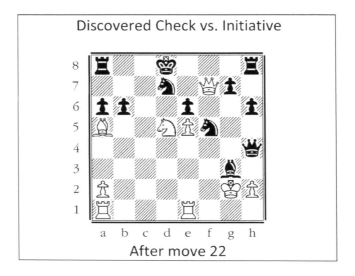

Discovered Check vs. Initiative

After move 22

If White had captured the bishop, then *Fritz* would have evaluated Qxh2+, Kf3 as (-/+ 11.62) in Black's favor. No immediate mate-threat but the material was overwhelming. Black continued to strip White's king of pawn protection, removing the pawn that was attacking the queen and threatening the pawn on h2. If h2 is captured, White's king would head out onto the open board.

Tactical Alert – Discovered Check

White could have protracted the contest, drawing out a few more moves by playing 23.Bxb6+ Nxb6 24.Qc7+ Ke8 25.Qc6+ Kf8, but the end result would not have changed. His fate was sealed. White sets up a discovered check, which would have devastated Black's position, but he was one move short, and it was never played.

23.Nxb6 Qxh2+ 24.Kf3 Qf2+

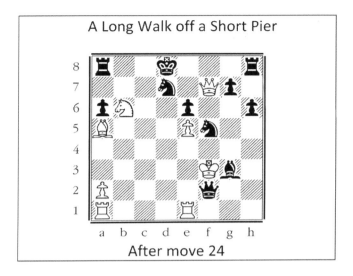

A Long Walk off a Short Pier

After move 24

Black had captured the last piece and stood $5 ahead while White's king walked right in front of the firing squad. White's king had to decide to take a long walk or a short one.

His candidate moves were:

- 25 Kg4, h5+
- ❖ 26 Kh3, Qh2#
- ❖ 26 Qxh5, Qf4+, 27 Kh3, Rxh5+ 28 Kg2, Qf2#
- ❖ 26 Kg5, Qf4+ 27 Kg6, Rh6# or Qg4#.

JIT was in force on the last move of the game. If it were White to play in this position, then Qxd7# would be checkmate for him. Black was able to checkmate first. Ironically, the castle move that was ostensibly made to protect White's king almost ended up trapping it. Black never moved his king into a castle, and though less protected, it was less constricted by surrounding pieces.

Instead of heading right, White heads his king left, which was a much shorter road. These moves were something out of the movie *Dead Man Walking*.

25.Ke4 Nc5# 0–1

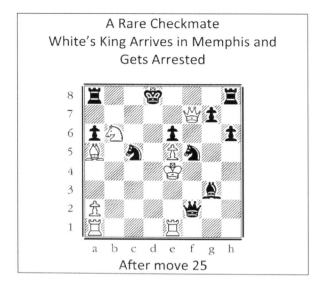

A Rare Checkmate
White's King Arrives in Memphis and
Gets Arrested

After move 25

Tactical Alert – Mating Net

A mating net is required to checkmate a king in the middle of the board. It's harder in the middle of the board because there are eight squares the king can move to at any given time. Most checkmates occur on the side of the board. White's king arrived in Memphis, and Black's troops promptly arrested him. In situational leadership, Magnus knew e4 was a good place for the endgame. In the middlegame, with so much material on the board, Memphis (e4) is not a favorable place.

Financial Analysis Using Technology

After my opponent moved his king to Memphis, I glanced up at him with the look of, "Are you sure you want to go there?" But it was played, and I had beaten a rated chess master. We went over the game for a few minutes while his international master friend watched, equally stunned. My opponent said he never foresaw 15…Qa5.

But what if other moves had been played? On move ten, White missed a promising continuation that led to a winning advantage with 10 Ncb5 instead of 10 Nxd4. On move eleven he missed the same continuation with 11 Ndb5 instead of the automatic recapture with 11 Bxc4.

The Final Auditor's Report

White liquidated $7 of Black's capital, and Black has $35 left, so $42 has been accounted. Black liquidated $12 of White capital, and White has $30 left, so his $42 of working capital in accounted. Accountants have made the appropriate entries, and material assets end in Black's favor.

White – 7 Black – 12

On move thirteen, White chose to invest a $3 bishop for a $1 pawn with an ROI (return on the investment) yet to be determined. In the actual game, he never got his money back during the game's remaining moves. Did that mean it was a bad investment? Did he throw good money after bad? The soundness of a sacrifice is determined by the "best moves" from both players. If the players made the best moves and it led to a winning competitive advantage for the sacrificing player, then the sacrifice was sound. Clearly 15 b3 was too slow; Black played solid defense and won. But what if 15 Nd5+ had been played instead?

Our grandmaster-level chess engine can check our logic and generate some improvements. Table 1 has four columns, the first with moves fifteen to twenty-seven for both players. The second column is *Fritz's* recommended move. The third is the accounting cash flow after the move from White's perspective. The fourth column indicates how *Fritz* evaluated his move. White's value columns become progressively more positive as his game gets better.

Move	White Black	Cash Flow	*Fritz* Eval
15	Nd5	-2	+1.49
15	exd5	-5	+1.49
16	Qxf5	-2	+1.58
16	Qa5	-2	+1.59
17	Be3	-2	+1.75
17	Rc8	-2	+1.49
18	b4	-2	+2.83
18	Qb5	-2	+2.93
19	e6	-2	+3.13
19	Nf6	-2	+3.18
20	Bc5	-2	+3.22
20	Rxc5	-5	+3.27
21	bxc5	0	+3.27
21	Qa5	0	+3.28
22	Rab1	0	+3.50
22	Kd8	0	+3.47
23	Qf4	0	+3.57
23	Qc7	0	+3.55
24	e7	0	+3.57
24	Bxe7	-1	+3.57
25	Qxc7	+8	+3.58
25	Kxc7	-1	+3.73
26	Rxe7	+2	+3.73
26	Kc6	+2	+3.76
27	Rxg7	+3	+3.77
27	Ne4	+3	+3.74

Table 1

276

Let's assume the moves suggested by *Fritz* were the best available for both players. Not unlike JPM using models to analyze VaR at their bank or AIG models analyzing housing values for their policies, *Fritz* is quantitatively able to model and predict what the future may hold. *Fritz* might even supply or suggest moves a human would never consider. It's where technology complements human analysis to reveal the truth in a position, or vice versa, as when *Fritz* had to be fed the sacrifice that it didn't want to consider. Cross-fertilization between the computer and human brains is an interesting phenomenon that seems to hold a lot of promise for many fields. Financial metrics are shown in Table 2.

The Investment (Sacrifice) was Sound

The long-term liability of Black's king in the center of the board caused by the bishop sacrifice on 13 Bxe6 was justified, and the investment was sound. If the "best" order of moves had been played, White would have gone ahead on move 26 Rxe7+ shown in the next diagram. Black is down the exchange, his g7 pawn is going, and the one on b7 is lost.

Fritz said all along that White was up $3 at the breakeven point on move twenty-one. It was not until move twenty-seven that the evaluation approached the actual cash flow totals represented on the board. If the computer model is to be believed, cash flow and the *Fritz* evaluation should eventually approximate each other.

This is the same type of analysis arbitragers look for in market inequity conditions. Mr. Weinstein and his hedge-fund colleagues knew that eventually the London whale's trades mathematically had to come back to a rational point as time progressed. They just had to wait him out. Here it took twelve agonizing moves. For the hedge funds, it took weeks. The challenge with chess is that visualization of future moves must be done in the player's head—no use of sophisticated models or software. *Fritz* can provide that but only after the fact.

Metric	Analysis
Cash flow	Turned positive on move 26 Rxe7.
Breakeven	Occurred on move 21: Black sacrificed the exchange of a $5 rook for a $3 bishop, returning the $2 gained from move 15.
Cost/Benefit	The cost of $2 yielded $3 of benefit.
The Return on Investment (ROI)	After move 27, White was up $3; $3 returned on $2 invested or 3/2 is 150% ROI.

Table 2

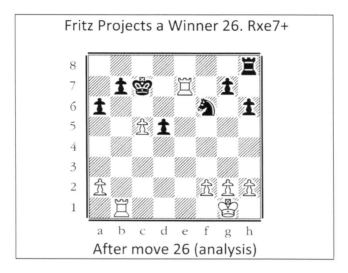

Fritz Projects a Winner 26. Rxe7+

After move 26 (analysis)

Putting Up Resistance

How often is a combination played that wasn't forced or when there were in-between moves? Or the moves were played out of order and the result turned into ruinous defeat instead of victory? History can demonstrate a few examples.

Napoleon at Waterloo attempted a divide-and-conquer strategy against the duke of Wellington and the English before Bucher and Prussians arrived. Due to torrential rains the night before the battle, Napoleon's army was not in a position to fight until afternoon, which gave Prussian reinforcements plenty of time to arrive.

General Custer utilized troop combinations during the Battle of Little Bighorn that offered a good chance of success, attacking the Native

Americans from one direction and anticipating they would retreat in the opposite direction where he was waiting. The victory was there for both of them, but they played their moves in the wrong order and suffered the consequences.

Business Applications

Just in Time

This case illustrated JIT concepts as an application of inventory, time, and space. Every time Black needed a resource he was able to find it. Manufacturers require production materials just in time to make the operation a success. Decision-making is another aspect of JIT. In business, timing is everything. Are you ready to launch on minimal information, or must you hold back until you have all available data?

Risk Management

Neglecting the risk management of his king, Black became immobilized in the center when attacking broke out that should have cost him the game. The complexities of the position helped Black stay the course and turn the game in his favor. White had a pristine row of pawns in front of his king. Black's king was stuck in the middle, operating on the edge, running for cover. Within a matter of moves, White's castle lost every pawn he owned, and White had to march his king to the middle of the board where he met his fate.

Perseverance

Ben Franklin believed that chess teaches perseverance by encouraging its players not to give up in dim circumstances and to continually strive to improve one's position. Franklin also believed chess teaches foresight, which is to look at long-term consequences of your actions—like not tending to king safety.[6]

The element of surprise with the sacrifice on move 13. Bxe6 became the game's inflection point. White's move was sound and could have won the game. Black persevered with a tenacious defense, keeping the contest alive until he could regain the initiative.

Practice Decision-Making under Stress

Keeping your cool under extreme pressure is a hallmark of a good leader. While you may not enjoy a pressure-cooker environment, it does prepare you for a bigger role in your career.

Decision-making under duress, when practiced in an over-the-board chess game, is like life's flight simulator. Staying calm under extreme stress helped United Airlines safely crash land flight 232 in Iowa, with survivors in a plane that had no hydraulics. The stressful feat was repeated when US Airways performed a "Miracle on the Hudson" by landing their plane successfully after bird ingestion caused engine failure during takeoff. Reacting favorably to unexpected situations is nothing more than turbulence to most chess players.

Play the Board, Not the Opponent

Playing an unfamiliar opening against a master chess player was a poor strategy. After the game, Mr. Bachler said he never foresaw 15...Qa5 preventing his attack from succeeding. It helps to know your opponent's rating, but if they have a bad day and you play the best moves available, "Caissa," the goddess of chess, may shine upon you.

Looking Back—Moving Forward

➢ Play what you know, using past valuable experience.
➢ Leadership styles can change on a single move.
➢ Not all businesses or games make it to the endgame.
➢ Like Enron's demise, this game was a middlegame checkmate.
➢ Going from defense to offense is a delicate operation.
➢ Tactics appear in strategically superior positions.
➢ Appreciate the devastation of a tactical combination.
➢ Analytics using technology can help frame the situation.
➢ Financial models/ratios can determine whether an investment/ sacrifice is sound.
➢ Use technology to detect the defects in your thinking.

The Next Game - It's Your Move

"One Door Closes, Another Door ..."

One game ends, another starts. If you are convinced that my business talent development methods can help improve your team's leadership skills, please contact my office at **1-800-785-0420**, to schedule an appointment on getting started.

Together we will determine the best way for you and your team to begin building strategically stronger and tactically sharper leaders.

For others that want to continue on the path of learning more about business leadership using chess, I recommend becoming a complimentary "Inner-Circle" member of The Business on the Board™ community. By enrolling in our member registration at www.businessontheboard. com/enroll, you will receive occasional e-mails with new and insightful perspectives on how the games of business and chess relate. The growing list of "Inner-Circle" membership materials available on the website include:

- A downloadable PDF file of all the links used in the book available by chapter. This eliminates unnecessary time spent typing and following the training material links.

- Videos that explain strategies and tactics used in business and practiced on the chessboard.

- More business strategies and tactics presented from other J.K. Egerton games against chess grandmasters, masters, and strong players from hundreds of games over forty years of competition.

- Training materials and handouts for teachers and trainers who teach "Chess for Purpose".

- A forum for staying connected through social media news and events on LinkedIn, Facebook, and Twitter.

- White papers and award winning articles published by the author.

- A feedback feature with the ability to leave a review on Amazon about your experience with the book.

If chess has helped you get ahead in your career, I would love to hear from you. Your story could become our next blog post helping other members share successful strategies and tactics they can use in their lives and careers.

It's Your Move

Better decision-making will improve your life. My intention was to demonstrate that business leadership, and its attendant decision-making, is vastly superior when it is strategically stronger and tactically sharper using chess. Practice the game of business on the field of your choice. I hope that by sharing my story, your story includes the desire to use "chess for purpose" as a deliberate practice facility.

If during your read, you paused and thought, "I didn't know that," then I have succeeded. I managed to connect the dots between business and chess. If George Bernard Shaw had been able to connect the business-to-chess dots better, he might not feel that "chess is a foolish expedient for making idle people believe they are doing something very clever, when they are only wasting their time." I'd like to think I could convince him otherwise.

J.K. Egerton
Business on the Board

Appendix
How Do I Get Started?

Active businesspeople have asked me where to start. They may be absolute beginners or say, "I know the moves, have played in the past, but have little or no time to study chess. What is the quickest way to make progress?" You may have already invested time and energy into developing a tool that can empower your strategic thinking and decision making. You just don't see how it applies to your business or your career. Having read up to this point in the book, you have a solid foundation upon which to build your leadership skills.

Improving in any endeavor involves deliberate practice, playing, and instruction. If you are a member of our "Inner-Circle" community, download the PDF file of all the links used in the text. It's time to investigate the Technology section in chapter 8. There you will find the available links to online playing sites, many for free. Sign up to play and don't worry about your results. You are using chess for purpose to help you practice and improve your decision-making.

For studying, there are more books on chess than all other games combined. You have seen five games in this book that amount to no more than a snowflake on the tip of an iceberg. You want to start with books that divide the game just like a business into the opening (entrepreneurial/ start-up), middlegame (growth), and endgame (mature) phases. To stay focused on what to do, follow these nine strategies that were introduced in chapters 4-6:

Opening – Start-Up	Middlegame – Growth	Endgame – Mature
C - Center	A - Attack	K - King
D - Develop	W - Win	P - Promote
C - Castle	E - Exchange	C - Checkmate

Use the first four moves I call "Playing the Pyramid" which follows the project plan in chapter 8. Starting with my moves will prevent a quick checkmate. Two games worth reviewing that utilize "the Pyramid" formation are at the following links:

Lautier, J (2570) - Shirov, A (2580) [E63] Manila Interzonal Manila (11), 1990

At the end of this game, White resigned in view of the lack of a defense against the advancing Black pawns.

http://www.365chess.com/game.php?gid=2116831

Use This at Home

One thing I would hate is to have an opportunity to play a great player, like a world champion, and get blasted off the board in nine moves. A much stronger opponent has the advantage of experience so why let them overwhelm you with their ability. Take a different approach and make them work to beat you. This is the opening formation I recommend for casual chess players, novices who don't want to get wiped off the board by a grandmaster or below. These moves take a slower positional route to the start where it will take some time for action to develop. Neither player aims their attacking intentions directly at the opposing king because it is too challenging to attack such a well-fortified, powerful pyramid structure.

If you play chess on your mobile device, you can record the moves in .pgn (pretty good notation) format. Input those moves into a computer using software that plays at a grandmaster level ability like *Fritz* to quickly improve. Go over your games as if you were running a company. Evaluate your strategies to determine their effectiveness. Learning from the previous game, especially a loss, will pay dividends in the next game. Whatever it takes, just get started.

Smyslov, V (2560) - Sax, G (2590) [B07] Tilburg (4), 1979

http://www.365chess.com/game.php?gid=2503999

By a transposition of moves, we have reached the exact same position after five moves of the previous Lautier vs. Shirov game. Here the White players went a different way. Lautier played c4 in his game, and Smyslov played Nc3. A chess position can be reached via certain move order transpositions. It doesn't always occur from just one sequence of moves; however, the end result could be the exact same position on the board. All of these moves illustrate good strategic opening principles of playing for the center of the board, developing the pieces, and castling with the king.

If you are chess curious and want to go further into the moves, for an excellent treatment of both of these games explained on a move-by-move basis by a world-class grandmaster, I recommend *Understanding Chess Move by Move*, by Dr. John Nunn, Gambit Publications, games 27 and 28.

If you are business curious and want to go further into practical advice for leading and managing real employees, I recommend *The Managerial Leadership Bible*, by Dr. Jeffrey Magee, Pearson Education Publications.

The games of business and chess can be maddeningly difficult to master. Chess knowledge provides powerful insights into business practices. One paying-it-forward consideration for sharing your business/chess knowledge is through a lunchtime mastermind group. A carefully chosen chess position could involve a strategy or tactic that applies to a current business situation. After all, leading a company doesn't come with a user's manual.

The "**About The Training**" tab at www.businessontheboard.com has more information about our instructional offerings.

Contact me at **1-800-785-0420** or use the **CONTACT** tab on our website, or email directly at jkege@businessontheboard.com. I look forward to hearing about the business success you deserve.

Notes

The First Move

1 Colvin, Geoffrey. *Talent is Overrated*, The Penguin Group, New York, 2008, Page 1

2 Beck, Randall & Harter, Jim. "Why Great Managers Are So Rare," *Gallup Business Journal*, March 25, 2014 http://www.gallup.com/businessjournal/167975/why-great-managers-rare.aspx

Chapter 1 Leadership

1 Lencioni, Patrick. *The Five Dysfunctions of a Team*, Jossey-Bass, San Francisco CA, 2002

2 Conger, Jay A. & Benjamin, Beth. *Building Leaders How Successful Companies Develop the Next Generation*, Jossey-Bass, San Francisco CA, 2002, Page 58

3 Pandya, Mukul & Shell, Robbie. *Lasting Leadership, What you can learn from the Top 25 Business People of our Times*, Wharton School Publishing, Upper Saddle River, New Jersey, 2005, Page 239

4 Bazerman, Max H. *The Power of Noticing, What the Best Leaders See*, Simon & Schuster, New York, 2014, Page 33

Chapter 2 Human Resources & Organizational Behavior

1 Vance, Ashlee. *Elon Musk, Tesla, SpaceX, and the Quest for a Fantastic Future*, Harper Collins Publications, New York, NY, 2015, Page 86

2 Buckingham, Marcus. *The One Thing You Need to Know …About Great Managing, Great Leading and Sustained Individual Success*, Free Press, New York, 2005, Page 83

Chapter 3 Strategy – Strategic Thinking – Tactics

1 Mintzberg, Henry & Quinn, James Brian. *The Strategy Process*, Prentice Hall, Englewood Cliffs, New Jersey, 1991, Page 5

2 Magee, Jeffrey. *Your Trajectory Code, How to Change Your Decisions, Actions and Direction, to become Part of the Top % High Achievers.* John Wiley & Sons, Hoboken, New Jersey, 2015, Page 114

3 Agassi, Andre. *Open*, Alfred A. Knopf, New York, 2009, Page 164

4 Mintzberg, Henry and Quinn, James Brian. *The Strategy Process*, Prentice Hall, Englewood Cliffs, New Jersey, 1991, Page 6

5 Korn, Melissa & Gellman, Lindsay. "Should Harvard Business School Hit Refresh?" *The Wall Street Journal*, February 4, 2015

6 Davis, Ann., Sender, Henry & Zuckerman, Gregory. "What Went Wrong at Amaranth," *The Wall Street Journal*, September 20, 2006

7 Stevens, Scott. *Games People Play*, The Teaching Company, Chantilly, Virginia, 2008, Page 38

8 Lowenstein, Roger. *When Genius Failed, The Rise and Fall of Long-Term Capital Management*, Random House, New York, 2001, Page 235

9 Patterson, Scott., Ng, Serena. "Deutsche Bank Fallen Trader Left Behind a $1.8 Billion Hole," *The Wall Street Journal*, February 6, 2009

10 Ahmed, Azam. "The Hunch, the Pounce and the Kill," *New York Times*, May 26, 2012

11 Ibid.

12 McNulty, Lucy & Zuckerman, Gregory. "London Whale Breaks Silence," *The Wall Street Journal*, February 23, 2016

Chapter 4 Opening – Leadership Phase

1 Kosur, James. "GE runs an intense 5-year program to develop executives, and only 2% finish it," *Business Insider*, October 10, 2015

2 Beard, Alison. "Life's Work: An Interview with Andre Agassi," *Harvard Business Review*, October 2015

3 Lipton-Dibner, Wendy. *Focus on Impact*, Morgan James Publishing, New York, 2016, Page ix

4 Sadgrove, Kit. *The Complete Guide to Business Risk Management*, Gower Publishing Company, Burlington, VT, 2005, Page 1

5 Frock, Roger. *Changing How the World Does Business, FedEx's Incredible Journey to Success – The Inside Story*, Berrett-Koehler Publishers, San Francisco, CA, 2006, Page 196

6 Thiel, Peter. *Zero to One*, Crown Business, New York, 2014, Page 10

7 Ibid., Page 107

8 Miller, Mark. *Chess not Checkers, Elevate Your Leadership Game*, Berrett-Koehler Publishers, Inc., Oakland, CA, 2015, Page 116

9 Ibid., Page 26

10 Ibid., Page 79

11 Loehr, Dr. Jim & Schwartz, Tony. *The Power of Full Engagement*, Free Press, New York, 2003, Page 4

Chapter 5 Middlegame – Managing Phase

1 Glazer, Emily, Byron, Ellen, Berman, Dennis K., & Lublin, Joann S. "P&G's Stumbles Put CEO on Hot Seat for Turnaround," *The Wall Street Journal*, September 27, 2012

2 Charan, Ram. *The Attacker's Advantage, Turning Uncertainty into Breakthrough Opportunities*, Public Affairs, New York, 2015, Page 31

3 Ibid., Page 7

4 Lucchetti, Aaron. "Facebook's Next Fight: Suits, and More Suits," *The Wall Street Journal*, September 26, 2012

5 Clausewitz, Carl Von. *On War*, Princeton University Press, Princeton, New Jersey, 1976, Page 359

6 Ries, Al & Trout, Jack. *Marketing Warfare*, McGraw-Hill, New York, 1986, Page 33

7 Tichy, Noel M. *Succession Mastering the Make-or-Break process of Leadership Transition*, Portfolio/Penguin, New York, 2014, Page 38

Chapter 6 Endgame – Expertise Phase

1 Greenspan, Alan. Letter to Senator Alfonse M. D'Amato, October 20, 1998

2 Lowenstein, Roger. *When Genius Failed, The Rise and Fall of Long-Term Capital Management*, Random House, New York, 2001, Page 230

3 Terlep, Sharon. "New CEO at P&G Vows to Lift its Standards," *The Wall Street Journal*, February 19, 2016

Chapter 7 Power of Tactics

1 OIG report, http://www.sec.gov/spotlight/secpostmadoffreforms/oig-509-exec-summary.pdf Page 21

2 Ibid., Page 21

3 Ibid., Page 20

4 http://www.iawatch.com/docs/Richards_testimony.pdf, Page 4

5 *Computerworld*, August 31, 1988

6 *DailyMail.com*, October 6, 2014, http://www.dailymail.co.uk/news/article-2824580/Witness-s-testimony-powerful-forced-9-billion-settlement-JP-Morgan-reveals-bank-giant-s-schemes-swindle-investors-selling-worthless-mortgages.html

7 Viswanatha, Aruna, Barrett, Devlin, Matthews, Christopher M. "Executives at RBS, J.P. Morgan Probed," *The Wall Street Journal*, November 18, 2015

8 *DailyMail.com*, October 6, 2014

9 News conference with Steve Ballmer, chief executive officer of Microsoft Corp., and Tony Bates, chief executive officer of Skype technologies SA, announcing Microsoft's $8.5 billion acquisition of Skype on May 10, 2011, in San Francisco

10 "Whistleblowers: Veterans Affairs inspector general a joke," *Chicago Tribune*, September 22, 2015 http://www.chicagotribune.com/news/ nationworld/ct-whistleblowers-veterans-affairs-20150922-story.html

11 Ensign, Rachel Louise. "SEC Probes Companies' Treatment of Whistleblowers," *The Wall Street Journal*, February 25, 2015, http://www.wsj.com/articles/sec-probes-companies-treatment-of-whistleblowers-1424916002

Chapter 8 MBA Using Gamification First Sememter

1 Mintzberg, Henry, Ahlstrand, Bruce, Lampel, Joseph. *Management, It's Not What You Think*, AMACOM Publishing, New York, 2010, Page 59

2 Ibid., Page 65

3 Mintzberg, Henry. *Managing*, Berrett-Koehler Publishers, San Francisco, 2009, Page 229

4 Korn, Melissa & Gellman, Lindsay. "Should Harvard Business School Hit Refresh?" *The Wall Street Journal*, Feb. 4, 2015

5 Verzuh, Eric. *The Fast Forward MBA in Project Management*, John Wiley and Sons, Hoboken, New Jersey, 2005, Page 12

6 Barrow, Colin. *The 30 Day MBA*, Kogan Page, London 2011, Page 13

7 Kark, Khalid, White, Mark & Briggs, Bill. *2015 Global CIO survey - Creating Legacy*, Deloitte University Press, November 3, 2015 http://dupress.com/articles/global-cio-survey/

8 Parker, Sybil. *Dictionary of Engineering*, McGraw Hill, New York, 1997, Page ix

9 Grosvenor, Gilbert. *The Builders, Marvels of Engineering*, National Geographic Society, Washington, DC, 1992, Page 206

Chapter 9 MBA Using Gamification Second Semester

1 Chase, Richard B., Aquilano, Nicholas. *Production and Operations Management*, Irwin, Homewood, IL, 1989, Page 7

2 Ibid., Page 8

3 Ries, Al & Trout, Jack. *Marketing Warfare*, McGraw-Hill, New York, 1986, Page 7

4 Kotler, Philip. *Kotler on Marketing*, Simon & Schuster, New York, 1999, Page 30

5 Ibid., Page 31

6 Ostrower, Jon. "Jet Prices Take Center Stage in Boeing Job Cuts", *The Wall Street Journal*, Apr. 1, 2016

7 Jan ten Geuzendam, Dirk. "Ken Rogoff: My life would have been just fine if I'd stayed a chess player," *New in Chess*, The Netherlands, January 2011, Page 34

8 O'Connor, David E. & Faille Christopher. *Basic Economic Principles, A Guide for Students*, Greenwood Press, Westport, Connecticut, 2000, Page 1

9 www.investopedia definitions

10 Stevens, Scott. *Games People Play*, The Teaching Company, Chantilly, Virginia, 2008, Page 1

11 O'Connor, David E. & Faille Christopher. *Basic Economic Principles, A Guide for Students*, Greenwood Press, Westport, Connecticut, 2000, Page 1

12 Ibid., Page 31

13 Ibid., Page 36

14 Ibid., Page 41

15 Jan ten Geuzendam, Dirk. "Ken Rogoff: My life would have been just fine if I'd stayed a chess player," *New in Chess*, January 2011, Page 33

16 Ibid., Page 33

17 Ibid., Page 33

18 Stevens, Scott, *Games People Play*, The Teaching Company, Chantilly, Virginia, 2008, Page 109

19 Bernanke, Benjamin. *The Courage to Act*, WW Norton & Company, New York, 2015, Page 215

20 Ibid., Page 222

21 Per discussion with Greg Lyle

22 Per discussion with Jeffrey Dixon

Chapter 10 – The Rich versus the Powerful

1 Buckingham, Marcus. *The One Thing You Need to Know...About Great Managing, Great Leading and Sustained Individual Success*, Free Press, New York, 2005, Page 275

2 Ibid., Page 276

Chapter 11 – Operating on the Edge

1 http://www.businessdictionary.com/definition/just-in-time-JIT-inventory.html#ixzz3pgwdgG8D

2 DeFirmian, Nick. *Modern Chess Openings 13th Edition*, David McKay Company, New York, 1990, Page 171

3 Clausewitz, Carl Von. *On War*, Princeton University Press, Princeton, New Jersey, 1976, Page 198

4 Chandler, David. *The Military Maxims of Napoleon*, Macmillan Publishing, New York, NY, 1987, Page 62

5 Ibid., Page 134

6 Franklin, Benjamin. "The Morals of Chess," *Columbian Magazine*, December 1786

About the Author

J.K. Egerton is the CEO and founder of Business on the Board™, a leading-edge talent development company that uses gamification to teach business strategies and tactics. He is a respected author, teacher, coach, manager, and entrepreneur whose work has impacted the lives of thousands. His management, information technology, and training experience come from serving in the health care, energy, and finance industries.

Business on the Board™ tailors its services to meet the needs of business clients looking to improve their leadership skills through better strategic thinking and decision-making. Corporate university classes, conference meetings, executive retreats, hands-on workshops, breakout sessions, exclusive private lessons, and keynote speeches are part of his wide array of services. By combining MBA-level business content and "chess for purpose," Mr. Egerton builds a mindset of skills his clients can use for a lifetime. His book, *Business on the Board,* supplements and expands on the training provided by the company.

His corporate clients include Federal Express, RR Donnelley & Sons, and Wrigley Corporation, among others.

He has a Bachelor of Science degree in mathematics from Northern Illinois University and an MBA degree in finance from Illinois Institute of Technology. He started his career teaching mathematics and has spent his entire working life teaching and improving the lives of others.

Acknowledgements

This book in large part would not have been possible without the invaluable coaching and editing skills of Paul R. Lloyd. Lynn-Zuk Lloyd provided the graphics for the book. A chess-mom extraordinaire and a truly professional editor, Rene Pas reviewed everything and wrote the words to end the book.

To Robbin Simons and her entire Crescendo Publishing team, Chris Collins for branding and cover design, Jason Webb for legal advice and marking the brand, and the entire CEO Space team for helping me take an idea and make it happen. To the staff at the Glen Ellyn Public Library for chasing down all the books I needed for my research. To Pat LaSpesa for her review and advice on promotions. To the following for reviewing the manuscript and providing invaluable feedback: Jeffrey Dixon, Annie and Peter Myung, Greg Lyle, Brian Smith, Jim Michalski, Christian Vieira, Scott Hanley, Nancy Egerton, Daniel Egerton, Constantine Anaiadis, Sherrin Ross-Ingram, and Lois Frankel.

In Gratitude

To my readers, thank you for taking your time, effort, and money to purchase, read, and learn about a game that can change your life. Please share your comments on our website and consider leaving a review for *Business on the Board* on the Amazon website. With social media available, someday we will meet across the board from each other, working on our plans for a better future.

23316861R00175

Printed in Poland
by Amazon Fulfillment
Poland Sp. z o.o., Wrocław